T0365162

The Miracle Children

GERALD MICHAEL DALY

SPIRITUAL ADVISOR: SONIA ORELLANA

WESTBOW
PRESS
A DIVISION OF THOMAS NELSON

WestBow Press books may be ordered through booksellers or by contacting:

WestBow Press
A Division of Thomas Nelson
1663 Liberty Drive
Bloomington, IN 47403
www.westbowpress.com
1-(866) 928-1240

ISBN: 978-1-4497-0502-2 (sc)
ISBN: 978-1-4497-0503-9 (e)

Library of Congress Control Number: 2010935778

Scripture quotations marked KJV are taken from the King James Version of the Holy Bible. Scripture quotations marked NLT are taken from the Holy Bible, New Living Translation, copyright 1996. Used by permission of Tyndale House Publishers, Inc., Wheaton, Illinois 60189. All rights reserved. Scripture references not marked KJV or NLT are the author's edit.

Printed in the United States of America

WestBow Press rev. date: 9/21/2010

Contents

The Miracle Children

Dedicated to God, the Encourager of us all,

And to Sonia Orellana,

Kaisha Kelly-Mozee,

And Jasmine Nicole Kelly,

The women God sent to encourage me.

Special Thanks To: John Bryant, Jacqueline 'Nia' Carter, Gilbert 'Hassan' Daly/On behalf Karnak Daly, Nathan 'Hakim' Daly, Melvin Lorenzo Downing Jr., Indira dias Gurley, Jasmine Kelly & Markeya Scaife, Joanne & Sidney Logan, Jamar & Kaisha Mozee, Pedro 'Rollie' Munson & Susan F. Talbot, Irving Parham, Elvin Spencer, Deryn Warren, Donald Wheatland, and Tina Williams.

To All, I pray your many years of support will finally bear fruit.

Author's Introduction

The story for 'The Miracle Children' was born out of my morning prayers asking God to bless children with gifts and talents to uplift the world and bring Glory to Our Father.

In the Beginning, the God SPIRIT of our vast Universe, entrusted hopes, dreams and encouragement to every child born into the world. However, many children grow up and never realize, take advantage, or even open the gifts, talents and hidden treasures embedded within their godly spirit.

Only a few really believe that God's Holy Spirit would encourage them to become the best doctors, scientists, adventurers, teachers, preachers, and world leaders. Most schools and educators don't teach our children that the wisdom of spiritual enlightenment, combined with world knowledge and discernment, would enable their young spirits to travel far beyond their circumstances to accomplish great feats, discover new technologies, write great stories, sing songs of empowerment, and dance through the stages of life, while sharing the glory of their godly adventures with the world.

As mentioned, Father God embedded these great gifts, talents, hopes, dreams, and encouragements in every newborn, nevertheless; over the years, the words of religious zealots, political hustlers, and usurpatory talking heads have become so destructive in their self-importance, that they've created a world of greed, separatism, distrust, suspicions, and age-old prejudices.

So my prayer for the children was for something a little more **High-Minded!** Which brings to mind, "Be careful what you pray for, because you just might get it."

One morning during this inspirational 'Prayer for the Children' a voice spoke to me, "Do you really want to help the children?"

"Of course," was my response, not wanting to be found guilty of praying for something I really didn't care about! You know, saying stuff that sounded good, but in actuality you know it reaches far beyond the Realm of Human Possibility.

Now that my answer was in the affirmative, I waited for the conversation to proceed. Nothing. Silence. Throughout the rest of the day my thoughts wondered who had spoken to me? Was it my own voice, or did I hear the true voice of the Holy Spirit? Dealing with our inner spirit always comes down to a question of faith, and my inquiring mind created no answers.

A number of weeks later, during this same 'Prayer for the Children,' the still small voice spoke again, saying, "You're a writer, tell the story!"

Though small in sound, the words carried enough power to awaken the writer within me. I've been writing stage and screenplays for over forty years, and to toot my own horn, it has been a successful struggle. So that's where I put my new adventure in writing. A screenplay!

Completing a Story Outline, the next task was the actual writing of the screenplay titled, 'The Day.' The story flowed like a gift from 'Writer's Heaven.' The second draft, 'The New Day' came together in a few weeks, and my third draft became, 'The Miracle Children.'

To my joy, the screenplay won 2nd prize in the Christian Screenwrite Competition. The prize came with cash, a certificate, and lots of acknowledgement.

A year later, my friend, Sonia Orellana told me I should write the story as a novel, because movies come and go, but stories last forever. She talked about how the world needed spiritual stories to share as gifts to family, friends, neighbors, and co-workers. She talked as if her spirit was possessed, and I'm convinced she was, because I've never heard Sonia be so concerned about my work as a writer before. Anyway, she touched my spirit when mentioning all the horror movies I wrote for the dollars. Plus, writing horror movies created a number of nightmares for me, since I was opening up my mind into a dark underworld that needed to be destroyed, and not used for financial gain.

So, I was quite thankful that the Holy Spirit, and now Sonia's challenge, would take me into a writing experience that would bring praise, honor and glory to Father God.

I shared Sonia's challenge with my goddaughters, Kaisha and Jasmine. They also agreed with Sonia. Thank God, now there were two others in agreement with Sonia; and Christ Jesus says in Matthew 18:19-20 (KJV) "Again I say unto you, that if two of you shall agree on earth as touching any thing that they shall ask, it shall be done for them of my Father which is in heaven. For where two or three are gathered together in my name, there am I in the midst of them."

I felt good about the assignment, but what did I know about writing a novel? My life experience was writing stage and screenplays, not authoring a novel at this late stage in my life.

My morning prayer was for God to bless the children, not for me to author a novel. In essence, "Be careful what you pray for, because God always has an answer: "You're a writer, tell the story!"

Sonia blessed and honored me again by taking time out of her busy life to do a spiritual edit of the manuscript. God surely places the right people in your life when they're most needed. And though my visual writing is more prominent, I pray you'll enjoy the journey. The story is now in your hands, so turn the pages, and pray along with me, that 'The Miracle Children' will move our Religious, Political and World Leaders to **Seek First the Spiritual Wisdom of God,** before they take their words onto the World Stage!

Revelation 21:1-2 (KJV) says; "And I saw a new heaven and a new earth: for the first heaven and the first earth were passed away; and there was no more sea. And I John saw the holy city, new Jerusalem, coming down from God out of heaven, prepared as a bride adorned for her husband." Let's pray the New Jerusalem into our world!

Peace and Love,
Gerald Michael Daly

The Miracle Children – Part 1

The prayer that opened my ears to hear, "You're a writer, tell the story."

Prayer For the Children

I pray, We pray, All pray
For The Kingdom of God
The Kingdom of Heaven
To Bless the Children of the Earth
Bless their body, mind, and spirit
And open their eyes to see,
Their ears to hear,
And their hearts to reveal God's Glory

And our special children,
The Miracle Children,
Who hear the call of the Holy Spirit
And walk in His Light,
Doing the will of Our Father
Becoming obedient to the Word,
I pray, We pray, All pray
That the spirits of Elijah and Elisha
Be upon their lives
And that they will do
Great work in the world
And bring Great Glory
To You, Our Father. Amen.

1

Rememberance

Then the Lord said to me, "Write my answer in large, clear letters on a tablet, so that a runner can read it and tell everybody else."

(Habakkuk 2:2 NLT)

In front of his home digital camera, Isaiah read aloud from his stack of hand-written pages:

"I, Pastor Isaiah Hillman, record this for those in the future who haven't heard the words of Christ Jesus stating: **"I am the way, the truth, and the life: No man cometh unto the Father, but by me."** (John 14:6 KJV) God proved it to me, and now I hope to encourage you to listen and learn what truthfully happened to us, and to our world, these last few years: It all began on the morning of Wednesday, December 12th, 2012, when three invisible whirlwinds of light, sound, and energy raced against time an into our world."

Isaiah stopped and replayed what was recorded. Satisfied with the picture and sound, he began recording again:

"The realization of what happened was not heard, or experienced by anyone, but the children involved. Yet, within a few hours, everyone knew that numerous miracles had occurred amongst many children throughout the world, and even though no radar screens lit up, no radio waves went haywire, and there were no disruptions of television signals, everyone knew something strange had happened. Many crazy ideas, and thousands of untruths were delivered through the media during the years that followed, but only the Miracle Children's spiritual message for the world spoke the real truth. One and all, the children said the same thing; they were blessed by God to prepare the world for a New Day. A frightening concept many didn't want to hear, or think about. And as the days unfolded, I've learned that the vibrations of light, sound, and energy were always flowing through the Universe. A Universal Force driven by the powerful voice of God, sending trillions of thoughts, ideas, messages, and dreams into the earth realm every hour, minute, and second of the day to communicate with human spirits seeking answers. For thousands of years, people listened and reaped the rewards of God's love. However, in this Day of Our Lord, human spirits became so misguided - they only heard the noise they themselves made. God's words of inspiration were dismissed as meaningless, and human words of self-importance became more useful, and after a while, these words got mixed up with thoughts from a dark underworld. God knew mankind was surely rushing toward a path of certain annihilation, and since mankind pushed the 'True Voice of Wisdom' into the dark corners of their soul, communication with the Kingdom of God was at the point of being terminated forever."

Isaiah stretched, and took a deep breath, before continuing his reading:

"Words of the World, became so infused in people's hearts and minds that only "Earth Words" created the new truth in the world, and words from the Holy Bible, such as: Psalms, Proverbs, and Scriptures were given little thought.

In His final attempt to save mankind, God, the Supreme Voice of the Universe, blessed the Miracle Children, with guidance from His Holy Spirit, to prepare the world for the 'New Day' on the horizon!"

~

2

Miracles

**You are the light of the world,
like a city on a mountain,
glowing in the night for all to
see.** (Matthew 5:14 NLT)

OOOOOOOMMMMMMM…a great whirlwind of sound raced into the earth's hemisphere and created a bright light of Golden Splendor on a hillside.

A company of soldiers stepped out of the light, and though their faces were of many skin tones, they shone with one purpose as they marched toward a vine-covered tomb and rolled away the large stone that sealed it.

The Prophet Elijah, wearing the white robe of a priest, with gold trim at the collar, cuffs and hem, stepped out from amongst the soldiers and walked into the tomb. Though thousands of years old, his physical image was a heavenly age of only thirty-three years.

"Does anyone know what this mission is about?" Axon whispered, and like Elijah, his true age was undetermined, which was the same for all the other soldiers whose spiritual bodies were less, or no older than thirty-three years.

"I've heard the earth is going to be given a last chance," Zavis answered. "But man will fail. It is written!"

"Zavis, that's not true. If humans are being given a last chance, then failure isn't written!"

"Axon, let me put it simply. Man will fail, the world will end, and the Prophet Elijah has come as a confirmation to my words."

The soldiers stared at Zavis, not sure if they should take his "End of the World" proclamation seriously. Not having a better response to Zavis' words, they laughed.

The Captain raised his hand to quiet the soldiers, and then spoke, "There must be somebody quite old in that tomb. Most bodies are cremated or buried in the ground now."

"It's probably Moses!" Axon said, though unsure.

"Abraham!"

"They're in heaven, not buried in a dark tomb!"

"Their bones are still here."

"That's true, so whoever it is, must be special. Elijah doesn't like coming here. Too much...er..."

"Don't be afraid, say it. Too much ignorance." Zavis said, receiving nods of agreement from everyone.

The Captain's tone was pleasant as he spoke up, "We all know the history of the world, and we've all been here many times before, though never with the Prophet Elijah. I suggest you stay alert and stop all the speculations. We will find out soon enough why we're here."

Inside the tomb, a ray of light flowed out of Elijah's body covering dry bones inside a stone sarcophagus.

"A New Day is coming into the earth," Elijah announced, and watched as the bones take on sinews, eyes, ears, a mouth, and then the flesh of a man. At that moment, the spiritual body of Elisha appeared in the tomb, and then, became one with the body inside the sarcophagus.

Elijah waved his right hand, and Elisha's aged and ragged burial robe was replaced, and he was adorned in a gold priest's robe, with white trim at the collar, cuffs and hem.

A flash of light startled the soldiers outside the tomb, as Elijah and Elisha suddenly appeared in front of them.

"Today, Elisha's spirit has been made one with his body," Elijah said, and looking up at a bright morning star, he closed his eyes, and lifted up his right hand as a sphere of light glowed on his palm.

The soldiers stared in wonder, as Elisha lifted up both his hands, and spheres of light appeared on his palms.

The three spheres, reflecting the beauty of precious stones, glistened in a rainbow of colors that represented God's jewels on the earth, the human seeds that are His children.

Elijah, Elisha, and the soldiers vanished from the hillside; the three rainbow spheres lingered, and then took off at ultra-light speed, as a ticking of clocks echoed from within them. They circled the earth, crossing paths from different angles and directions, and flashing rainbow points of light down on cities, towns and villages throughout the world.

~

In Nairobi, Kenya, a little boy, born with only one arm with two fingers on his hand, struggled to draw water from the village well.

Suddenly, a rainbow of light, unseen by the other children at the well, surrounded the boy's body causing a miraculous growth of a perfect second arm and hand.

The children, terrified at what they witnessed, dropped their wooden water buckets and ran off to the village yelling for the elders.

Alone at the well, the little boy cautiously touched his new arm, and then burst into laughter.

~

In Copenhagen, Denmark, in a hospital for burns, an eight-year-old girl covered in scars, tried, but failed to sit up in bed to greet her family. For a fraction of a second, her scarred body is covered in a rainbow of light, and though she saw the light, her family didn't. However, the family did witness a miracle flowing over the girl's body as her mother cried out, "My God…My God…"

Everyone in the room watched in amazement as the girl's face and body is covered in new, smooth skin with no visible scar tissue remaining.

~

Throughout the earth, the rainbow spheres of lights raced about covering boys and girls from every nation around the world. The rainbow lights encircled their young bodies while they were sleeping, at school, or at play.

The light healed sick bodies, opened blind eyes, awakened deaf ears, and unveiled paths of communication into a spiritual dimension beyond the earth.

Three minutes later, the ticking clocks within the spheres stopped, and the rainbow spheres vanished, returning to whence they came.

~

In Studio City, California: Pastor Isaiah Hillman awakened with a sudden jerk of his foot. He sat up and looked around his bedroom, he glanced at his bedside clock that glowed 3 a.m., while the clock's calendar showed 12-12-12.

Isaiah, six feet tall, clean-shaven with brown, curly hair, appeared skinny beneath his navy-blue pajamas. As he slipped out of bed, his young wife, Evelyn, sat up.

"Another bad dream?"

"Different."

"Different good or different bad, Isaiah?

"Felt like somebody grabbed my foot."

"Scary. Must be those faceless people you're always dreaming about."

"The dream was spiritual, the foot grabbing woke me up."

"Maybe an angel grabbed your foot, as a way of telling you we're heading down the wrong road, and you've made a bad decision about leaving the church? "

"Evelyn, my dream didn't have anything to do with my job."

"Being a pastor is not a job. It's a Calling from God."

"I thought we made this decision together."

"Because, I'm your loving wife, and because you are the man of the house, I agreed with your decision. Your decision!"

He turned and looked at her, but remained silent.

"Maybe your dream was telling you…excuse me, telling us that we're making a bad decision."

Isaiah smiled, reluctantly, "It's a good decision, Evelyn. I don't feel called to pastor an empty church. Our church has lost its power, we need a better future, and so does Baby Paula."

"A future with faceless people? Honey, God is our future. I'm worried we haven't thought this through. Please apologize and take back your resignation."

"It's too late. My replacement is coming in two weeks."

"I see," Evelyn said. "Thanks for letting me know!"

She picked up her pillow, stripped a cover off the bed, muttered under her breath, and walked out of the bedroom dragging the bed cover behind her.

Isaiah stared out the bedroom window. "So God, you've heard the question. Is this decision good or bad?"

Silence.

Isaiah felt in his heart, he made the right decision, but Evelyn's doubt troubled him. One moment, she was by his side, and then a second later, she didn't want to be near him. He told himself, he had to get a new job, and quick, or he'd have her opposition staring him in the face twenty-four hours, every day of the week.

Evelyn sat on the living room sofa with the bedcover around her shoulders, holding Paula, their six-month-old daughter.

"Paula, I don't understand why your father is doing this, but don't you worry, I'll find us a new church home, okay?"

She hugged Paula, and then closed her eyes and prayed, "Hello, God. I know I've asked this a few times already, but are we...no, did Isaiah make the right decision?"

No answer came forth, but she knew God heard her, because, even though she was married to Isaiah, she also married Jesus when she was seventeen. She told Isaiah about her special marriage with the Savior, and Isaiah still agreed to marry her. Now, Isaiah's leaving the church, just wasn't acceptable to her. She told herself, she had to get Isaiah to make a recommitment to their marriage, where they would make decisions together, and then, she prayed, "Father God, please get Isaiah to marry Jesus, and open his heart to continue the Calling you've placed on his life! In Jesus name I pray, Amen!"

Isaiah, wearing a tan sweater with a pastor's white-collared shirt underneath, walked into the Victory Union church classroom for the 'After School Children's Bible Study.' Placing his Bible on an empty desk, he looked at the ten solemn faces of children ranging in ages from five to twelve.

"Good Afternoon," Isaiah said, cheerfully, but the children didn't respond. "Ahhh, it seems we have a standoff as to whether it's a good afternoon or not. Want to tell me what's wrong?"

Five year old, Susan Faraday raised her hand. Her other arm is wrapped around NuNu, her colorfully dressed stuffed doll. Isaiah often thought that if there were a prize for seeing the world through rose-colored glasses, Susan would definitely be the winner.

"Yes, Susan."

"Pastor Hillman, Kenny says you're walking out on us!"

"I was going to tell everybody the news today, but it looks like Kenny has inside information."

"My Father says you're flawed!" Kenny responded. The children stared at Isaiah, and though many didn't understand what flawed meant, they knew it didn't sound good.

"Kenny, haven't we learned that everyone is flawed. That we are all born into sin."

"I thought you were saved," Kenny said, sounding wary, but wanting to challenge Isaiah with what he heard his father say.

"Are you quitting God, Pastor Hillman?" Susan asked.

A hush came over the room as the kids awaited Isaiah's answer. He took a deep breath before answering.

"No, I have another dream. I want to help children outside the church."

"Bad kids?"

"No, not exactly, Susan. Children needing a guidance counselor, or someone to coach them at sports."

"My father says you want more money."

"Yes, Kenny, I have a baby daughter, so more money is needed," Isaiah smiled.

"We can give you our money."

"Thank you, Susan, but I was kidding. It's not about the money. We all have dreams in our hearts, and you can let your dreams stand still forever, or you can do something to make them come true. My advice to all of you is to never let your dreams escape out of your heart. Hold on to your dreams until you're able to make them come true!"

"My dream last night said for me to prepare everyone for the New Day."

Four other kids yelled out, "Me, too! Me too!"

Kenny, wanting to scare everybody, growled. "I'm preparing everyone for a new night."

"People of the night will die in the fire!"

"Susan, who told you that?" Isaiah asked.

Suddenly, the children gasped at the sight of Kenny clutching his heart, moaning, and falling out of his chair. Isaiah rushed over and knelt at Kenny's side. When Isaiah began artificial respiration, and pressed the palms of his hands up and down on Kenny's chest, Kenny giggled, and caused an expression of relief from Isaiah, and laughter from the children.

"Okay, Kenny, you've had your little joke for today. Take your seat. Susan, what you said was...interesting. Who told you in the dream to prepare everybody for this New Day?"

"The Holy Spirit."

Isaiah smiled, "Very good, Susan. Everyone open your study Bible to Mark 6:48. How many of you heard the story of Jesus, Our Savior, walking on water?"

Five-year-old, Timothy raised his hand.

"Yes, Timmy?"

"I can swim on water," Timothy announced, and when Isaiah and the other kids laugh, Timothy joined in.

~

"How's everybody doing?" Isaiah smiled, as he entered his living room. Evelyn was still sitting on the sofa with Paula sleeping next to her. Isaiah kissed Paula, and then Evelyn.

"Again, how's everybody doing?"

"Since Paula isn't going to answer you, I guess you're directing your question to me."

"Paula, wake up and help!"

I'm fine, Pastor Hillman. OOPS! I mean, Mr. Hillman!"

Isaiah felt the sting of her words, but not wanting an argument, he started to leave the room.

"Isaiah, have you heard the news?" Evelyn asked. "There are stories about healings everywhere."

Picking up the television's remote, she turned up the sound to hear a news reporter in the home of an African American family.

"I'm with eleven-year-old Carnetta Jackson. Three years ago, Carnetta was partially paralyzed from a drive-by-shooting. This morning, Carnetta woke up able to walk again. This is surely a miraculous healing. Truly amazing."

"Praise God," Mrs. Jackson rejoiced, dabbing at her tears of joy with a handkerchief.

Carnetta's younger brother spoke up, "Carnetta says she's going to prepare the world for the New Day!"

"I am! I am!" Carnetta shouted.

"I'm sure you will, young lady. Stayed tuned to Channel 2 News for more miracle stories. This is Danny Wynn, reporting live from the South Bronx."

Isaiah was startled and excited by news, "At Bible Study, five kids also said they were preparing the world for a New Day."

"Something strange is happening. There are over a thousand reported miracles in the last few hours."

Isaiah changed the station to Channel 4, as a television news host pointed to specks of lights on a world map, "We've received so many reports of miracles that it's become impossible to number them all."

Isaiah flipped to Channel 7, where a News Host was speaking to his associate.

"The amazing thing is that these stories all involved children, and the miracles happened within a time-frame of three-minutes."

The associate shook her head in bewilderment, "It's amazing, Steve, thousands of miracles in three minutes. We will follow this story throughout the day. In other news, a bomb exploded in Iran this morning, killing a number of students in a Bible Study Class…"

Isaiah changed the channel to Jan Summers' network television show, 'Talking With Jan.'

"The first report came in from a village in Central Africa," Jan reported, as the soft wrinkles at the corners of her eyes revealed her many years of experience as a television news host. She stood in front of a large monitor, while photos of children flashed on the screen.

"Reports of bodies being healed have come in from North Africa, Spain, France, and the Netherlands. Please understand, we haven't verified the reports, so some elaborate hoax, or possibly a movie promotion is behind this!"

"Ms. Summers," Rabbi Cohen interrupted.

"Yes, Rabbi Cohen," Jan answered, as she turned to face three religious leaders seated at a round table.

"Ms. Summers, this is too big to be a hoax, or a movie promotion. No, truth be told, the hand of Jehovah is all over this wonderful, spiritual awakening. Too many countries are involved for it to be anything else."

"Twelve Islamic countries. Allah is good!" Minister Kalif Amin announced.

"So is Jehovah," Rabbi Cohen said.

"Whatever caused these strange healings only lasted for three minutes. So, let's set religion off to the side for a moment and question how this was possible?"

"Ms. Summers," Cardinal Bynum said. The event appears to be a spiritual shift in the world. Miracle healings, and children preparing the world for something new, well… I'm sure scientists will have many answers, and they'll try to move us beyond the boundaries of religious dogma, but it won't be possible. What happened is impossible in our natural world, but not in the spiritual, supernatural world of God!"

"I agree, Cardinal Bynum. This is a super-natural explosion of Jehovah's healing power," Rabbi Cohen said.

"Don't forget, Allah's hand has touched many Islamic countries," Minister Kalif Amin states.

"We won't, Kalif," Rabbi Cohen smiled. "What do you think it means, Cardinal Bynum?"

Cardinal Bynum shrugged, "I don't think we can set religion off to the side, and this may not be about religion to some, but religion is about God, and when children say they're preparing the world for a New Day, well, I don't think it's not about electing a New Class President!"

"Allah, Mohammed, and the Holy Koran speaks to the New Beginning the children are talking about," Minister Kalif Amin announced. "It's called the Day of Judgment."

"The Day of Judgment and the End of the World' are also written about many times in the Bible, but a New

Day won't come into the world until all the terrorists are destroyed. Kalif, children were healed, not Islamic suicide bombers," Rabbi Cohen smiled.

Minister Kalif Amin smiled back, "I'm sure Israelis bombs weren't blessed, either, Rabbi Cohen."

Jan spoke up, "Gentlemen, have you, as religious leaders received an advanced warning about this event?" She knew the answer was no, but her producer wanted her to ask the question. "Cardinal Bynum, did the Pope forewarn Catholics about this New Day?"

"Many signs were in the world that a change was coming. However, the healings have taken the Pope, Jews, Christians, Muslims and everybody else by surprise! Though the healings are a godsend, we all have to agree that miracle healings won't stop people from warring with each other. Just listening to our conversation in this studio, forewarns me, that this New Day the children are talking about, may not be the answer we've hoped and prayed for!"

"After the attack on the World Trade Center, everybody claimed to have had forewarnings, but the only ones who really knew the truth were the terrorists,' Rabbi Cohen said.

Minister Kalif Amin spoke up, his voice calm, but full of authority, "Perhaps, in this New Day, the Holy Land will be a land of shared opportunities."

Rabbi Cohen nodded, and then surprisingly reached over and shook hands with Kalif, "I'll agree with that, Minister Amin. That surely would be a New Day!"

"We'll return with our guests after this important message," Jan announced, motioning to the stage manager to cut to a commercial.

During the commercial break, Evelyn turned to Isaiah, "I'm scared, this New Day stuff sounds like trouble."

"They're children. God healed their bodies. He didn't give them guns to fight a Holy War. What's to be afraid of?"

"It doesn't seem right for children to be preparing the world for a new anything. It's scary that little kids are in charge of what's coming into the world!"

"Adults haven't done such a great job," Isaiah said, as he changed to the cable channel, National News Network, and the News Host, Alison Hewitt.

"Three adults and five children were killed in that bombing in Afghanistan yesterday. In other news, Markeya Montes is reporting live from Brazil. Markeya what's going on in Rio?"

"Alison, as you can see, I'm on Corcovado Mountain, the site where Christ the Redeemer statue was voted in 2007, as one of the New Seven Wonders of the World. Standing with me, are some very special children who have experienced miracle blessings in their lives. Antonio, tell everybody about the words spoken into your spirit today!"

Antonio, instead of speaking, sang in Portuguese, as the seven other children sang along with him. Markeya listened to the song for a moment, and then whispered, "Alison, I don't know what this all means, but Antonio and the children are singing about a New World Order on the earth. If the New Day is as beautiful as their song, our world is going to experience heaven right here on earth. Live from Corcovado Mountain in Rio de Janeiro, Brazil, I'm Markeya Montes."

~

"Thank you all for coming out tonight," Isaiah said, as he presided over a packed church, where parishioners were loudly venting about what was going on in the world.

Mrs. Maddy Smith, while fanning herself, openly spoke of her disappointment; "God blessed those children in three minutes. I've made a count, and figured out that I've lived twenty-four million, seven hundred and three thousand minutes, and I'm still waiting for a half minute's blessing!"

"Perhaps you're wasting God's time by counting dust!" A man said, but loud enough so everyone heard, which caused laughter to echo throughout the church.

"Yeah, you joke, Mr. Funnyman, but everyone knows I'm telling the truth," Maddy replied.

Isaiah held up his hand to quiet the crowd. "Maddy, the past is dust, and even though we've heard only children were touched, we must be thankful."

"Why?" A woman yelled out from the back of the church. "My child is suffering from cancer, and he wasn't healed!"

"I don't want to sound bitter, but all those children being healed and not one from our church! Don't you see something wrong with that, Pastor Hillman?" a man shouted, as loud voices echoed his sentiment.

Again, Isaiah raised his hand to restore order. "Hello... Listen up! Last Sunday, only fifteen members showed up for church service, and no adults were at the mid-week service last week.

"Pastor Hillman, didn't you quit the church?"

"Sam, we all know that even good people have turned their back on the church. My resignation has nothing to do with quitting God; I'm just tired of trying to teach adults to be truthful about their spiritual walk. For the last twenty-four hours, I've listened to broadcasts of news anchors, talk show hosts, and civic and religious leaders arguing and professing things they know nothing about. The same thing is happening here. We don't know what this is about, but I do know our church has been blessed."

"Who, Pastor Hillman? Who's been blessed?" Sam asked.

"Sam, men, women and children around the world have been touched by the events that happened, perhaps not all of them physically, but surely spiritually. I know I've been.

19

What it all means, nobody knows? Only God knows, so let's wait and see what's being revealed to the world."

"I know I'll be waiting, watching, and trusting the Lord to plan the New Day for all Christians!" Mrs. Shepard called out.

"It's not just for Christians. It's for everybody. God welcomes everyone, Jews, Christians, and Muslims. Saints and Sinners. Right, Pastor Hillman?" a young man announced, which caused loud shouts to break out amongst the church members.

"No! You have to be saved! That's the only way."

"The Christian Way!"

The young man continued to make his point, "Getting saved is for all believers, and believers don't have to be Christians!"

"They have to be Christians! That's the only way for the whole world. *The whole wide world!*"

Isaiah shook his head in despair as he watched church members argue with each other. Closing his eyes, he raised his hands in Praise to God, and then sang a spiritual hymn.

One by one, others followed Isaiah's lead and sang along with him:

Isaiah/Congregation: "Hallelujah, Hallelujah
Hallelujah, Hallelujah
Thank you, Lord
For your light, so bright
In our lives
Hallelujah, Hallelujah
Thank you, Lord
By blessing, our children
You've blessed our lives
By blessing, our children
You've blessed our lives!"

"Praise the Lord," A woman shouted.

Isaiah watched as a large number of people exited the church. As he sang, he wondered if God saw him in the same light, a dissenting shepherd who was walking out on his flock.

~

Evelyn stopped reading her book when Isaiah walked into the bedroom. The sadness on his face was disheartening.

"Was the meeting helpful?" she asked, knowing full well it wasn't.

"There may be trouble ahead. Like you, they disliked God's plan even though they don't know what it is."

"Ouch, my ex-pastor husband is throwing stones!"

"Sorry, I was trying to be humorous. You're much better at it."

"Apology accepted, so what's the trouble ahead?

"Christians can be so selfish. Most of them see the children's preparations as something only for themselves. Everybody else better watch out!"

"That's why you're there, Isaiah. God anointed you to lead his sheep. You're their pastor even if it's only for another two weeks."

Isaiah sat in a chair and took off his shoes. "I know you disagree with my leaving the church."

"No, that's not true. I love you. I'm with you. We're in this marriage together. You, Paula, me. Us. We. Together. You don't know what's going on, and neither do I. What will be, will be. I'm not going to be scared anymore. I'm ready for whatever!"

"Good, but what happens if the world we know crashes and burns? Already in the meeting tonight, mothers and fathers were envious of what happened to a few children. I'm happy you're with me to the end, but what if the children are preparing the world for "The End?" America has never been the same after the World Trade Center buildings were destroyed, and today, terrorists are causing even more trouble."

"Sweetheart, you can't place children being healed in the same equation with devils doing evil acts."

"Yes I can! You can't. It takes a war to destroy evil. God has been warring with evil since the Garden of Eden. From what I'm hearing, over two thousand children are saying they're supposed to prepare the world for something new. New means getting rid of the old...the only way those children were healed was because God wanted it, and if they are going to prepare the world, then they must have been told something only they know. The scripture says: And no one puts new wine into old wineskins. The old skins would burst from the pressure, spilling the wine and ruining the skins. New wine must be stored in new wineskins. That way both the wine and the wineskins are preserved. (Matthew 9:17 NLT) These children represent the living water, that Jesus has turned into new wine..."

Isaiah looked at Evelyn who was smiling at him. He also smiled, "I can go on about storms, earthquakes, fires and brimstone, but it'll only sound like preaching to you!"

She laughed, "I'm looking forward to hearing your sermon on Sunday."

"Sunday! I hope we can get through tomorrow. Everything is spinning out of control. Then after tomorrow, there's Saturday breaking through the dawn."

Again, she laughed at his silliness, "Come to bed, and let me help you get through the night. Jesus says tomorrow will bring its own worries." (Matthew 6:34 NLT) She smiled and lifted the bedcovers for him to join her.

3

Trust

But without faith it is impossible to please Him: for he that cometh to God must believe that He is, and that He is a rewarder of them that diligently seek Him. (Hebrews 11:6 KJV)

"Everybody out," Isaiah announced, opening the church van's sliding door. Susan Faraday clutched her doll, NuNu, as she took Isaiah's hand and hopped out of the van. Next, seven-year-old twins, Leon and Alonzo Serna jumped out, their long ponytails bouncing as Susan playfully chased after them.

Eight-year-old, Michelle Spencer stepped out next, followed by her twelve-year-old brother, Michael. Like his sister, he's tall, but if Michelle's eyes expressed a heart full of love, Michael's eyes expressed a spirit of playful authority.

Isaiah removed picnic baskets from the van, while Michelle covered a table with a red and white-checkered tablecloth.

Later, while the kids ate their lunches, Isaiah brought up his reason for the picnic.

"God knew us before we were born, and He placed special gifts and talents in each one of us. Two days ago, God blessed you with a special purpose. Anyone want to talk about it?"

Silence.

"Anybody want to share their dreams? Michael… Michelle…Leon…? Come on, talk to me. Susan, at Bible Study you said something about preparing the world for the New Day, and I've heard other kids on television say the same thing. Tell me, how are children going to prepare the world?"

Susan giggled, but remained silent.

"Susan, are you kids keeping secrets?"

"Pastor Hillman, you know we're special, so there's no secret," Michael said.

"How do I know that, Michael?"

"We're here, Kenny and the other kids are not."

"So, you understand why I brought you here? Do you want to talk about this "New Day" you're preparing for the world?"

The kids look at Michael, but Michael remains silent.

"I'm asking about this because you're making a lot of people nervous," Isaiah said, but not getting a response, he softens his voice. "Listen to me, maybe not you kids, personally, however, special kids like you are being talked about around the world, and it's not all good talk."

Noticing that the children were comfortable in their silence, made Isaiah uncomfortable.

"Listen, guys. I'm feeling that your joy and peace is a good thing, but it won't make the growing fears in the world go away. I hope you aren't preparing the world for something to make people more afraid of your…your special preparations."

"No one needs to be afraid," Michael said.

"Michael, you say that, but I've heard people arguing about this on television and in church. Everyone is concerned about what a few kids can do to prepare the whole world?"

"Not a few kids!" Leon yelled, and then, Alonzo spoke in unison with his brother. "We are one million, five hundred and fourteen thousand children!"

"And that's an army!" Leon shouted.

"Wow," Isaiah said. How do you know the exact number? One million...er...?"

"One million, five hundred and fourteen thousand children all around the world. The Holy Spirit told us that," Michelle answered.

"You have direct communication with the Holy Spirit?"

"Don't you?" Michael asked, amused.

"Perhaps, not as immediate as you guys."

"That's because you're old," Alonzo said, causing laughter from the children.

"You like to control everything so it takes the Holy Spirit a lot longer to talk to you," Michelle said.

"The Holy Spirit told you that?"

The children laughed again.

"What's so funny?"

"The Holy Spirit says what we hear with one ear you don't hear with two," Leon joked. "So you..."

"Need to get more ears," Leon and Alonzo laughed together.

Isaiah joined the children's laughter. "Okay, okay. I'm twenty-five, I'm old, and my ears are clogged with gook. Question? How do you know the voice you're hearing is the Holy Spirit, and not some trick of the devil?"

"That's a question showing doubt!" Michael said. "And doubt won't get you the right answers from the Holy Spirit!"

"Michael, it may be a question of doubt, but it's still a fair question to get the truth. People who hear voices aren't always saints. Voices have talked people into committing horrendous sins, and you guys aren't fully aware of the history of this world. To you, I'm old. However, God has been in a war against wicked people and evil spirits since Adam and Eve had to leave the Garden of Eden. So, I ask you again, how do you know the voice you're hearing is the Holy Spirit?"

"The devil is as puzzled as you are," Alonzo answered.

"Great, but that doesn't answer my question."

"Satan isn't prepared for us!" Leon said.

"Nobody is, so you still haven't answered my question."

Silence.

"You don't know, do you?" Isaiah said, surprised that they heard a voice, but didn't know whose voice it was.

Susan raised her hand.

"Okay, Susan, prove it to me! How do you know it's the Holy Spirit speaking to you?"

"Because we can hear and you can't," Susan smiled, liking her answer.

"The Holy Spirit says your faith is weak. You need to stop questioning and just listen. You may like what you hear," Michelle said.

"I hope you're right!"

"You're still doubting," Michael informed Isaiah.

Isaiah sheepishly smiled, because Michael and the children were certainly right. He doubted what he was hearing from them, so he'd have to wait and see what God was planning on doing with the children. His thoughts were further confused when it seemed like the children knew what he was thinking and started singing:

Michael/Children: *"Listen to hear his voice*
The door will open for you
Be still and listen
Then you'll find your way..."

In his heart, Isaiah agreed and disagreed with the children. He admitted to himself that he might be a little controlling, but he did walk by faith. Why did they say he didn't hear? Did they really have a one on one conversation with the Holy Spirit? Isaiah always knew, or at least thought he had that same connection. Who was he hearing and talking to? His thoughts troubled him, so he told himself that if God wanted him to hear, then the Holy Spirit would have to make His voice clear and recognizable.

Isaiah's mind wandered, and his thoughts took him back to a sermon he had delivered about God wanting his children to have a relationship with Him. He remembered the Holy Spirit telling him that God liked his sermon. He felt blessed hearing that, and from that day his heart was opened, and he wanted to work with children, because the future belonged to them. As Isaiah came out of his reveries, he smiled as the children continued singing and dancing around him:

Michael/Children: *"Listen to hear his voice*
The door will open for you
Be still and listen
Then you'll find your way"

Once again, Isaiah wondered with whom the children were communicating. They heard something, or someone they all agreed about, but one million, five hundred and fourteen thousand children, and they all appeared to be in agreement, with not one dissention, well, he knew that couldn't happen. Praise God, but in this world, Isaiah knew there was always a Judas spirit.

~

"Your mother said that pastor at Victory Union Church, took you to the park today. He asked you about me, right?" Henry Spencer questioned, as he walked through a crowded Mini-Mart carrying a case of beer. Michelle and Michael walked with Henry carrying bags of potato chips and peanuts. Henry looked at Michelle. "Michelle, did the pastor ask you about me?"

"No."

"What do you mean, no? Michelle, I know your mother is always telling him stuff about me."

Michelle hunched her shoulders, while Michael looked away from his father's eyes.

"Why did he take you to the park, Michael?"

Michael remained silent, so Henry grabbed Michael's arm, "When I ask you a question, I want an answer! Do you hear me?"

A few Mini-Mart customers stared at Henry. He glared back at them. "This is my son! He will obey me. So mind your own business!"

Michelle gently removed Henry's clenched hand from Michael's arm and walked him toward the checkout counter.

"Dad, don't get upset. Pastor Hillman talked to us about the special children."

Away from Henry's eyesight, Michael placed a finger over his lips in an effort to silence her.

"Why Michael and you? Does that pastor think you're one of them? Are you? Yeah, your mother must have prayed you into those miracles, but Michael and you weren't sick or cripple, so what did God give you, Michelle? Did God give you something special?"

Silence.

Henry stared at a lottery sign with a prize of twenty-one million dollars. Leaving Michelle in the checkout line, he ushered Michael over to the lottery stand, and though he didn't read the Bible, he knew that it said something about asking and receiving, so he shoved the lottery playslip in Michael's hand.

"I'm not old enough to play," Michael said, to stop what his father wanted him to do.

Henry snatched the playslip from Michael and whispered, "You're not playing. I am! Michael, you know your mother and I are having problems. This will solve all of them. Son, use your special gifts, powers, and whatever God gave you…"

"Dad, I don't have special powers."

"The news reporters say the Holy Spirit talks to you. Talk to him and get me tonight's winning numbers."

"I don't have special powers."

"You're lying, and God doesn't like liars. Michael, if you do this for me, I promise, there will be no more fights with your mother."

As Michael walked away, Henry grabbed his wrist, "If you don't ask God, Jesus, or the Holy Spirit for this special request to save our family, I don't know what I'll do. I know the Bible says something about ask if you want to receive. (Matthew 7:8) Go ahead, ask, and see if God answers. If He doesn't answer, you'll know you're not preparing the world for anything!"

Michael nodded. Closing his eyes, he spoke, "I see the numbers three, twelve, twenty, twenty-eight and thirty-three."

Henry marked the numbers down on his playslip. "One more, Michael. I need one more number!"

"Number twelve, again."

Henry playfully ruffled Michael's hair. "Yeah, you're special, Michael. We're gonna go far in this world."

Henry hurried back to the checkout counter. Michael, left at the lottery stand, closed his eyes, and bowed his head in prayer.

~

"I thought I heard you. Want something to eat?" Evelyn asked, seeing Isaiah writing on a notepad in his study.

"There were too many people coming into the church wanting me to give them answers, so I came home to work."

Evelyn looked over Isaiah's shoulder at the open Bible. "Second Kings? I'd think a better sermon would be Jesus talking about the children: Suffer the little children to come unto me, and forbid them not: for such is the Kingdom of God. Verily I say unto you, Whosoever shall not receive the Kingdom of God as a little child shall in no wise enter therein." (Luke 18:16-17 KJV)

"I see you've been studying. I thought about that scripture," Isaiah replied. "But I'll be teaching from the Book of Second Kings, since I don't think we'll be packing our bags for a trip into the Kingdom anytime soon."

"You're not going to preach about the Miracle Children?"

"Where did you get that name?"

"On the news. Everyone has branded them with that name. Now back to "Second Kings," did the children reveal to you what their "Great Preparations" are all about?"

"They're being mysterious."

"Sweetheart, the congregation on Sunday, will want to know if the children are playing with heavenly flutes, violins and harps. They don't want to find out on the "Last Day" that the children will be throwing Adam and Eve's rotten apples at them."

"Did I ever tell you that you have such a lovely way of tossing words around to please yourself?" Isaiah joked, and though he always enjoyed her sense of humor, he wasn't really in the mood for it while he was trying to get his sermon out of his head and down on paper. Unthinking, he turned back to his notepad, which she felt was an act of being dismissed.

"Sorry, I didn't see the 'do not disturb' sign."

"I'm sorry, too. What did you want?"

"Isaiah, are the children being mysterious good, or mysterious bad?"

Isaiah looked up at her, "Whatever happened to what will be, will be?"

"Honey, I'm really excited about everything. You know I'm married to you and Jesus, and whatever God is planning for the world, I'm in agreement. So to really make our marriage work, have you thought about marrying Jesus?"

"A woman marrying Jesus is wonderful, but a man marrying a man, well…I have a problem with it. Sweetheart, when I get some free time, I'll read the scriptures you gave me."

"Jesus is the bridegroom that built the church. You're not marrying a man; you're marrying his Godly Spirit, the church!

"Please, we'll talk about it later. I'm busy trying to get this sermon written."

"Find, I'll read Second Kings, and maybe, someday you'll marry Jesus, and you'll find out how beautiful it is!"

He nodded and returned back to writing on his notepad.

"Would you like some rotten apples for dinner?" Evelyn asked, sweetly.

Not really listening, Isaiah nodded in agreement. She smiled, and then walked out of the study thinking that it would be fun to place a rotten apple on his dinner plate. She laughed at the thought.

~

"Michael, you're going make us rich with your powers," Henry said, slurring his words. He took another beer out of the refrigerator, and sat down at the kitchen table. As his wife, Sylvia walked passed him, he roughly fondled her backside in front of Michael and Michelle.

Sylvia shoved his hand away. "Henry, listen to me. Getting Michael to gamble is wrong. Our kids are blessed to do good."

"Shut up, Sylvia. God knows we need the money, and lottery money is good money," Henry said, and took a long swig from his beer bottle, looked at his watch, and then stumbled out of the kitchen to turn on the Laker's basketball game. He shouted out over the television noise, "Michael, it's after eight. The winning numbers come on this channel. Everybody, get in here. Let's see if Michael is our Golden Child."

Sylvia, Michael and Michelle walked in as the winning lottery numbers were highlighted on the television screen.

Henry wrote the numbers down on a newspaper. Three, twelve, thirty-three...His mouth dropped opened as the last three numbers came up...twenty-eight, twenty, and finally, twelve again. He jumped to his feet, staring at the numbers he wrote down, and the numbers on his lottery ticket. Three times, he matched the numbers, and then, he screamed, shouted and hollered, "I won! I won! Michael, I won..."

In his excitement, Henry fell over the coffee table onto the floor, which made him giggled even more. Still overjoyed, he stumbled to his feet, danced for a minute, and then flopped down on the sofa with his hand over his heart to stop his labored breathing.

"Great Hallelujah," Henry whispered. "I won...I won!

Bewildered, Sylvia took Michelle and Michael into the kitchen. "Why did you do it, Michael? What's your father going to do with twenty-one million dollars? Michael, more important, what about your walk with God and what you kids are preparing?"

Michael remained quiet.

"I know we should be happy, but I hope he leaves on the next train to hell...no, I don't mean that. Lord, I didn't mean that," Sylvia cried out, as Michael and Michelle did their best to comfort her.

~

Henry drove up to the Mini-Mart in his pickup truck, and looked out his driver's side window at the crowd of people, police cars, and emergency vehicles in front of the store. A traffic cop waved for Henry to drive away.

"What happened? Is it a robbery?" Henry asked.

"That's what I'd call it. Move on. You're blocking traffic."

Henry parked and walked up to the police barrier and watched riot police march men and women out of the Mini-Mart. The police pushed and shoved them into a police transport bus.

A street corner preacher, wearing an old, worn out black suit, tie, and shoes, and also had a piece of white cardboard, paper-clipped to his black shirt collar, approached Henry.

"Are you saved?" the preacher asked.

"Yeah."

"How do you know you're saved?"

"I'm still alive."

"Not for long. Last night, Friday, December 14th, 2012, I received word that the children have come for only those alive in Christ. Make a donation, and I'll pray to save you from the persecution coming into the world!"

"Go away!"

The preacher looked Henry over, and then pointed at the police and the noisy crowd. "Funny, isn't it, Brother?"

Henry wanted to be left alone, but decided, he didn't really want to offend anyone on his Lucky Day, including a street-corner preacher.

"Doesn't look funny to me, Preacher"

"Not the scene. The situation. They're being arrested for stealing from God. They should have invested their money in the church! Would you like to make a small donation to the church I'm building?"

Henry looked the street-corner preacher up and down, "Perhaps some other time, Preacher Man."

"An offering will bring a blessing into your home."

Henry lifted up his winning lottery ticket as he walked off, "I'm already blessed!"

"Okay, I'll stand here and watch them drag you into the paddy wagon like all those other losers with lottery tickets."

Henry stopped, "Okay, Preacher. I got it. You think playing the Lotto is for sinners, fools and losers. Well, let me tell you something, you're **WRONG!**"

"Talk to me after you've checked your numbers. This situation is heaven sent, otherwise, how could they all have the same winning numbers?"

"What?"

"Yep! I find it hilarious, but they aren't too happy about it. Friend, no man can cheat God. You cheaters won because those children made it happen. You know, those New Children of God."

"You're lying!"

"The scandal is on all the television channels. If they're lying, they're dying. It's on them, not me. I preach nothing but Good News!"

Henry hurried off to his truck in anger.

The preacher yelled after Henry, "The time is now for sinners to repent. God is trying to tell you something! The writing is on your television screen!"

A police officer walked up, "Okay, let's move away from here!"

The preacher hollered out, "Unless you become like little children again, you won't get through the eye of the needle! The children will inherit the earth, everybody else will die in the wilderness!"

"Move on, or you'll be placed under arrest!" the police officer stated.

One by one, the bystanders moved away from the preacher. Losing his audience, the preacher waved at the officer and walked off.

~

Isaiah watched Jan Summers' 'Special News' report, "So far, over six thousand people in California have Friday night's winning lottery numbers. The results aren't all in, but according to our estimate, the twenty-one million dollar jackpot will equal out to about three thousand, five hundred dollars per winner. The cash value is a little over fifteen hundred dollars. After taxes maybe seven hundred dollars. Those dollars will drop even lower when all the tickets are counted. Needless to say, lottery players are angry!"

A video clip came on of angry protestors throwing rocks and bottles at the police. Another news clip showed an angry loser starting a fire inside a Liquor Store, and when employees confronted the firebug, a scuffle broke out as the fire burned on.

"In other news, the Wicked Nurse of Memphis, Sybil Prue has been convicted to life imprisonment for the murder of five babies at Memphis City Hospital!"

~

Henry picked up a bottle of whiskey and poured the last trickle into his glass. In a drunken stupor, he did his best to watch and listen to a reporter talking about the lottery fiasco.

"What happened in California, has caused the Lottery Games throughout America, Canada, and the world to shut down until the problem can be solved," Danny Wynn announced, from the middle of Times Square in New York City, and then he questioned a pedestrian. "Sir, what are your feelings regarding the California Lottery Crash?"

"Those children are a curse."

"What makes you think the children caused it?"

"I know. And when I know, I know!"

A woman nearby agreed, "They need to be stopped. They're going to ruin everything in the world."

A man yelled out, "Yeah, everything! Horseracing, Las Vegas, Atlantic City, sports, legal gambling… **everything!**"

"You think the children have that much power?" Danny asked, staring at the large crowd of angry protesters.

"They don't play the lottery and they stopped that!"

"They have the power!"

"The devil is using those children!"

"Our hopes and dreams are gone!"

Danny Wynn stepped away from the crowd, and spoke into the television camera, "People are blaming the Miracle Children, even though they had nothing to do with the problem. The Lottery Board has issued a statement that a computer glitch caused thousands of lottery tickets, sold between five-thirty and seven p.m. yesterday to print the same numbers. Did the children do that? I don't think so. This is Danny Wynn, hanging out in Times Square with many, New Yorkers who think they know who caused the Major Lottery Glitch in California."

~

Michael and Michelle came home and saw their mother, lying unconscious on the floor, with blood on her forehead and in her hair.

Michelle screamed, "Mommie! Mommie...!"

Michael knelt down beside his mother. He placed his hand on her head, closed his eyes and prayed, "God, heal my mother...take us out of this house..."

Henry stumbled over and jerked Michael to his feet. Michelle tried to pull Michael away from Henry's strong hands, but he shoved her to the floor. Michelle scrambled to her feet and ran out of the apartment, screaming, "Help...Help...Help me!"

As Michelle ran down the stairs, she called out to the Holy Spirit asking why something so horrible was happening to her mother and brother. Though, the Holy Spirit answered and said that the violence was in her father's spirit, she didn't hear Him, because her own images of her father beating Michael invaded her thoughts.

Back in the apartment, Michael slipped from his father's grasp, and tried to escape, but Henry tripped Michael up and fell on top of him.

Henry punched Michael in the face and blood gushed from Michael's mouth and nose. Michael cried out, and pushed, shoved and kicked at his father, but Henry stumbled to his feet, choking Michael.

"You dirty, no good devil. I know you did this to hurt me. You're not my son! You're not my son!"

Henry tossed Michael through the plate glass window, and Michael hurtled down to the concrete pavement three floors below.

Michelle ran down the stairs and out of the apartment building. She screamed at the sight of Michael's lifeless body lying on the ground. She rushed over and shook him.

"Michael, wake up. Please, Michael, wake up. We have to get away."

A neighbor quickly wrapped his arms around Michelle, and lifted her away from Michael's bloody body. She struggled to free herself, but he held her tight.

"Calm down, paramedics are on the way," the neighbor said.

Henry stumbled out of the apartment building and announced to everyone, "He...fell...it was an accident. He fell, Michelle..."

Michelle broke loose from the neighbor and ran off down the street. Tears streamed down her cheeks, as she tried to think straight, but the images of her mother and brother's body filled her mind. Then thoughts of many horrors filled her mind until finally, she stopped and prayed, "Help me, Holy Spirit. Please God, help my mother and brother!"

Immediately, the image of her church filled her mind. Wiping away her tears, she thanked God, and ran off as fast as her young legs would carry her.

~

Isaiah and Michelle hurried down the corridor of Saint Mary's Hospital and stopped at the nurse's station.

"We're here to see Michael and Sylvia Spencer," Isaiah told the nurse, who typed the names into her computer.

"Are you sure you're at the right hospital? I don't have their names in my computer?"

Michelle begged, "Please, help us. We live at Twenty Morningside Avenue."

"An ambulance was dispatched to that address. Please, have a seat in the waiting room and I'll get you some better information."

~

"Michael prayed and asked God to make everyone who played the lottery, winners. He didn't want our dad winning all the money," Michelle said.

Isaiah placed his arm around her shoulder.

"Why would God answer Michael's prayer knowing that your father would hurt him?" Isaiah asked, but she remained silent. "Why, Michelle? I don't understand!"

After a moment, she answered, "We're not to question why something bad happens."

"Why not? If the Holy Spirit is really talking to you, then there must be a reasonable answer! Why is Michael being punished when he received the numbers from the Holy Spirit? Ask the Holy Spirit that!"

"He says faith is more important than reason."

"That's an unacceptable answer. My faith has nothing to do with this!" Isaiah said. No, his faith had nothing to do with a mother and son who were beaten by a drunk, but he didn't have time to question Michelle further, because a doctor walked into the waiting room an approach them.

"I'm Doctor Norman. You must be Michelle Spencer. Your mother is in recovery. You'll be able to see her in a few minutes."

"How's her brother, Michael?" Isaiah asked.

The doctor eased Isaiah away from Michelle and said in a lowered voice, "I'm sorry. He died."

"Oh God, no!" Isaiah cried.

"I'm sorry, there was nothing we could do."

"My brother is not dead. He's asleep," Michelle said, somehow overhearing the doctor's announcement.

"Michelle, he's not in a coma. The doctors would know if that was the case," Isaiah said, as he took her into his arms.

"God can bring back the dead. We've read it in the Bible. Remember the story about the little girl who was dead, and Jesus said she was asleep?" (Matthew 9:24 KJV)

"Michelle, this isn't the same situation."

"It is the same. Let's...wake him...before it's too late!" Michelle shouted, pulling Isaiah over to Doctor Norman. "We want to see my brother."

"I'm sorry, but that won't be possible. Children aren't allowed in the morgue," Doctor Norman answered.

Michelle shrugged, and then ran off.

"Michelle, come back here!" Isaiah yelled, as he chased after her.

Michelle raced down the hospital corridor; accidentally knocking over a food cart and bumping into a Hospital Aid, who dropped the food tray he was carrying.

Seeing a sign with directions to the morgue, Michelle hurried down some stairs into the basement.

Isaiah, Doctor Norman, and now, two security guards joined the chase into the hospital basement.

Michelle charged into the morgue, and rushed about lifting up sheets on dead bodies. When she found Michael, she lifted the sheet off his face, placed her hand on his bruised forehead, and turned and stared at Isaiah, Doctor Norman, and the security guards when they rushed into the morgue.

"We need your help, Pastor Hillman!"

"Michelle, you have to understand..."

40

Michelle yelled at Isaiah, "No, you understand! God healed many children around the world. Michael is the oldest of all of us. He's our leader. Help us or leave!"

Isaiah looked at her for a moment, her words had so much power that he could only nod in agreement. He whispered to Doctor Norman, "She wants me to pray for her brother. Is it okay? We're already in here?"

Doctor Norman agreed, and motioned to the guards that the situation was under control.

"Okay, Michelle," Isaiah spoke, gently. "Doctor Norman will give us a little time to pray for Michael."

"No! First lay your hands on him. We need to do this together. You too, Doctor Norman!"

Doctor Norman nodded, and along with Isaiah, he laid his hand on Michael's body.

"Now pray with faith," Michelle instructed.

Isaiah's hand trembled as it lay on Michael's body. Michelle placed her hand over his to calm him.

"Father God, it's not by our might, nor by our power, but by your loving Spirit," Isaiah prayed, with his eyes closed and head bowed.

~

"We've just received confirmation, that Michael Spencer, the young boy who fell from his third floor window, died on the way to the hospital. Mr. Henry Spencer, the boy's father claims it was an accident, however, police have taken him into custody to answer further questions. There are many reports about children being abused by parents who thought the children caused the lottery crash. Channel Eleven News has reported many stories of children being healed, but no stories have surfaced that these children have special powers to see into the future, and get winning lottery numbers. I'm Jan Summers, stay tuned for more news at six p.m."

The television station goes to a commercial break.

"Joe, what's so special about this story that you dragged me in here to report it?" Jan asked, sharply.

"Word is that the boy was one of those Miracle Kids," Joe answered.

"And...come on, there must be more."

"Since our viewers already have your lovely face on the children's story, management wants to continue using you to report it."

"I see. Well, was he?"

Joe shrugged his shoulder, "It hasn't been confirmed. We're checking it out."

"An accident, police taking the father into custody, and children shutting down gambling. Thanks, Joe. Channel 11 is first with the news even if it hasn't been confirmed!"

"Not Channel 11, Jan, you're first with the news even if it doesn't pan out."

Joe grinned, as the rest of the television crew laughed.

~

"I know what I'm talking about, Katie. You live in Boise. It's not the same here in Burbank," Jan said, as she talked to her sister on the phone. "I'm fifty-eight years old and they want me out of here. I don't want to retire...I'm not going to let them push me out, so they're making me do this story of that boy being killed, and saying he's one of those special kids, because they know how I feel about God, churches, and religion...Katie, we were Mormons, because Mom and Dad were Mormons. You need to start thinking for yourself..."

~

"God, our pastor said that we couldn't do anything without you. Show them your power, Father God," Michelle prayed, as Isaiah fidgeted, and Doctor Norman removed his hand from Michael's body.

"Amen," Doctor Norman said. "I have to go. I'm so sorry about your brother, Michelle. I truly feel how much you loved him."

"The Holy Spirit said for you to stay! God, I trust you to wake up my brother. Pastor Hillman and Doctor Norman will never doubt your power again. Thank you, Father God! We truly love your Mighty Power of Life!!!"

Michelle backed away from Michael's body. She motioned to Isaiah and Doctor Norman to do the same. Unseen by Isaiah and Doctor Norman, a bright rainbow light appeared in the morgue. As the light faded, Michelle stared at the spiritual bodies of Christ Jesus and Michael Spencer.

"Jesus is here. He's bringing Michael back!" Michelle announced with excitement, which caused Isaiah, Doctor Norman, and a morgue attendant to look around the morgue for Jesus, but they couldn't see His Spiritual Body, towering over Michelle at a height over eight feet tall; if there were once giants in the land, Jesus was surely the tallest. The scars from His nailed crucifixion on the cross were visible on his palms, and when He touched Michelle's face, she smiled in pure joy.

Isaiah, Doctor Norman, and the attendant stared at Michelle, who had a bright, happy smile beaming from her face.

"Michelle, Dr. Norman has to leave. We have to go," Isaiah said, his spirit filled with doubt and sadness.

"Wait, stop doubting! Jesus is speaking to Michael. He's telling him to continue preparing the world for the New Day."

"Michelle! It's not real, you're hallucinating," Doctor Norman said.

"It's real. Jesus heals. It's real!" Michelle spoke out in the authority of her conviction. "Watch God's Power!"

Michael's spiritual body hovered briefly, and then disappeared into his physical body as the Spirit of Jesus, became a bright emerald light and vanished from the room. Suddenly, Michael's heart started thumping, his eyes opened, and the bruises on his face and forehead faded away.

Isaiah, Doctor Norman, and the morgue attendant, looked on in astonishment as Michael sat up and slid off the table.

Isaiah touched Michael, "Are you...alive? Talk to me."

"I'm alive," Michael grinned at Isaiah.

"Hello, Michael. I'm Doctor Norman. I'd like to check your pulse."

Michael held out his arm. The doctor felt for a pulse, and then using his stethoscope, he checked Michael's heart. He turned to Michelle and Isaiah, his voice quivering at first, but quickly became filled with joy as he announced, "It's...it's a...a miracle. He's alive!"

The attendant ran out of the morgue, shouting, "It's a miracle, I've seen it happen. The boy came back to life. A miracle right before my eyes!" A minute later, he returned with doctors, nurses, security guards and others on the hospital staff.

Everybody stared at Michael with excited wonder. They touched his body, shook his hand, and spoke to one another that Michael was indeed alive.

~

4

The Dream

The prophet that hath a dream,
let him tell a dream; and he that
hath my word, let him speak my
word faithfully. What is chaff to
the wheat? saith the Lord.
(Jeremiah 23:28 KJV)

Stationed outside the Hillman house are numerous news trucks, cameramen and television reporters.

Inside the Hillman house, Isaiah picked up the phone, quite irritated that it's the tenth time it rang in the last hour. "Hello…no, I'm sorry, the kids don't want to be interviewed. No they don't want to go on television. Thanks for calling."

Isaiah hung up the phone, but when he sat back down at the dinner table the telephone rang again.

"I'll answer it," Evelyn said.

"No, let it ring."

"Isaiah, please answer the phone," Evelyn frowned, upset about the ringing phone, her husband, and the News Crews camped outside their home.

"It'll stop, Evelyn," Isaiah said.

"You want me to answer, Pastor Hillman. It's probably for me," Michael said.

"What would you say?"

"Boo," Michael grinned.

Isaiah and Michelle laughed, and even Evelyn smiled because she agreed with Michael. She wanted to scare everybody away from her home with a powerful lightning strike. She smiled again, and then wondered if God was going to rain down fire and brimstones on the earth.

"Are you all right?" Isaiah asked.

"Yes, I'm fine." Evelyn answered.

"You were smiling like you were planning something angels would think twice about."

"It's my way to stop my heart from being troubled," Evelyn smiled, and carried Baby Paula out of the kitchen.

"Mrs. Hillman doesn't want us here," Michelle said.

"That's not true." Isaiah said, defensive, but sensing that the kids knew what was true, he relented. "Why did you say that, Michelle?"

"The Holy Spirit says you need to talk to her about being married."

"Excuse me…" Isaiah said, but before he continued the telephone rang again. He ignored the phone, but couldn't ignore what Michelle said. He wasn't sure if the Holy Spirit wanted him to talk to Evelyn about their marriage, or being married to Jesus and the church. If it was Jesus and the church…well, it was too late. He already made his decision to leave the church and move on with his plans. However, why was he straddled with Michelle and Michael? Michelle said at the hospital that Michael was the oldest Miracle Child, and their leader, and now that he's brought the kids into his home, Evelyn would have to mother them. He told himself, when he got some free time, he would talk to God about it.

"Let's get you ready for bed," Isaiah said. He walked out of the kitchen and removed a futon from a hall closet. He carried it off to Paula's bedroom, where Evelyn was preparing a bed.

"I'm feeling you're not totally in agreement with my bringing the kids into our home, but please, try not to show it in front of them."

"What did I do in front of them, Isaiah? If you want to know the truth, I think your own consciousness is troubling you about leaving the church. Especially at this time when so many children were blessed by God."

"So you're not upset about me bringing the kids home?"

"No, but I think we need to talk about it."

"Then you do have a problem with it?"

Michael and Michelle walked into the room wearing their pajamas.

Evelyn looked at the toothbrushes the kids were holding, "You should have left your toothbrushes in the bathroom."

"We didn't want them in your way," Michael said.

"I'll take them back," Isaiah said.

"No, I'll do it. Isaiah, move Paula's crib into our bedroom."

Michael and Michelle turned and stared at Evelyn. Their unblinking eyes made Evelyn shudder.

"I don't want Paula disturbing you during the night," Evelyn said.

Michelle smiled, "She's a beautiful baby. She won't disturb us."

"She will. She has a loud cry."

"Better she disturbed the kids," Isaiah joked.

"Isaiah, please, move the crib. Michelle and Michael had a long day and they need a good night's sleep."

Isaiah rolled his eyes for Michael and Michelle to see. Their muffled laughter alerted Evelyn that something happened behind her back.

"Isaiah, I know when you make funny faces behind my back!"

Isaiah sheepishly grinned, while Michelle and Michael laughed out loud.

"Look, Paula is smiling!" Michelle said, as she lifted Paula up into her arms.

Evelyn smiled, but removed Paula from Michelle, "You kids say your prayers and get ready for bed."

Michael and Michelle nodded. Later after the children were tucked in, Evelyn brought Isaiah a cup of hot tea into the study, but remained standing over him.

He looked up at her, "Everything okay?"

"You've decided you wanted to take your life on a different journey, and leave the church..."

"You agreed with me...it wasn't my decision alone. Didn't we have this same conversation five times already? Why are you bringing it up again?"

"Cameras are pointed at our home, and throughout the evening our phone didn't stop ringing. People are knocking on our door for you and the kids to heal them. Isaiah your journey now consists of turning our home into some kind of public spectacle."

"So I should have locked the kids in the church basement?"

"No, but you could have asked my feelings about it!"

"I didn't think you'd object."

"It's not a problem, but when I asked you to move Paula's crib into our bedroom, they looked at me as if I was frostbite."

"They may have sensed your fear."

"I'm not afraid of them. I just want Paula with us until other arrangements are made."

"A polite way of saying you don't want them here. You sound like a lot of other people who fear the children!"

She glared at him, "I told you, I don't fear them! But, when they leave, the News Crews leave. Honey, I'd like to remind you, that their father tried to kill Michael and his mother. If Michelle hadn't run away, who knows what he would have done to her."

"He's in jail."

"For how long? A week? Until his lawyer posts bail, or his wife refuses to press charges?"

"Stop being so worried about everything!"

"I'm not worried, but there are other Henry Spencers in the world who'll want to harm these children. You said you saw trouble ahead, and then you bring the trouble home! What's wrong with you?"

"I understand you're feeling nervous about it…but you should understand their situation."

"I understand you want to help them, because it's God's plan…"

"Pastor Hillman."

Evelyn and Isaiah looked around and saw Michelle standing in the doorway.

"Yes, Michelle, is something wrong?" Isaiah asked, embarrassed.

"Is it all right if we watch television?"

"There's nothing on television for children at this hour."

"We want to watch the news."

"No, go to bed. We'll be getting up early in the morning for my last day at the church."

"Okay," Michelle said, however, as she walked away, she stopped and smiled at Evelyn. "Don't be afraid, Mrs. Hillman, Jesus gave us new powers to walk on snakes and scorpions, and over all the powers of the enemy: (Luke 10:19 KJV) and nothing will hurt you. Don't fear, we all have new powers."

As Michelle walked off, Evelyn whispered to Isaiah, "She's eight years old and talking about having new powers! What powers is she talking about? Who gave them to her?"

"I heard her say the name, Jesus."

"I heard her, too, but don't you think you should find out the truth before they use this "New Power" and cause more trouble?"

"I'm sure she's talking about all the angels protecting the children."

"It didn't sound like that to me! Find out what she means, Isaiah!" Evelyn said, and stared at Isaiah, and hoped in her heart that he understood her new apprehensions.

"I'll talk to them in the morning. Is that okay with you?"

"Fine," Evelyn said, as she walked out of the study, her hands trembling. She took a deep breath and leaned against the hallway wall. It didn't take long before tears formed in her eyes. These new powers, Michelle talked about troubled her spirit. Why was God using her home as a safe house? She understood Isaiah taking them in, because, he always talked about wanting to help children, and that was his main reason for leaving the church, but now that God answered Isaiah's dream, she felt alone, and had a selfish feeling that she lost him to the children. She then told herself to get a better attitude. God was planning something beautiful for the world, and Isaiah and herself played an important role in it. Realizing this, she wiped away her tears, and decided to watch, wait, and see what this New Day was all about.

~

"For God so loved the world, that he gave his only begotten Son, that whosoever believeth in him should not perish, but have everlasting life. John 3:16," Isaiah preached, as he looked out at the overcrowded church, full of members, visitors and media persons. "Today, Sunday, December 16ᵗʰ, 2012, that Son is still, Jesus! And Our God, loved us so much, His Spirit filled the hearts of Abraham, Isaac and Jacob. God's love for us anointed preachers, teachers, messengers and prophets to speak to His children. First Kings in the Bible reveals the life of the prophet Elijah, who performed countless signs, wonders and miracles during his lifetime. In Second Kings, when Elijah came to the end of his days, he spoke to his servant, Elisha: "Ask what shall I do for thee, before I be taken away!" (2Kings2:9KJV) Elisha requested a double portion of Elijah's spirit, (2Kings2:11) and when Elijah was taken up in a whirlwind to heaven, Elisha was given that double portion of Elijah's anointed spirit. Elisha then performed twice the amount of the miracles Elijah had performed. And Elisha did them all with God's blessing."

Isaiah stared out at the congregation and the news media with their cameras. There's complete silence in the church.

"I'm sensing my sermon has put my six-month-old daughter and all of you to sleep. Make some noise to let me know you're still alive up in here!"

The congregation laughed and shouted out to Isaiah.

"We're alive, Pastor!"

"Tell us what you know?"

"What are the children preparing?"

Isaiah nodded, "Thank you. Today that question resounds in all our hearts. What are the Miracle Children preparing the world for? I'll get to that in a minute. I was speaking on Elisha's double portion. The special anointing poured out on him, awakened my own spirit since the Miracle Children have been revealed to the world. The anointing of Elisha rings many bells in my mind? Bell number one; when Elisha died, why did he take his anointing to the grave with

51

him? Bell two, why didn't he pass it on as Elijah did for him? Bell three, why did...?"

Samuel, a member of the congregation, yelled out, "Tell us why? Bells are now ringing in my head!"

Laughter filled the church. Even Isaiah broke out laughing.

"I'm getting to why, Samuel. But it's my last sermon at Victory Union Church, so I want to preach for a few more hours."

There's more laughter, but everyone was anxiously anticipating the answers to Isaiah's questions.

Isaiah continued, "Yes, Elisha was a great prophet, but the question that still rattles my brain is why did he take his great anointing to the grave with him? We know he took it there, because in Second Kings 13:21, some soldiers dropped a dead man on Elisha's bones, and the dead man immediately came back to life. Now that's a powerful anointing wasting away in a tomb! Was there no one else in the world he could pass it on to? The answer is, YES! The morning the children were being blessed, a dream woke me up. I didn't know what it meant at the time, but now I know that it was a revelation. God had a special plan for Elisha's double spirit, and we see God's plan coming together in our world today. In my dream, by the Grace of God, I had a vision of three rainbows of light circling the earth. The rainbows were a reflection of God's special jewels in the earth, His children. Each and everyone of you are precious seeds, jewels in God's eyes, and on Wednesday morning, December 12th, 2012, I saw Elijah's single anointing, and Elisha's double-portion anointing being imbued into the spirits of the Miracle Children."

Murmurs of voices echoed throughout the church. Isaiah held up his hands for silence.

"Stay with me, I know this sounds simple, crazy...weird... but I've been thinking about it for while, and it appears that God has placed a triple anointing on, **One million, five hundred and fourteen thousand, Miracle Children around the world!"**

Many in the church gasped, while others shouted out praises, "Glory to the Lord!...Jesus Saves!...Hallelujah!"

Isaiah's powerful voice thundered throughout the church, "God poured out the triple anointing on the children for a special reason! The children will become great teachers, preachers, doctors, scientists, adventurers, artists, and world leaders. God has blessed all the people of the earth with the potential to fulfill great purposes. However, God placed into the spirits of these special children, a knowing that their first mission is to prepare mankind for a **New Life! A New Beginning!! A New Day!!!"**

The piano player pounded the piano keys as Isaiah's words took his congregation up to a Higher Level.

"A New Day, that God and his Miracle Children will bring us into, whether we like it or not!"

The piano man caused a thunderous roar of excitement throughout the church, by once again pounding the piano keys.

"Yes, I said whether we like it or not! This New Day will come upon us regardless of our hatreds, envies, and jealousies. When God opens a door, no man... let me say this stronger, ***When God Opens A Door, No Man Can Close It!"*** (Revelation 3:8)

Tears rolled down the faces of many parishioners as Isaiah preached about the Miracle Children.

"To open our eyes, the Miracle Children received the same Pentecostal blessing of the Holy Spirit, that the disciples received seven weeks after the Resurrection of Christ Jesus. (Acts 2:1 NLT) The windows of heaven are open today. God is watching us! Jesus is watching! The angels are watching! The prophets are watching! The eyes of our ancestors are watching!

The New Day is coming upon us, so we have to step out of our own self-importance and wash our spirits in the blood of our Savior, Jesus the Christ. The Miracle Children have lifted their hearts up to God, so now it's our time to follow their rainbow lighted path, and open up our hearts to the Lord. Now, that the doors and windows of heaven are open, let's pray, that the New Day the Miracle Children are preparing for the world, will bring great peace, love and joy into our lives!"

The small church band played loud and strong, which excited the congregation to shout, dance, and joyfully celebrate of the New Day coming into the World.

Afterwards, a crowd gathered around Isaiah, Evelyn, Michael and Michelle as they stood at the church altar.

"A wonderful sermon, Pastor Hillman. Overflowing with new understanding. Just wonderful!"

"Thank you, Doris."

"Too bad the rest of the world didn't have a chance to hear you!" an older man said.

Isaiah laughed, "Well, Mr. Wilburn, they can hear you. Go out and spread the word."

"I will. Your dream was full of great revelations."

"So it was to me, too. But remember, Mr. Wilburn, God still conceals his true plans in mystery. Not everyone wants a truthful relationship with God."

A woman held Isaiah's hands in hers, "You're so right, Pastor Hillman. We accept bad relationships, and then we wonder why our life ends up in hell." She turned and spoke to Evelyn. "You must be thanking God everyday for all the blessings being brought into your home."

Evelyn smiled, shook the woman's hand, but remained silent.

Everyone was filled with joy as they exited the church.

"I'm impressed," Evelyn admitted. "You never told me you had that dream."

"I know how much you like the unexpected. The unknown," Isaiah laughed, handed his papers to Michael, and picked up Paula in the bassinet. He wrapped his arm around Evelyn's shoulder and walked with her out of the church.

A crowd of news media reporters and cameramen converged on Isaiah and Michael, and in the melee, Evelyn and Michelle were pushed aside.

"Michael, what was your death experience like?"

"Did you have an out-of-body experience?"

"Pastor Hillman, you were in the morgue when the miracle happened. What was that like?"

"Michael, tell us about the New World!"

Isaiah pushed through the crowd with Evelyn and the kids close behind, "I've said what was needed inside the church. I have no further comments. Neither does Michael."

"Why are you keeping the world from this news?"

"I'm trying to protect my family from being shoved around. Let us pass, please!"

The reporters and cameramen made a path for Isaiah and his family to get to the church van.

~

"Pastor Hillman," a woman's voice called out, when Isaiah arrived at his home and stepped out of the church van.

Isaiah, Evelyn and the kids turned and recognized the host of 'Talking with Jan,' Jan Summers. She's with Brian, her cameraman.

"Hi, I'm Jan Summers."

"Yes, I know. Ms. Summers, we've had many news crews camping out at our home. Perhaps, because it's Sunday, they've given us a day of rest. In other words, we're happy they've left, so I'll pray you'll do the same."

"Sorry, of course we will. I just wanted to offer you an opportunity to come on my show," Jan answered, as she shook hands with everyone, but when she came to Michael, she smiled, "Hi Michael, everybody's talking about your miraculous life and death experience."

"I know," Michael said.

"Ms. Summers, please honor our privacy," Isaiah frowned.

"Again, I'm sorry. Brian, turn off the camera. Pastor Hillman, I'm sure you know that none of the children are talking to the media. Come on the show and speak on their behalf."

"Like you, I have no idea what's going on, so speaking for the children would come from ignorance."

"You sounded pretty sure of your message today. Was it inspired from the heavens, or was your dream something you thought up to get your congregation dancing?"

"Excuse me, we need to feed the children." Isaiah smiled, and walked away, followed by Evelyn and the children.

"Pastor Hillman...The children are in danger!" Jan said.

Evelyn turned and looked at Jan.

Jan talked fast, knowing she had Evelyn's attention, "The Bible talks about a land of milk and honey, but that land is not here in America. Not now, and I'm guessing it won't be here tomorrow. The world needs to hear from someone with wisdom and understanding. Some common sense, otherwise, television news producers will put on a lot more commentators, talking heads, and religious fanatics wanting to push their personal spin on the children's mission. Judging from what's going on in the world today, this isn't a time for more fools and foolishness!"

Isaiah looked at Michael and Michelle, but they remained silent.

"Do it, Isaiah," Evelyn whispered to Isaiah. "Tell the world about your dream. It'll help a lot of people understand."

Isaiah whispered back, "It's well known she's an atheist."

"So what? You're leaving the church. What does that make you?"

"I'm never going to hear the end of this, am I?"

"Not while I'm alive," Evelyn smiled.

"Pastor Hillman," Jan said. "You're in a position to be a part of the children's preparations. Think about it, you said there were one million, five hundred and fourteen thousand children, and you've become a significant part of their preparation. You saw Michael come back to life, right?"

Isaiah remained closed mouth.

"Ahhh...I hear you're quitting the church. Are you also going to turn your back on this wonderful opportunity? Are you going to quit the children, too?"

After a long pause, Isaiah reluctantly nodded, "I'll do your show."

"I'll get my producer to send out a press release that you'll be speaking about the children on my show. You've mentioned that you have to feed the children, please join Brian and me for lunch. The children can play games at the restaurant's amusement center, and we can talk about the show and get to know one another. I promise, Brian won't invade your privacy with his camera, and Mrs. Hillman, you won't have to cook."

"I'm sold, how about you, Isaiah?" Evelyn said.

"The news media will be all over Michael," Isaiah said.

"I'm sure media people are enjoying brunch right now, but they'll be arriving here soon. We leave, and they'll be left here all alone. Come on, get back at them for disturbing your peace," Jan cajoled, walking Evelyn over to her car.

~

"I like Jan Summers, she's quite friendly and knowledgeable. It was a nice of her to invite us here," Evelyn said, as she sipped her lemonade and watched Michael and Michelle sitting on a bench in the amusement center.

"When she didn't get a news exclusive from Michael or Michelle, she left. What's nice about that?" Isaiah said.

"You can't blame her. They wouldn't answer her questions, or talk about what they were preparing. Look at them; they just sit there staring off into space. You think they're making plans to blow up the world?"

"Probably," Isaiah laughed.

"I don't understand. They don't play. They don't answer questions, or do anything different or special. How is that making preparations to change the world?"

"The Holy Spirit talks to them, so I guess they have to be quiet to hear."

"Why don't you ask some questions?"

"Why don't you?" Isaiah said, amused.

"You're right, we best not go where angels fear to tread."

"But, you want to know what's going on, but only if you can find out by getting me to question them, and then freeing yourself of any responsibility of getting me thrown into the hellfire with the rest of the world?"

"That sounds reasonable," Evelyn laughed.

Isaiah took her hand in his as he called out, "Michael, Michelle, come over here."

Michael and Michelle walked over and sat down at the table.

"Were you guys talking with the Holy Spirit?"

"Why," Michael and Michelle answered together.

"I'd like to know if the Holy Spirit has any suggestions about what I should say on Jan Summers' television show?"

"Why don't you ask him?" Michelle said.

"You guys have the ears to hear, remember?

"We're children, not private detectives," Michael joked.

"Very funny, Michael. Michelle what should I say on the show?"

"I'd suggest you talk about your dream," Michelle answered.

"Is that it?" Isaiah asked.

"Pastor Hillman, if you don't want to talk about your dream, then ask the Holy Spirit for your message, not us," Michael said, amused that the Holy Spirit wanted him to push Isaiah to start listening.

"I don't think the ex-Pastor, Isaiah Hillman is standing on firm, sacred ground with the Holy Spirit right now," Evelyn said, now also amused.

"Evelyn, have I ever told you that you have such a lovely way with words. Okay, never mind, I'll get in touch with the Holy Spirit, and I'll get my own answers. You all will hear what I've found out on Jan Summers' special interview with the ex-pastor, Mr. Isaiah Hillman," Isaiah said, and walked off to the restroom.

"What chance does he have that the Holy Spirit will respond to him?" Evelyn asked.

"The Holy Spirit will answer, but Pastor Hillman won't hear," Michael said.

"Why won't he hear?"

"He doesn't listen."

"Now that's a true statement, though we all have our own thoughts getting in the way of our hearing," Evelyn said.

"We don't," Michelle announced.

"You don't have your own thoughts?"

"They don't get in our way."

Evelyn sat in silence as she wondered what Michelle meant. Didn't they think for themselves? If their minds were being controlled, even spiritually, she knew that would be dangerous. What if one child rebelled, and used this new power Michelle talked about for evil purposes?

"Mrs. Hillman, the Holy Spirit said for you to stop creating worries you don't want to deal with."

"I'll deal with them," Evelyn said, but as she prepared to leave, more worried thoughts invaded her mind as to why the Holy Spirit shared her personal thoughts with Michelle, and why didn't God forewarn the world about the children, and why didn't she feel at peace with what was being prepared for the world? She wondered, where was Jesus in all this? She knew the Holy Spirit was the Comforter, and was the one talking to the children, but where was Jesus? Jesus knew how to talk to people, and as her mind raced on, fear took over, and her thoughts became filled with life on earth coming to its end. She stopped, and told herself not to let her heart be troubled, because God was preparing something beautiful and wonderful for the world, and she'd just have to keep the faith to find out what it was. Saying that, she felt a peace coming into her heart. She then prayed, that the peace would last forever, and even though some new worries tried to fill her thoughts, she remained steadfast to not let her heart be troubled.

~

"I'm going shopping. I know what Isaiah and Paula like, but is there anything special you want?" Evelyn asked, with pen and paper in her hand.

"I'd like an orange," Michael said.

"One orange?"

"That's all. One orange."

"How about you, Michelle? You want an orange, too?

"No, I want a flower."

"One of these days, I'm going to get all the pieces of the puzzle you two enjoy creating," Evelyn said, she looked at Isaiah, but he shook his head in bewilderment, so she walked out of the room talking to herself, "One orange. One flower. One orange, one flower…"

Isaiah looked at Michael and Michelle, "What's with the orange and flower?"

"She asked us what we wanted. It's what we want," Michelle answered.

Isaiah knew it must be for something special, so he questioned Michael, "Why one orange, and one flower?"

"We didn't want bicycles!"

Michelle laughed, but quickly became serious, "Michael, stop joking…Pastor Hillman, you'll understand later why we asked for the orange and flower."

"Then it is a puzzle!" Isaiah said.

"No, it's something our mother needs. She doesn't need a bicycle," Michael joked.

Isaiah, annoyed with Michael's smugness, turned and looked at Paula, "Watching Paula, I get the feeling she knows what's coming into the world. Is she a Miracle Child?"

Michelle looked to Michael. He remained silent, so she did the same.

"Okay, I understand you can't talk about it. Perhaps you can wink, or do something to show me whether Paula is a Miracle Child. Come on, I really want to know. I won't tell Mrs. Hillman."

Michael saw Paula's baby rattle on the coffee table. He picked it up and handed it to Paula, who then shook the rattle to Michael and Michelle's hand clapping. Soon, Paula shakes the rattle faster and faster, causing Michael and Michelle's praise dance to pick up speed. The three children became so absorbed in their spirit, that their joy, rapture and wild abandonment gave Isaiah true a vision of their spiritual freedom.

"Wow!" Isaiah said, as he watched wide-eyed for a moment, and then removed the rattle from Paula's clenched fist. Michelle and Michael stopped their dance, while Isaiah lifted Paula out of the playpen and stared into her eyes. Paula smiled.

~

Sylvia sat up in her hospital bed and sniffed a yellow rose. "It smells so beautiful. Thank you, Michelle."

Michael handed his mother a slice of orange.

"Hmmn, what a wonderful taste."

Michelle kissed her mother, "The orange and flower are blessed to heal your body, mind and spirit."

"You'll hear and see clearer if you don't go backwards," Michael warned.

"Backwards?" Sylvia asked, as Michael and Michelle sensed Henry's spirit in the area, and at that exact moment, Henry entered the room with a dozen red roses, a box of chocolates, and a large teddy bear that he handed to Sylvia.

Isaiah walked into the room and saw Henry. There was a momentary silence as the two men stared at each other.

"Michael, Michelle, its time to go. Tell your mother goodbye.

"So you're the preacher?" Henry asked.

"Yes, I am Isaiah Hillman."

"I wasn't sure it was you. Thanks for taking care of my kids, but they can come home with me now." Henry took his wife's hand in his, "Honey, I promise, I'll never hurt you or the kids again. No more drinking, I promise. It's going to be like when we first met."

Michael walked out of the room, but as Michelle tried to leave, Henry grabbed her wrist. She touched Henry's hand, and he immediately jerked his hand away, and stared at the burnt skin on the back of his hand!

"Michelle, you burnt my hand!" Henry said, a little scared, but he calmly tried to grab her wrist again.

"Jehovah Koah!" Michelle yelled.

Henry's body is flung backwards. The force caused him to crash into a window. The glass shattered, but Isaiah grabbed Henry a second before he's about to tumbled out of the window.

Isaiah screamed, "Michelle, what's come over you?"

Michelle walked out of the room as two nurses rushed in, and attended to the bleeding scrapes and scratches on Henry's arms.

"Kids, I'm sorry...come back home," Henry called out, and when he slumped down on the edge of the bed, Sylvia's hand reached out and touched him.

"I'm sorry, Sylvia. I really messed up this time," Henry moaned.

"Henry, it's okay, I understand. It was a lot of money to lose."

Embarrassed by what he saw and heard, Isaiah hurried out the room and ran up to Michelle and Michael in the hospital corridor.

"You could have killed him! What were you trying to do?"

"I wanted to show him that our power will protect us, but I didn't know he would be moved that far."

"Because you don't know what you're doing. I don't want you to use that power again. You hear me?"

"Our words have the power to protect us. Michelle didn't do anything wrong," Michael said.

"Protect you! Nothing wrong? Michael, you didn't see what she did. If anyone finds out what she did it'll only cause more trouble. The world will turn on you, and believe me it will destroy you. I know more about people and this world…"

"Pastor Hillman, why do you keep forgetting God's power over life and death?"

"So you can't be destroyed…killed?"

"We won't be stopped!" Michael answered, with finality.

Isaiah stared long and hard at Michael, "What kind of new world will this be if you're willing to kill people to make it happen?"

"It'll be a world being prepared for the New Day. Jesus died to save us. He won't die again," Michael answered, took Michelle's hand, and they walked off together.

Isaiah whispered, "God, I'm not sure I liked that answer. What about you, God? Are you in agreement with Michael?"

No response came to Isaiah.

"Does anybody hear me? Jesus! Holy Spirit! I need to have some answers. Hello!"

Silence.

Isaiah knew the children told him to listen, and he did his best to listen, but he didn't hear anything. Matter of fact, he only heard his own thoughts, so he told himself he needed time to be still, contemplate, and pull wisdom from his sub-conscious to conscious mind…no, he needed time to rest, meditate, think, pray, and read the Bible. He needed time to work everything out, but time was moving too fast for him to keep up.

"I need help, Father God, Christ Jesus, Holy Spirit…I need help!" Isaiah called out, and rushed off to catch up with Michael and Michelle, while at the same time, he promised himself he would take the time in prayer, to listen.

~

"No, Isaiah! Hell no!"

Isaiah reached over and locked the bathroom door. "Lower your voice the children will hear you."

Evelyn yelled, "I'll lower my voice when you understand me! She can't stay here! I had a few doubts about the children staying here, but I've accepted it as the will of God and your desire to work with children. Now you want to move their mother into our home? No, No, No!"

"Evelyn, listen. Henry is staying in the apartment and Michael doesn't want his mother to go there. I've spoken to Henry and he's agreed to spiritual counseling."

"Put her in a hotel. House her at the church!"

"My pastoral duties are coming to an end, and you know we can't afford a hotel for them."

"Doesn't she have a family somewhere? Send her there. Put her in an Abused Women's Shelter."

"They should stay together as a family."

"She can take her children with her. They allow children in shelters."

"Evelyn, be reasonable."

"No, you be reasonable! You want to keep their family together and break up ours. Those kids don't trust their father and neither do I. Who knows when he'll go crazy again and come into our home in one of his drunken rages. I'm sorry, but I don't feel comfortable about this. I'm scared about the future problems this might cause, so please don't bring more trouble into our home. I'm sorry, Isaiah. You move her in here, Paula and I will have to leave. I'm worried about this house being a safe place for us!"

Evelyn walked out of the bathroom disappointed and sad.

~

"Are you okay?" Isaiah asked, when he walked into the bedroom and sat down next to Evelyn.

"My decision is made."

"I know."

"You're bringing trouble into our home."

"Evelyn, I'm their pastor."

"Oh, so now you're a pastor again? You're confusing me with your off and on ministry!"

"Honey, I want to see this through. I'm not going to abandon them now. I saw God's power bring Michael back to life. I can't act as if it didn't happen. Trust doesn't come easily to them, but Michelle came to me when the trouble started. They trust me, and God has placed them into our care."

"Your care. Paula will be in my care...Isaiah, try to understand. I watch the news shows and there's a great fear regarding what the children are bringing into the world."

"Who cares what the world fears? I fear God's wrath if we throw them out! Haven't you learn to trust God's decisions? You're married with Jesus, so you should know his power! Why have you become so obstinate, so uncaring? What's happened to you?"

"Your spirit sees God's Glory coming into the earth. I see evil forces mounting up against God, the children, and you for getting involved!"

"I don't deny the evil. Michael's father is a prime example of anger out of control. I also know the children have power to fight the evil forces."

"What? You saw their powers!"

Isaiah realized that he spoke without thinking. He took a deep breath, and readied himself to change the subject about what he witnessed.

"They really have powers? Oh God, what's going to happen?"

"I don't know. Sweetheart, I told you I wanted to help children when I left the ministry. You agreed and wanted to be involved."

"I didn't know it would be like this. I didn't know it would be the children over our family," Evelyn cried, and when he put his arm around her, she cried even more.

The next morning, Evelyn cooked pancakes for Isaiah and the children. Michael hung up the phone and sat down at the table.

"What did your mother say, Michael?" Evelyn asked.

"She's happy and getting out of the hospital tomorrow."

"Is she going home to be with your father?"

"Evelyn, let the boy enjoy his breakfast," Isaiah insisted.

"She's going back home. I'm going back too. I need to be with her," Michael said.

"I'll pack our things," Michelle said, as Michael and her rose up from the table.

"Sit back down! You're in my care and you'll stay here. I'll talk to your parents. They need some time away from each other," Isaiah said, his stern voice declared his charge and control over the situation.

Evelyn glared at Isaiah, "Where will their mother stay?"

"Here with her kids!"

Evelyn walked out of the kitchen, her thoughts expressing her hurt and disappointment. She knew in her heart, Isaiah was right in what he was doing, but no matter how many times she prayed to support his decisions, she couldn't shake the horrible thoughts that crowded her spirit. Trouble was ahead and she knew it. She then reminded herself she was married to Jesus, and she had to trust Him. She spoke out in prayer, "Jesus, your peace you leave with me, your peace you give to me: not the peace the world gives, you give to me. I won't let not my heart be troubled, neither will it be afraid." (John 14:17)

After saying her prayer, Evelyn knew Jesus was with her, because Jesus spoke into her spirit, telling her to stop blocking God's plans. Yes, she had to guard her heart, something she could control, but let Father God control everything outside her spirit. She had to get out of the Holy Spirit's way, and let God's preparation for Isaiah and the Miracle Children become fulfilled. Wiping tears from her eyes, she thanked Jesus, and prayed for God to hurry up in preparing the world for His New Day. She then entered the bedroom and started packing.

Meanwhile, in the kitchen, Michael, wanting to be at the apartment when his mother came home, spoke up, "We have to leave, Pastor Hillman."

"The decision isn't yours to make. You're still a child. Eat your breakfast and respect my wishes," Isaiah said, and doing his best to stay in faith, he silently prayed for God to save his marriage. He didn't want to care for the children on his own, but if Evelyn was so convinced that trouble was coming into their home, he agreed with her to take Paula to a safe place.

"Pastor Hillman, the Holy Spirit will guide, provide, protect and direct all our lives," Michael announced.

Michelle added, "Let your faith trust God. He knows the beginning and the end."

Smiling, Isaiah hugs Michael and Michelle, "Thanks, I needed that. Your wisdom will surely be a blessing for the whole world."

"It's not our wisdom, it's the Holy Spirit," Michael said.

Isaiah nods in agreement.

~

5

Power

**The truth is, anyone who believes
in me will do the same works I
have done, and even greater works,
because I am going to be with the
Father.** John 14:12 NLT

It's snowing in Philadelphia, as two bank robbers, seventeen-
year-old, Streetlife, and his fifteen-year-old brother, Jovan,
ran out of a bank as the alarm blared. A security guard
chased after them, firing several shots. Pedestrians ran
and ducked behind cars, as Streetlife and Jovan blasted off
rounds from their guns. The guard is shot, but as he fell to
the ground, he fired off a final round.

Jovan dropped the canvas bag of cash, stared at the
blood under his overcoat, and cried, "Streetlife, I'm shot.
I'm bleeding…"

Streetlife fired off a number of rounds, and one of
his bullets ricocheted off a building and pierced the neck
of a little girl. The girl toppled slowly into her mother's
arms.

"Vanessa...Oh my God! My daughter is shot, help!" Vanessa's mother shouted and screamed as she held her hand over her daughter's neck to stop the blood flow. "Help, help, my daughter's been shot. Somebody help my daughter!"

Streetlife ran over and grabbed the canvas bag of money.

"Jovan, let's go. Run to the car!"

Jovan painfully crawled on the ground to follow after his brother, but unable to continue, he started weeping.

Streetlife stopped, and ran back to help his brother, but at that moment, two police cars with sirens wailing converged on the area. Streetlife stood in the middle of the street and dropped his gun to the ground; he then put his hands on his head and knelt down.

Paramedics attended to the bank guard and the little girl, while Jovan squirmed in the snow in a pool of his blood, as three police officers stood over him with their guns drawn.

Handcuffed, Streetlife yelled out, "Somebody help my brother. Help my brother!"

A mother said to her eleven-year-old son, "Akeem, go help those people."

Akeem walked over and knelt next to the paramedic that was helping Vanessa.

The paramedic hollered to a police officer, "Get this kid out of here!"

A police officer grabbed Akeem's arm, but the officer jerked his hand away when a minor electrical shock ran through his body.

"It's okay, we have power from Jesus," Akeem informed the paramedic and officer. The paramedic nodded, and watched as Akeem removed the bandage from Vanessa's neck. He placed his hand over her wound, closed his eyes, and prayed in tongues, "Jehovah Koah, thelema, Jehovah Koah, thelema..."

As Akeem prayed, the bullet that was in Vanessa's neck was drawn out and into his hand. He handed the bullet to the open-mouthed paramedic, and then placed his hand over Vanessa's wound, and as he spoke in tongues again, a white light, unseen by the paramedic and the police officer, flowed out of his hand and miraculously healed her wound.

Vanessa sat up and smiled as her mother cried out, "Thank you, Jesus. Thank you for your Miracle Children!"

Akeem walked over to the security guard and placed his hand over the guard's shoulder wound until the bullet was in his hand. Once again, he prayed in tongues, "Jehovah Koah, thelema," and as before, the white light flowed from his hand and caused another miracle healing.

A police officer handed Akeem a wet towel to wipe the blood off his hands.

The security guard shook Akeem's hand, "Thank you, young man."

"Thank God. He worked His power through me."

"Thank you, God, heaven...thank everybody!"

Akeem laughed and walked back to his mother, who hugged and kissed him as television news reporters captured everything on film.

"What about my brother? Do something for him!" Streetlife hollered out to Akeem.

A bystander yelled out, "Let him die!"

"Yeah, let him die," hollered another bystander.

Akeem walked on with his mother.

"You're gonna let him die! God have mercy on my little brother!" Streetlife yelled.

Akeem's mother stopped and spoke to him. Akeem shook his head in a negative manner that he was against helping the bank robber.

"You do as I say, Akeem. You go back there and help that boy!" the mother scolded. Akeem resisted at first, but reluctantly, walked over to Jovan, knelt at his side, and though he spoke in tongues and removed the bullet, he didn't heal the wound like he did for Vanessa and the security guard.

"God loves you, but He doesn't like what you and your brother have done. You understand?" Akeem asked, and Jovan nodded he understood.

"Good, your body will heal if you turn your life to Jesus. If you don't, the sin in your spirit will kill you!" (Romans 6:23) Akeem said, with spiritual authority and knowledge.

Akeem left Jovan in the care of the paramedic. A few people in the crowd clapped their hands, as news reporters ran up and talked to Akeem and his mother.

～

Jan Summers is 'ON THE AIR' with Isaiah.

"Pastor Hillman, everyone is talking about that incident in Philadelphia yesterday."

"And they should be talking about it. God performed some great miracles through that boy, Akeem Wallace."

"However, without his mother's insistence, he would have let that boy, Jovan Sullivan die. And Akeem only removed the bullet, he didn't heal him like the others."

"Jovan Sullivan committed a crime."

"So these children are judge and jury over our lives?"

"I didn't say that."

"He didn't want to save him. He was willing to let him die."

"The paramedic was helping the boy, and perhaps, Akeem knew the boy didn't have a bright future, or a miracle healing wouldn't heal his spirit."

"So let him die?"

"I don't think what the children are preparing the world for...will be full of...how shall I say this; I don't think sin will be tolerated."

"Now I'm surprised. I don't know why Akeem didn't want to help that kid, but you being a pastor, aren't you supposed to be forgiving sin?"

"No, the truth is that when you accept Christ Jesus as your Lord and Savior, your sins are forgiven because of his blood sacrifice on the cross. Pastors teach about sin and how sins are forgiven in Christ. It's up to you to accept or reject."

"Okay, sins are forgiven if you want to accept theological understandings, but wasn't Jesus about saving lives? Akeem Wallace was not interested in saving that boy's life."

"I can't speak for Akeem, but I'll say the church is about teaching people how to be saved. Sadly, the world isn't."

"What do you mean by that?"

"We live in a world where neighborhood gangs kill for the silliest of reasons, where our government kills with capital punishments, we allow Third World babies to starve to death, though there's warehouses full of food stored up in fear it'll run out, and let's not forget mercy killings, wars, abortions..."

"We don't have enough time to discuss all that in this program."

"My point exactly. You don't even want to talk about it for fear you'll upset your sponsors, or some other group. Let's not hide our heads in the sand. We're living in evil times and terrorist bombings are occurring all around the world. Today, God is speaking to the world through the Miracle Children, and I'm sure everyone has heard that the children were told by God to prepare the world for something new!"

"I've heard new revival...new start...new beginning. The children are confusing everyone."

"It's not the children's fault that the words being translated are confusing to some people, but most of us realize that the children are all saying the same thing. In Genesis, which is about the beginning of life in the Holy Bible, the scriptures revealed a truth about people, speaking a single language, building the Tower of Babel. (Genesis11) They became so absorbed in their own greatness that they dismissed their relationship with God. God knew that they were being led astray by their own self-importance, so he confused their language so they wouldn't be able to understand each other. The Miracle Children don't have that language barrier with the Holy Spirit, and neither will we if we change our minds and renew our relationship with God."

"The children told you that?"

"No, God told us that. It's written in the Bible. Genesis also tells the story about Adam losing his relationship with God, and the rest of the Bible speaks about prophets trying to get people to renew that relationship. A relationship you have the choice to accept or reject. The Miracle Children listened, and accepted the voice as truth. Now it's time for people to make a choice."

"Make a choice because some children hear a strange voice? You'll have to give people something more than some old stories! Tell me, how will children stop terrorism, evil forces, and whatever else that needs to be done to change our world?"

"God's Grace is still in the world, and in the scripture, Ephesians Six, it calls for us to put on the whole armor of God to resist the devil's tricks. (11 KJV)) We're not fighting against flesh and blood, but against evil rulers, against mighty powers of darkness that rule this world and against wicked spirits in high places. (12) Put on God's armor and you'll be able to stop the fiery arrows aimed at you by Satan.

(16) The children are wearing that armor, and that's how they'll fight evil. That's how they'll still be standing after the battle is over. I can go on and on, and even though it's the truth, it'll only sound like preaching to unbelievers."

"Why children? Why is God using children?"

"I've asked myself the same question, and then I've searched the Bible for an answer. Now, what I'm about to say isn't going to fill your audience with joy, so perhaps, if somebody doesn't like what I'm about to say, they have the right to turn off their televisions."

"My audience members are adults, and I'm sure they'll want to know what you've discovered."

"Okay...I've read that children are the sources of over eighteen hundred verses in the Bible. In Isaiah 3:2-3, God said he will destroy the entire nation of leaders, the heroes, soldiers, judges, prophets, diviners, skilled magicians, and expert enchanters. In verse 4, God says he will appoint children to rule over them, and anarchy will prevail. Going to Isaiah 44, verses 18 and 19, God says... "Remember ye not the former things, neither consider the things of old. Behold, I will do a new thing; now it shall spring forth; shall ye not know it? I will even make a way in the wilderness, and river in the desert." Miss Summers, it seems to me that God has a problem with the old ways and people who put themselves first. It also seems God has a great love for children and new, younger visions!"

"Interesting, but do those scriptures really mean children, or is it about the men and women that the Bible calls, Children of God?"

"If you look around the world you'll see that the Miracle Children are not men and women, they're children!

Jan nodded, but she knew Isaiah was the same as all the other preachers who used age-old scriptures, because they had no real answers for life in the Twenty-First Century.

"Pastor Hillman, please talk about your dream and the prophets."

"Prophets Elijah and Elisha!"

"Yes, them. Tell everybody about the dream you had about the triple anointing being placed on the Miracle Children."

Isaiah turned from Jan and spoke into the television camera, "My dream was the very morning of the children's anointing. An anointing is a Holy Consecration to make something sacred..."

~

Evelyn sat with her parents, Richard and Thelma Downing in their living room filled with old-fashioned, antique furniture and oil paintings of peaceful landscapes.

"Is Isaiah saying God is going to use children to destroy everybody?" Thelma asked.

"He's saying the children are being used to wake up the world before it's too late," Richard answered.

"Well, I don't like God using children to wake up the world, either," Thelma countered.

Richard pointed his finger at Thelma, "Who then? The President. Who, the Congress, businessmen, lawyers? Ha! Thelma, get real!

"Richard, my comment wasn't open for argument. I was stating my opinion that it's wrong to use the children!"

"Thelma, God doesn't do wrong. A few weeks ago they were normal children, and then, suddenly, a bolt of lightning hits them, and they've become a light out of darkness. Imagine being hit by lightning. It's a miracle those children are still able to feed themselves."

"What you've just said has nothing to do with anything. Absolutely nothing!" Thelma scoffed, and turned her attention to Evelyn. "Would you want Baby Paula to be one of those kids?"

"It would be such a blessing, but she's to young to understand."

"I agree, but you do understand all the evil Isaiah is talking about will soon come down on those children! People killed Jesus, and they'll have no problem finding a reason to kill children who think they're above everybody else. I see it coming."

Evelyn and Richard stared at Thelma.

Thelma nodded, "I do. I see it coming. Am I the only one who sees the future?"

Richard responded, "Thelma, I hope you see Isaiah wearing a Superman costume in your crystal ball, because he's living with two of those children you see being hunted down and killed!"

Tears gathered in Evelyn's eyes.

"Don't worry, sweetheart. I was just joking," Richard said. "Isaiah and the children will be fine. Just fine. God protects his own."

~

"Pastor Hillman, you have taken two of the children, Michael and Michelle Spencer into your home. Michael is the boy who was in the morgue and came back to life. Was his death misdiagnosed?" Jan asked.

"No, I was there. God raised Michael back to life. He was dead!"

"Why is that so important? Other people have been brought back to life after being diagnosed dead."

"True, but the importance was that his sister, Michelle actually saw Jesus bringing Michael back into the world."

"I'm sure it was a wonderful, mind experience for her, but she may have been hallucinating."

"I'm sure many of your viewers would love that hallucination!"

"Touche! Pastor Hillman, bringing Michael and Michelle Spencer into your home has caused your wife to leave. Was it your choice to choose those kids over your own wife and daughter?"

"No."

"The children are resisting questions about what they are preparing the world for. Your wife must be worried about something more serious than a lottery crash."

"I've already stated my personal understanding. The Miracle Children are anointed, and they'll become great leaders, doctors, scientists, preachers, and teachers."

"Is it possible they can cause financial ruin to institutions, such as the lottery?" Jan asked, to relieve her viewer's fears, or at least get Isaiah to fan them for a television rating's bonanza.

"Their special gifts will be a blessing to the world," Isaiah answered. "Powers of healing have been well documented for centuries, some true and some unscrupulous, but nothing anyone should be afraid of."

"Are you the leader of the Miracle Children?"

"I'm caring for two kids and their mother. That doesn't make me a leader of over a million children around the world."

～

"Isaiah, should be caring for Evelyn and Paula, not some other kids and their mother!" Thelma said, once again to offer her valid opinion, at least, valid to herself.

"Isaiah did the right thing."

"Richard, I know you just didn't say that!"

"I did, Thelma, and I'll tell you why! Isaiah let Evelyn and Paula leave home and come here where it's safe. At the same time, he kept those kids with their mother."

"Oh, I see. Well, you're so high and mighty on Isaiah's righteousness, why don't you pay for those kids and their mother's stay at the Beverly Hills Hotel? That way, your daughter and granddaughter can go home and be a real family!" Thelma waits for Richard to answer, he doesn't. "What happened, Poppa? Did you lose your wallet?"

Thelma and Richard laugh, but Evelyn walked out of the room. Her parents stared at one another in puzzlement.

"She used to have such a wonderful sense of humor," Thelma commented.

"Don't worry, she'll be back to herself in no time. God isn't going to let Isaiah lose his family over this."

"I know that's right!"

~

Jan escorted Isaiah down the studio corridor; she's still angling to get a more controversial story.

"Pastor Hillman, I haven't confirmed this story, but do the children possess some sort of electrical energy that can kill people."

"Does that sound like a loving God? Blessing children with gifts and talents to electrocute people!" Isaiah said, not wanting to bring people's fears down on the children.

"If they are going to fight the evil in the world you've talked about, I don't think they'll stop it with peace and love. You must know something more than the rest of us. You have a child in your home that has come back from... maybe from death, and his sister trusts you enough to tell you he's the oldest of all the children, and that he's their leader."

"I rather you didn't repeat that," Isaiah whispered, sorry that he blurted out that information during a commercial break.

"What are you afraid of?"

"That kind of information may be harmful to Michael."

"Yes, of course, but he isn't afraid of being the leader. I bet he'd welcome the chance to speak to the whole world! Talk to him. A television interview would answer a lot questions. Don't you think it'll be good for the world? Talk to him, Isaiah. Talk to him."

~

Isaiah stepped out of the church van and stared at the long line of men, women, boys and girls from all cultures, races, and nationalities that were entering his backyard in wheelchairs, on crutches, and using walkers. There were also the blind, mentally stressed, a number of alcoholics, drug addicts, and others who lacked social skills in the line.

Isaiah walked into his backyard and looked around at Michael, Michelle, the twins, Leon and Alonzo, and little Susan as they laid hands on the sick. Many wept, while others shouted and yelled out praises to the Lord. When Michael, or one of the other children laid hands on someone, a white light, invisible to everyone, flowed from a child's hand and caused a miraculous healing.

"Thank you, Jesus. Thank you for giving me back my strength!" an elderly woman tearfully said over and over. "Thank you! Thank you, Jesus!"

"I always knew I'd walk again," a man wept, as he pushed his wheelchair aside.

Sylvia walked over and stood next to Isaiah, "It's been going on for almost two hours. They're so blessed. God is really bringing a New Day into the world."

Susan waved to Isaiah, and then placed her hand on a man's closed eyes that was kneeling on the ground. She spoke with authority as a white light flowed from her hand, "In Jesus' name, I pray that you see again!"

The blind man's eyes were miraculously cleansed with his tears, and when his vision cleared, and he saw Susan, his voice joyfully sang out, "It worked. Oh, my God, I can see! I can see you!" He hugged Susan, "You're so beautiful. Thank you, Lord. Thank you, thank you, My Lord!"

In the next few hours, thousands of sick, crippled, and people with mental problems lined up around Isaiah's home to receive the miracle healings that God sent through Michael, Michelle, Leon, Alonzo and Susan.

~

"We can't let this continue," A hospital administrator said, as he stared at Board Members, drug company representatives, doctors, and lawyers who sat at a large conference room table. "The same way they destroyed the lottery, those children's miracle healings will bring our walls tumbling down just like Jericho."

A Board Member spoke up, "Our main problem is the hundred million dollar building debt hanging over the hospital!"

The Drug Representative spoke up, "I agree, the children have to be turned around! Also, the News Media has to be more responsible in reporting this. If this story spreads, it'll be devastating to doctors and medical science around the world. Who knows where all these children are hiding, or what they are planning to do next? I love children, but let's be serious, these children are a threat to the medical profession!"

"Miracle healings are great. Wonderful, but there's something wrong with children having that much power," another Board Member acknowledged.

Once again, the Drug Company Rep agreed, "Phieffer Industry has more than a billion dollars in inventory of medicines, drugs and supplies. Our research dollars are rising higher than that. These children have to be taught that healing everybody will cause financial ruin to America, Europe, and everywhere else!"

"We could get a court-ordered injunction to stop them," a lawyer said. "But it would only be temporary, and the public outrage would create some very bad press."

A doctor fearfully announced, "In twenty-four hours, other hospitals, health centers and clinics will have the same problems we're dealing with, so we have to contact them..."

The Administrator disagreed, "That'll take too long! We have to act fast, and now!"

"I have a long standing friendship with Mayor Gillard," the Drug Company Rep said.

"Get him on the phone!" the Administrator shouted. "I know how to resolve this!"

The rep took out his cell phone.

~

An hour later, police cars screeched and stopped in front of Isaiah's house, and riot police moved in and dispersed the long line of sick and indigent people.

"The kids are being escorted to Saint Anthony Hospital. If you're sick, the children will be able to help you there!" the Police Captain shouted into a bullhorn, as his officers lined up Michael, Michelle, Leon, Alonzo and Susan.

"I'll go with the children," Isaiah said, taking hold of Susan's hand.

"I'm sorry, our orders are to escort the children, not the sick," the Police Captain said.

"I'm their Pastor."

"Pastor, I'd advise you to pray that no one gets hurt."

Sylvia rushed over and grabbed Michael and Michelle, "I'm their mother. You're not taking my kids anywhere!"

"Release them, Ma'am, or I'll have you arrested."

"What kind of country is this?"

"Let them go, Sylvia. The kids will be all right," Isaiah said, with as much calm as he's able to muster.

Sylvia reluctantly released Michael and Michelle as the riot police marched Michael, Michelle, Leon, Alonzo and Susan out of the backyard. A few people shouted and protested, and some raised their fists, but most of them were too sick to express their anger.

~

Doctor Lauer entered the conference room and looked at Michael and the other children wearing Laker T-shirts, "I guess being little missionaries has great rewards."

The children didn't respond.

"Hi kids, I'm Doctor Lauer, and I've been chosen to bring you some good news. First, I'd like to know what it feels like to have such wonderful, healing powers?"

Silence.

"Somebody has to talk or people won't understand your supernatural powers."

Susan raised her hand.

"Okay, I see one hand raised. What is your name?"

"Susan Faraday."

"Hi, Susan Faraday. So what is it like being you?"

"It's like having fun all day."

"Then your mother calls you home for dinner," Leon said.

"And you have to stop your fun for spinach," Alonzo joked, making the children laugh.

Doctor Lauer laughed as well, and when the laughter faded away, he said, "So you think we brought you here to eat spinach!"

He thought he would get a laugh, but the children didn't respond. Finally, Susan spoke up.

"Are we going to jail?"

"No, Susan. We don't put kids, or anyone else in jail for healing people." Doctor Lauer sat down at the table. "And we surely don't want to stop your fun. Listen up…I want you to hear a story of why I became a doctor. When I was twelve years old, Doug, my good friend, started smoking. Doug was very smart in school, but he thought smoking cigarettes made him look tough. I told him that smoking cigarettes caused cancer and many other illnesses. Doug laughed, and said he was only thirteen years old, and by the time he got cancer there would be a cure for it. He died last year."

Doctor Lauer poured himself a glass of orange juice and continued, "Your miracle healing powers will make smokers laugh at cancer and say that when they got sick the Miracle Children would heal them. People with serious health problems, alcoholism, gambling, drug addictions…"

"What are dictions?" Susan asked.

"Susan, addictions are when people eat too much candy, cake and apple pies, and they continue eating these foods, full of bad sugar and fats, until they no longer have the will power to quit. It's the same with cigarettes, alcohol and drugs, and when people wake up and continue doing the same bad habits everyday it becomes an addiction. These addictions will eventually cause people to put on too much weight, which will cause heart disease, and many other medical problems. I'm sure you know the human body is God's temple, and that we must respect it. Healing these problems is great, but it's also a quick fix. Quick fixes don't solve the serious problems these people refuse to face up to."

"You want us to stop the healings."

"I know who you are. Hi, Michael."

Michael nodded.

"In answer to your question is, no. Michael, we don't want to stop the healings. We just want you to stop the backyard healings. Come into the hospital after school. Come in on weekends and special holidays..."

~

"That's a great idea," Isaiah said, while he drove the children home. "There are so many people around the world you can help. Don't you agree, Michael?"

"He was honest that's why they used him."

"Used him? Who? The hospital?"

"Everybody. Their plan is to take away our time."

"Our time after school," Leon said.

"Weekends and holidays," Alonzo complained.

"No way," Leon and Alonzo said at the same time.

"You're not going to do it?" Isaiah asked.

Michelle answered, "God blessed us to prepare the world for the New Day. We don't have time to visit hospitals."

"Doctors have to heal sick people and dictions," Susan added.

"We have to do what the Holy Spirit says," Leon said.

"And that's the end of that," Leon and Alonzo said, and closed the subject.

Susan smiled at Isaiah, "But is was fun!"

"And much better than spinach," they all harmonized together.

Isaiah, though he smiled, felt uncomfortable when he noticed the children's ability to say the same thing, at the same time. He understood Leon and Alonzo doing it, because twins were able to think alike about many things, but five children thinking alike wasn't normal.

"Then you'll never understand one million, five hundred and fourteen thousand children thinking alike," Michael commented.

"Michael, how do you know what I'm thinking?" Isaiah asked.

I don't know how, but sometimes we can hear you."

"Hear me?"

Leon cut in, "Hear your voice inside."

"We're all connected to the Holy Spirit," the children said together.

"Don't be afraid, we're still people," Susan said, and smiled to ease Isaiah's discomfort.

"I'm not...not afraid. I'm just amazed at your gifts."

Michael explained, "We have to be connected to prepare. If we're not together our thoughts would be scattered and the Holy Spirit would be at his..."

"Wit's End!" everyone said at the same time, and then laughed at Isaiah's blank expression. Then, once again, they harmonized together, "And that's the end of that!"

Isaiah looked at Susan, "Do you have the slightest idea what wit's end means?"

Susan reached over and rested her hand on Isaiah's shoulder, "Pastor Hillman, it means the Holy Spirit would go crazy."

The children chuckled at Susan's answer, but Isaiah, while he knew in his heart that they said the right thing, he wondered what had happened to their individual free spirit.

"We can think together or apart," Michael said, as he stared at Isaiah. "We're all connected, so the Holy Spirit can talk to everyone at the same time."

"When we hear his voice, we know its time to listen and not think about other stuff," Michelle said. "Being connected together teaches us many things about each other."

"What is the Holy Spirit telling you now?" Isaiah asked, hoping to find out what they were preparing.

Silence.

"Come on, I want to learn."

"You'll hear when it's your time."

"My time for what, Michael?"

"To learn what you want to know about us."

Silence.

"You hear anything yet?" Michelle asked.

"No, nothing," Isaiah said.

"Then it's not your time!" Michelle joked, and laughed along with the others.

⁓

Michael sipped from his cup of hot chocolate, while he played a video game on Isaiah's computer.

"It wouldn't be good for me to go on television. I would only make things worse."

"That's not true. Your appearance would open people's hearts and minds. It'll calm their suspicions about you!" Isaiah answered, trying to assure Michael.

"You went on television, and you didn't open people's hearts and minds, or stop their suspicions, and you're a preacher!"

"I didn't have the answers you have. Anyway what's the big secret?"

"It's not time for people to hear about the...the New Day."

"You were about to say something else. What aren't people ready to hear about?"

"God knew we all agreed to prepare the earth before we came here."

"Came here...from where?"

"We're told people are born with a purpose to do something good in the world, but once they get here they forget their purpose. God knew us before we came here, and He knew we would choose Jesus and not the world." Michael said, as he focused his attention on the video game.

"That's very nice, Michael, but you're not telling me what's going on?" Isaiah said, but Michael remained silent. "I see, whenever you and the other children don't want to answer a question you become silent, or you laugh, and do something else to evade answering! What are you hiding?"

Michael turned and faced Isaiah, "Okay, what's the question?"

Isaiah knew he opened Michael's heart to answer the Big Question! "Are we at the End of the World?"

"I'll do the television show."

"Are you doing it to prepare people for The End?"

"I'm doing it because the Holy Spirit said it's okay."

"The Holy Spirit wants you to prepare the world for The End, right?"

Michael stood up to leave, "I have to go."

"Go where?"

Michelle came and stood in the doorway, "Michael, the news is coming on television now."

"Told you," Michael said to Isaiah.

"Michael, answer me truthfully, did you just talk with Michelle spiritually, telepathically, or whatever way you communicate...did you tell her to come in here to get you, so you wouldn't have to answer my questions?"

"No, I asked her before to come and get me when the news was coming on the television."

Feeling foolish, Isaiah walked with Michael and Michelle out of the study, "What are you expecting to come on the news?"

"I'm expecting the news to come on the news," Michael laughed.

"You know what I mean!"

"I'm sure everyone is watching the news to see what's going on."

"Don't you know?"

"No, I don't know what's coming on the news. I wouldn't have to watch it if I did."

Michelle interrupted Michael's fun, "Michael, stop playing. Pastor Hillman, we know you're interested in what we're preparing, but we're not allowed to tell you. Yes, we know what we're preparing, but we want to see what the world is saying about us. God has chosen us to prepare the world for the New Day, and it's really exciting to be us."

"Exciting for you, not for everyone else. Michelle, when did God choose you?"

"I'm sure it was the same time He chose you," Michelle shrugged, but her voice is warm and friendly. "Stop worrying so much. When it's your time to know everything, you'll know, okay?"

Isaiah nodded, returned to his study and sat down at his desk. He thought for a moment, and then knelt down and prayed, "Holy Spirit, you know I've been asking you to talk to me. I rebuke the fears grabbing my thoughts. I rebuke my suspicious heart. I rebuke everything and everyone that's standing in my way of hearing you. Father God, Christ Jesus, Holy Spirit, I've been placed into this situation, and I don't know why I'm here, or what I'm supposed to do. Michael said you knew they agreed to prepare the world before they came here. Talk to me like you talk to them. Guide me into your will, and I'll be able to understand, and not feel like an outsider. What are they preparing? Why am I in the middle of all this? Why don't I hear...?"

6

The Answer

*It is the same with my word.
I send it out, and it always
produces fruit. It will
accomplish all I want it to,
and it will prosper everywhere
I send it.* Isaiah 55:11 NLT

A fourteen years old girl, walked onto a New York City subway car. The car was crowded with men, women, and children. She moved through the crowd and stood at the center of the car, and then pressed a button that ignited the explosives she wore under her overcoat.

Blood splattered, and howling cries of horror came from passengers as the subway car, filled up with black smoke and fire.

The subway train was in the station, and the passengers that were still alive, banged on windows and doors, crying for help. Passengers that stood on the station's platform, yelled and screamed for the train's conductor to open the subway car doors. The conductor tried, but was unsuccessful, and passengers, inside and outside the car, broke windows and squeezed open one door.

~

"Twenty-five men, women and children were killed this morning when a suicide bomber entered a subway car and set off her explosives. Will the Miracle Children be fighting a war against the children of terrorists?" Jan Summers questioned her guests.

Pastor Arnold responded, "No, that isn't biblical, so children won't be fighting..."

"Excuse me, Pastor Arnold," Jan apologized, as the station's news director handed her a slip of paper.

"I've just received a late breaking news report," Jan announced. "Michael Spencer will appear on our network this coming Friday, December 21st, 2012, and you all know that date ends the Mayan Calendar. I'm not supposed to say this, but Michael Spencer is the oldest, and leader of the Miracle Children. I apologize for stopping you, Pastor Arnold, please continue."

"I'm sorry, I got caught up in your announcement. What...what was your question?"

"You were saying it wasn't biblical that children would be warring against other children."

"No...I don't think God is preparing the children to fight a war...Miss Summers, isn't Michael Spencer the child who died and came back to life?"

"Yes, he's twelve years old, and he will appear on my show this coming Friday, two days from now. I've had the honor of interviewing him, and Michael has so much information regarding what the children are preparing to bring into the world," Jan said, over-exaggerating her connection to Michael, and excited about promoting her upcoming event with the world. "Pastor Isaiah Hillman is caring for Michael and his sister, Michelle. As mentioned before, I wasn't supposed to let the cat out of the bag, regarding Michael's leadership of the Miracle Children, however, everyone needs to know how important his appearance will be, especially on that date..."

~

"You told her all that stuff?" Michael questioned Isaiah.

"Yes and no, she's using something I said to create a big news ratings, and get people around the world to tune in and hear what you have to say. Michael, you don't have to do it. The choice is still yours."

"The Holy Spirit said it was okay for me to do the show. He doesn't change His word, why should I change mine."

Michael turned his attention back to the television as Michelle changed channels.

"It's been reported that the Miracle Children's leader, Michael Spencer will prepare the world this coming Friday, December 21st, 2012, on another network, and Jan Summers, the host of 'Talking With Jan' will allow us to broadcast her show here at Channel 2," a News Host announced.

"It's going to be real big, Michael," Michelle said, as she flipped to another channel.

"The Miracle Boy is preparing the world for the New Beginning they've been promising. A Great Change is coming into the world, and we'll be broadcasting a live-feed on the All Saints Network!"

"Turn to that comedy channel, I like them," Michael requested.

On the comedy station the host, Joey McGuire joked, "Dead Boy has decided to talk on Friday, December 21st, 2012, and we all know why he picked that date. He's going to Shake up the World. Wall Street will be bracing for The

Great Market Crash of 2012, because they know God doesn't like greed, then again, God doesn't like pride, covetousness, lust, anger, gluttony, envy and sloth. I don't know about you, but I'm running for the hills, and well, you gluttons best lie low because you can't run fast enough to escape the coming punishment!"

Isaiah took the remote from Michelle and turned off the television.

"Michael, did you pick that date to end the world?"

Silence.

"Michelle, do you know what's going on?" Isaiah asked, and though his voice was calm, inwardly his heart was filled with apprehension.

Michelle shrugged, "Only God knows when the End will come." (Mark 13:32)

Isaiah sighed, and inwardly prayed to not let his heart be troubled or afraid, because the peace that Jesus gave him was greater than the peace the world could give. (John 14:27)

~

Richard changed the television station, "Look, they're filming on Venice Beach. Now you know it's the end of the world when they put Hare Krishna people on television: Hare Krishna, Hare Krishna, Hare Krishna, Hare Krishna..."

"Okay, Daddy, change the channel, please," Evelyn prompted, unhappy with the news.

"You know it's a fact that chanting God's name leads to enlightenment. You'll feel a lot better, Evelyn, come on chant with me, Hare Krishna, Hare Krishna."

"Richard, we'll all feel a lot better if you go to Venice Beach and chanted with the Krishna's," Thelma snarled sarcastically. However, she noticed Evelyn smiled for the first time in days, and when Richard saw the same smile, he took Evelyn's hand and led her in a dance around the living room.

"Though your mom is full of sarcasm, she is right. The beach will be a wonderful place to spend the day. The ocean has a way of relaxing and taking all the stress out of your thoughts."

"Daddy, I'm fine."

"No, we're not staying in the house. Let's go. Thelma go get, Paula."

"I'm going to get my razor to shave your head so you'll feel real enlighten while chanting, Hare Krishna, Hare Krishna..."

~

"More champagne, please," Jan laughed, and looked at her crew of coworkers gathered in the studio's monitoring room. She smiled at everyone beaming with happiness at her accomplishment.

"Trust me, this will be a ratings blockbuster. Children will stay home from school, everyone will call in sick, everyone except you, of course!"

Jan pointed a warning finger at the staff of producers, editors, and studio personnel who laughed along with her.

"Look...Look, monitor one, the London Bells are ringing with the story of Michael Spencer appearing on 'Talking With Jan.' Brian, read that newspaper headline on that monitor over there."

Brian, Jan's cameraman, looked at monitor 4, "It's from the Daily Sun, and it reads: 'Miracle Boy Prepares The World For The End."

"Monitor 5, Brian," Jan yelled, as she pointed and sipped her champagne.

"It's that London 'Blue News' Television Show, and its flashing photos of Michael Spencer's dead body lying in the morgue," Brian reported. "The photos are doctored, but Londoners don't care. Blue News is the most watched television show in all of England, France, Belgium..."

"Brian, you're a cameraman, not a reporter," Jan said, somewhat annoyed. "We all know Blue News is a top rated show in Europe, but after Friday, 'Talking With Jan' will be the most watched show in the whole world. I've lined up some very important guests to come on my show."

Ronnie Roberts, Jan's Executive Producer, asked, "Do you have any idea what Michael Spencer is going to tell the world, Jan?"

"Ronnie, none of the children are talking, so whatever he says will be news. Hey, he's a kid, what can he talk about besides how he hears voices from another world," Jan laughed, and held out her champagne glass for a refill. "Ronnie, everybody, listen up, Michael, his sister and all the other children are just that, children. They're going to go to Disneyland like everybody else."

Lots of laughter came from the crew, and as Jan enjoyed the limelight, she continued, "They're going to draw and paint silly pictures for refrigerators. They're going to put on Superman and Wonder Woman costumes, jump out of trees, fly out of playground swings, and do whatever else children do that's news worthy, because we're going make it newsworthy. Is everybody in agreement?"

Jan beamed, as she raised her glass to toast everybody, while everyone in the monitoring room shouted and cheered.

"Hooray."

"Bravo, Jan. We're number one with the news!"

"So Mr. Roberts, in answer to your question about what Michael Spencer is going to tell the world, **who cares?**"

Hands clapped and more cheers echoed around the room, "Whoop, Whoop, Whoop..."

Ronnie Roberts frowned, "Jan, I don't like being in the dark about what that boy will say. For many years that date has been announced, predicted, and shoved into people's minds through movies, books, and documentaries about the Mayan Calendar, Hopi Indians, Nostradamus..."

"Ronnie, I agree, the whole world knows that date, and everybody will be watching 'Talking With Jan,' and our ratings will be through the roof. Relax, it's going to be great!" Jan laughed, and held out her glass for more champagne.

~

"Evelyn, look at these news reports of over a hundred thousand Christians and Jews visiting the Wailing Wall to pray. In Mecca, Saudi Arabia, thousands of worshippers are walking around the Mosque. People in Montreal, Canada are dancing in the streets. Everybody's hugging and kissing. Michael Spencer will shake up the world tomorrow!" Richard announced.

Thelma spoke up, "People getting drunk, breaking windows and stealing stuff doesn't look like anything new for the world."

"Yes, there are still idiots running loose, but my point was that Isaiah has stumbled into the biggest story in all our lives and Evelyn shouldn't be upset."

"I'm not upset!"

"You should be," Thelma warned. "Those children are trouble, and Isaiah has left the church, Paula, and you to hang out with them."

"Mom, he was leaving the church before all this happened."

"And that's exactly how the devil works. He takes you out of the Lord's House, so he can use you in his evil deeds."

Richard and Evelyn stared at Thelma as if she's lost her mind.

"You know what I'm talking about. Isaiah had a dream the morning it all happened, right? Well, he's not the only one who has dreams, and let me tell you two something, people better pray long and hard, because there's trouble on the way."

"This is Breaking News! What did you dream, Thelma?"

"Richard, God knows you can't bring a New Day into this world without ***Raising Cain!***"

"So you saw Cain rising from the grave and going on a rampage killing his brothers and sisters?"

"People will be raising hell whether it's good news or bad, and your mocking grin won't stop that."

"Thelma, the news reports are showing people praying in Times Square. Buddhists, Mormons, Seventh Day Adventists, and many other religious sects are weeping, praying, and calling the world to fast and repent. God is preparing something wonderful for the world."

"I agree with, Daddy, and I'm sure you didn't dream anything, Mother!"

"Sweetheart, you're staying here because you know it's not all rosy out there in the world. Most smart people are in their homes watching the news twenty-four seven, because they want to see this new world the children are preparing from a safe distance. Am I the only one aware of this?"

No one responded, so Thelma picked up her pocketbook, "Anyone want to go back to Venice Beach and sing along with the Hare Krishna people?"

Silence.

"Anyone want to let the Pacific Ocean calm his or her spirit?" Thelma asked, and once again there's silence, so Thelma pointed her finger at Evelyn and Richard, and smirked, "I've proved my case."

~

Jan Summers glowed with anticipation as she spoke into a hand mike, "I'm so happy to have as our guest today, Michael Spencer. It's my pleasure to let you meet and hear him for yourself. Michael Spencer is the Miracle Boy who came back from the dead, back from the other side of life, and he's here to speak to the world. He's told me, this is his one and only appearance, and it'll help everyone prepare for the New Day. Ladies, gentlemen, boys and girls of all ages, my studio audience, and viewers throughout the whole wide world, here is the leader of the Miracle Children, Michael Spencer!"

A studio monitor flashed on and informed audience members to applaud. However, audience members remained still and quiet, and focused all their attention on Michael as he walked onto the set. Jan, not anticipating the audience's reaction, became somewhat rattled, "This wasn't the response I expected. I thought everyone would stand and greet you with loud applause. I was wrong. Actually, the complete opposite has happened. Total silence. Amazing. You can hear a pin drop in this studio!"

Jan took a deep breath to calm down, and then smiled for the cameras. "Michael, first let me start by welcoming you to our studio with a big hug."

As she hugged Michael, the show's news director clapped his hands, forcing the studio audience to do the same.

"Michael, lets start with the question, I'm curious to know, and I'm sure everyone else in the world wants to know the words of wisdom, words that the Miracle Children hear and want to share with Americans, and all the other Nations around the World. What have you been told, as a Leader of the Miracle Children, to get everyone ready for the 'New Day' you're preparing?"

Everyone waited in silent anticipation, as Jan held her hand mike for Michael to speak. Michael's young face had neither a frown, nor a smile when he spoke one word.

"Believe!"

Michael, then turned and walked off the set. His action caused everyone's mouth to drop wide open in shock! Jan looked dumbfounded as she stared into a television camera, unmoving, and frozen in time.

Ronnie Roberts, the executive producer, made a motion to symbolically slash his finger across his throat.

"Cut! Cut!" the news director yelled out.

Meanwhile, Jan gathered herself and rushed backstage over to Michael.

"What kind of stunt was that? Why did you do this to me?"

Michael remained silent.

"Believe...Millions of people were hoping for answers and all you gave them was one word!"

"It's the only word I was given."

"Who...who gave it to you? Him?" she said, pointing at Isaiah.

"No," Michael answered.

"Who then?"

"Who do you think?"

Jan is taken aback, she patted her chest to calm herself, and then, knelt down in front of Michael, "I'm sorry, I got upset. Michael, come back into the studio and explain your word to everyone."

"I was given one word to say. Saying it a hundred times would lose its power. Once is enough, and if their ears were open, they heard," Michael said, as he walked away.

"I'm sorry," Isaiah said and followed after Michael.

For a moment, Jan stood motionless, furious, but then she returned to the studio. A makeup person powdered her forehead and face, while the news director yelled out, "On Air...five, four, three..."

Jan held up her hand and shouted! "Stop the show! I'm not ready. Do another commercial! Go to commercial!"

~

A mob of media reporters, photographers, and cameramen surrounded Michael and Isaiah when they came out of the studio. One news reporter shoved his mike at Michael, "Why only one word, Michael?"

"It's hard to mislead the world with one word," Michael answered, with finality as other reporters yelled out more questions.

"What is God preparing, Michael?"

"When is the New Day?"

"Did you ruin Jan Summers' show because she's an atheist?"

Isaiah spoke up, "Have faith that what Michael told the world was from God!"

Isaiah and Michael pushed and shoved their way pass the crowd of media men and women to the church van.

~

Isaiah was asleep when shotgun blasts shattered his bedroom window, and then gun blasts shattered more windows around his house. Isaiah heard Sylvia's screams in the hallway. He ran out of the bedroom and hurried over to her in the upstairs hallway, where Michael and Michelle were doing their best to comfort her. When Isaiah took her in his arms, the sound of more shattered windows exploded downstairs.

"It's Henry, he's drunk…he's going to kill us!" Sylvia screamed, as tears rolled down her face.

"Sylvia, Henry wouldn't do this," Isaiah said, and then raced downstairs, banged open his front door and yelled at a red pickup truck as it peeled rubber and sped off, "You cowards. You're nothing but a bunch of cowards!"

A minute later, a fire truck roared by Isaiah's home with it's siren howling in the night.

Isaiah looked down the street and saw fire and smoke coming from a few blocks away. In a panic, he ran off, and arrived as a raging fire engulfed his church.

~

Sorrow filled Evelyn's heart as she fed Paula and watched television with her parents.

News Reporter, Danny Wynn announced, "I'm here in Times Square, New York City, and riot police have their hands full with this angry crowd that erupted from Michael Spencer's One Word from God. The police are firing rubber bullets, tossing tear gas canisters, and they've been carrying and dragging people off to prison transport buses, but it still hasn't stopped the rock and bottle throwing."

A rioter grabbed Danny's mike and yelled, "We want the truth. Tell us the truth about what you're preparing. We want the truth!"

Another rioter shook his fist in anger, and shouted into the camera filming the riot, "Tell us it's *The End*, or shut the hell up."

Other enraged men and women, took the opportunity to take Danny's hand mike to rant and rave.

"Those children are false witnesses."

"They're demon possessed."

"They have to be stopped!"

Evelyn turned off the television, but Thelma turned it back on. "You can't hide from what's going on, Evelyn."

"Isaiah is caught up in this, Thelma," Richard said.

"I know that, and perhaps, when Isaiah sees all the trouble that boy is causing, he'll understand why Evelyn is here."

"That is so dumb! What does Evelyn watching television have to do with anything?"

Evelyn started walking out the room.

"Where are you going?"

"I'm going to call Isaiah."

"You've talked to him three times already, sit down and learn something about marriage. Richard, go call Isaiah and tell him to bring the children and their mother here."

Evelyn and Richard stared at Thelma in shock!

"Just do it, Richard, or move your stuff out of my bedroom!" Thelma stated, and winked at Evelyn, and then, turned her attention back to a round table discussion on television.

"Michael Spencer gave the world a powerful message. Believe…a word of pure beauty," Minister James Brothers stated as a member of the round table.

Author, Angel Bonds disagreed, "Perhaps a word of beauty to you, but to everybody else in the world, it says little. Very little! Michael Spencer may have thought one word would suffice, but as an author of spiritual novels, one word won't sell books. It won't get people to change their lives."

Minister Brothers then defended his position, "Hello, Michael wasn't writing a book, he spoke a prophetic word from God!"

"You believe that?"

"How else could a twelve year old boy be so profound?"

The television host offered his thought, "I think his one word was enough."

Then a youth minister spoke in a calm voice, "I agree. The world was supposed to end yesterday, it didn't. Though our world is dying from viruses, diseases, poverty, and so many natural disasters, including horrific television shows, movies, and music videos that are destroying children's innocence with visions of sex, drugs and overpriced toys, we've been given an opportunity to change our lives! Mankind has lied, and lied, and lied some more, to push their ungodly policies on our lives. Michael Spencer's word should shake us awake; God is in charge, and you better "Believe" that His children are preparing the world for a New Day. You may not like it, but you better find some sort of belief in your spirit that'll comfort you through these Last Days!"

The host, author, and minister stared at the youth minister in bewilderment. The youth smiled back at them.

"Richard, do like I told you, call Isaiah. I believe it's the End of the World, so we might as well go out as a family," Thelma said, as she changed the television station again.

"Believe, Michael Spencer's prophetic word has many beautiful connotations," Charles Gerard, Bishop of Life Church, preached. "Believing opens doors into faith, and without faith it's impossible to please God!" (Hebrews 11:6 KJV) Inside a believer's heart lives the Holy Spirit of hope, love, forgiveness, mercy and grace. Believe!"

The congregation then shouted out, "Believe! Believe! Believe!"

Bishop Gerard continued, "Michael's one word spoken, "Believe" is a divine inspiration from God. Believe, a glorious word that shines a bright light into our lives. If a light isn't shining from you, it's because the devil has hung a dark cloud over your heart. Believe, and remove that dark cloud from your life, and all the evil forces within you will take off running, because the light of God drives them crazy... BELIEVE!"

~

The congregation of believers joined in and shouted, cheered and clapped their hands, as Sylvia cleaned up broken glass and watched Bishop Gerard on television. Michelle was helping in the clean up, and Michael assisted Isaiah in nailing a large wooden board over the living room's missing window.

"I'm sorry about the trouble I've caused you, Pastor Hillman," Michael said.

"You warned me you would only make things worse and I didn't stop you. There's nothing for you to be sorry about. The reaction to what you said should make the protesters feel sorry."

"The Holy Spirit says everyone received the word."

"I'm sure they did. So are we to believe God's plan for us is coming soon?"

"We know what we're preparing for, and when it's your time to know you'll be called."

"Is it soon?"

"God will open your eyes and ears and you'll see and hear what we do. Do you believe that?"

"Is it beautiful, Michael? What you see and hear, is it beautiful?"

Michael smiled, which radiated joy in Isaiah's heart.

"It'll be a wonderful surprise."

"I'll answer the call when it comes," Isaiah said, realizing everything that transpired since God blessed the children, he couldn't back away. His heart had to stay pure. He had to guard his heart with all diligence; for out of it flowed the issues of life. (Proverbs 4:23)

The Sunday after Michael's appearance on Jan Summer's show, Isaiah and Sylvia were at the Burger House Diner with Michael and Michelle. At six p.m., Michael stood and spoke to Isaiah, "The Holy Spirit wants you to read Acts 2, starting at number 17. Excuse me, I have to go to the restroom."

"Me too," Michelle smiled, as she placed her small pocket Bible in Isaiah's hand, and then took Michael's hand and walked off with him.

"I'm so happy God chose my kids. Is your daughter a Miracle Child?" Sylvia asked.

"Paula has shown me signs my wife doesn't know about."

"I won't say anything. I know it must be hard on her being away from you. God will work it out. Do you know the scripture Michael told you to read?"

"Not right off," Isaiah said, as he flipped through the pages of the pocket Bible, and then read aloud, (Acts 2:17 NLT) "In the last days, God said, I will pour out my Spirit upon all people. Your sons and daughters will prophesy, your young men will see visions, and your old men will dream dreams. (18) In those days I will pour out my Spirit on all my servants, men and women alike, and they will prophesy. (19) I will cause wonders in the heavens above and signs on the earth below, blood and fire and clouds of smoke. (20) The sun will be turned into darkness, and the moon will turn blood red..."

Sylvia's heart was suddenly filled with fear, "Please stop, Pastor Hillman. I don't want to hear anymore."

Isaiah nodded, and closed the Bible as a wall clock moved three seconds backwards in time, and Isaiah is once again reading from the Bible, (Acts 2:20 NLT) "The sun will be turned into darkness, and the moon will turn blood red..."

"Please stop, Pastor Hillman. I don't want to hear anymore," Sylvia said, in fear. Isaiah nodded and closed the Bible.

"Do you believe it's, The End?"

"I don't know, but whatever it is, the children seem to be quite happy about it," Isaiah remarked.

"That's true," Sylvia said, as she stood and looked around the restaurant. "Where are they? Haven't they been gone a long time?"

Isaiah also stood and looked around when a mother, a few tables away, stood up with an empty blanket in her hand and screamed out in horror.

"My baby, she's gone. She was in my arms...She's disappeared!"

"She disappeared from your arms?" Sylvia cried out, and then hurried off in a panic and banged open a restroom door and yelled, "Michelle, are you in here. Michelle!"

Isaiah rushed inside the men's room, and one by one, he banged open the doors to the stalls and found them all empty. He ran outside where other parents were in a panic, looking for their sons and daughters in the giant playhouse, up in the trees, behind bushes, inside and under cars, and wherever else children could hide.

"Tom Tom, Fern, Linda, Kelly, Marvin..." shouted parents in tears.

Isaiah ran over to help a mother who fainted, and while he dealt with her, he glanced up at the red glow from the sun's reflection that made the evening moon appear blood red.

~

"Paula's gone. She's been taken away with the other children!" Evelyn cried, as she ran into Isaiah's arms when he returned home and entered the living room with Sylvia.

Isaiah nodded, and Evelyn glared at him, "You just nod like everything is okay. Our daughter is gone! How could you be so uncaring?" Evelyn stopped and stared at Isaiah and Sylvia. "You knew, didn't you? You knew she was one of them and you didn't tell me!"

Evelyn pounded her fists on Isaiah's chest until he wrapped his arms around her.

"Honey, there wasn't anything we could have done about it. Paula was chosen along with the other children. Our wishes and desires were not considered."

Sylvia started to sob, "I know my marriage was rotten, and I had two beautiful children, and God took them from me, and He's only one who knows why!"

"Everybody, let's not die in faith before we know what's going on, right, Isaiah?" Richard said.

"Yes, let's wait and see what God's is doing. I'm sure an answer is coming!" Isaiah said, as the front doorbell rang, which caused Evelyn and Sylvia to shudder in fear, but even in fear they followed Isaiah, Richard and Thelma to the front door. When the doorbell rang again, Evelyn and Sylvia shuddered even more, but they stood close behind Isaiah as he opened the door. The women stepped back in shock when they saw Henry Spencer in the doorway, with his head bowed and eyes lowered.

Henry's voice is almost tearful as he spoke, "I didn't want to be alone."

"I wouldn't want to be alone either. Come in, Mr. Spencer," Isaiah said, as he stepped aside and Henry entered the house. Isaiah did his best to comfort Evelyn, but her body still trembled as she stared at Henry.

"I wanted to be here with you, Sylvia. You're always forgiving me and it's time for me to be here for you." He looked at Isaiah and Evelyn, "Pastor Hillman, Mrs. Hillman, thank you for taking care of my wife and children. Because of you, I know they are safe."

"They're gone, Henry. They've been taken!" Sylvia cried out.

"I know, but I also heard Pastor Hillman on television saying the children were preparing the world for something new."

"The Last Days. The End!"

"Sylvia, preparing doesn't mean, The End. If they are preparing something, then they have something they want to show us. Pastor Hillman, I've thought about this, and my mind is made up. I want to prepare myself."

In puzzlement, Isaiah questioned Henry, "Prepare yourself?"

"Yeah, you know, get saved, my sins washed in the blood of Jesus. (Ephesians 1:7) I want that relationship with God you've talked about."

Sylvia cried out, "Praise the Lord! Hallelujah!!!"

~

"Lord James, the Bible says in the Final Days people will be raised up. Something the Christians call the Rapture. Do you feel that the Rapture has come and gone, and those still here are lost?" Byron Sanders asked his guest, as Jan Summer sat on her sofa and watched the telecast from London, England.

"No, we are not lost, and we are not in the Last Days," Lord James stated, with authority.

"Explain, what do you base your opinion on?"

"If it were the Last Days, then the Rapture would have also taken men and women believers, not just a few children!"

"Earl McMillan, what do you think the Miracle Children's mysterious disappearance is about?"

Earl McMillan, short of breath, wheezed as he spoke, "I don't think...we should get...caught up in anything...except the message...the boy...delivered!"

Lord James groaned, "What message, "Believe," that's no message. Believe what? He didn't say, so we're still in the dark as to what they're preparing to do! Believe whom? The Baptists? Catholics? Jews? Who, the Muslims?"

Earl McMillan shrugged, "I'll assume...the young lad was referring to...Jesus...remember after his crucifixion, Jesus disappeared from his tomb...appeared...before the two Mary's...appeared before his disciples, and appeared and disappeared on the walk to Emmaus. Elijah disappeared in a whirlwind..."

Lord James smirked, "So you want us to assume the child was telling us to believe and we'll disappear, too!"

"No, we...don't have that triple...anointed spirit that... that pastor in California said...was poured out on the Miracle Children. So...I believe we need...to look...at the life, the death, and the resurrection...of the Savior, Christ Jesus."

"Sir, let me remind you that the children weren't all Christians. Some were Jews, Muslims, and many other religions!" Lord James said, in prideful triumph.

"Exactly, Michael didn't say...anything, except for us to... believe. It appears...to me that all the Miracle Children are in accordance...with that since they all disappeared together. It also tells me that...everybody is welcomed to believe and become like the little children. Of course, I'm paraphrasing Jesus words...from Bible scripture." (Matthew 18:1-6 KJV)

"Man wrote all those scriptures in the Bible. So why should we believe it's true when we all know that man is corrupt, evil, and devious? Even God knows that!"

Earl McMillan smiled, "So...you...believe...that there... is a God?

Lord James frowned, "I'll agree with that in the abstract."

"The lad, dies...comes back to life and tells you to believe...then he disappears with over a million and a half of our children, and you're still in the abstract? No wonder the boy only delivered one word to the world. Two words would have caused suspicions. Three words, I perceive would cause World War III!"

Host Byron Sanders and Lord James stared at Earl McMillan in amazement, because as he talked, there was no more heavy breathing and wheezing in his powerful voice.

"You want three words, I'll give you my three words, "Believe! Believe! Believe! I believe God. I believe He's bringing a New Day into the world, and I also believe you, me, and the rest of the world have no power to stop it!""

Byron Sanders commented, "Well, that's the end of our broadcast today. I hope you, our viewers, will make the right choice during these Days of the Unknown. Thank you, Lord James and Earl McMillan. Join me, hopefully, tomorrow, when my guests will be Prime Minister Blackmoor, and Author, Maggie Warren."

Jan mixed herself a scotch and milk, and changed the channel to Danny Wynn who did a live broadcast on the corner of Broadway and Forty-Second Street in New York City.

"Sir, many religious leaders prophesied an answer would come in three days. The Miracle Children disappeared on December 23rd, and now seven days have passed and nothing. No signs and no news. Nothing! What do you think is happening?"

The man answered in bitterness, "Only God knows where the children are, and this has been the worst Christmas ever for families everywhere, so your question is a waste of time, because nobody knows what the hell is going on! Get out of my face and leave me alone!"

The grumpy, old man walked off in anger, but Danny smiled and stopped another person, "Sir, some people are saying the missing children are a sign that "The End" is near! What do you think it means?"

The man laughed and joked, "It means the end of McDonalds Happy Meals!"

"A sense of humor will help us all," Danny said, and smiled again through a bad situation, but stopped a young woman who was walking her poodle, "Hi, would you like to say something to New Yorkers regarding the missing Miracle Children?"

"I believe the children are safe with God, and now it's up to us, every one of us need to get our lives in order. The boy said for us to believe, and I believe God has the children preparing something wonderful for the world! New Yorkers, let's show the world how we will receive it!" She knelt down on the pavement, bowed her head, and then looked at her poodle, and said, "Kiwi, let's pray!"

The poodle laid down on the ground and crossed her paws on top her tiny nose. Danny laughed; however, many other New Yorkers, one by one, men, women and children knelt down and prayed.

Jan picked up her phone and called her cameraman, "Brian, pick me up...I'm sorry, I didn't know your daughter was one of the children. Brian, your wife will just have to understand you have work to do...Pick me up, or I'll get another cameraman...I'm not drunk, and don't you talk to me like that...Brian, I've had a few to calm my nerves...I'm warning you, I'll get Bobby to...Don't you hang up on me..."

Jan screamed, as she tossed her phone across the room, and then stumbled over to her bar and mixed herself another drink.

~

"Since the missing children are from families of believers and unbelievers, we must all come together and pray for the safe return of our children. At noon everyday, let's pray for their safe return and for God to remove crime, greed and terrorists from the face of the earth. Yes, it's a big prayer, but we serve a Big God, and I'm sure that the enemies of God, are in a panic and doing everything they can to stop this New Day. So we have to do everything we can, through the power of prayer to keep the Miracle Children and God's New Day alive in our spirit. As Michael Spencer's word said, believe…well, I believe. What about you? I'm Markeya Montes, live from Brazil."

"Amen," Isaiah said, and then spoke to Evelyn, Thelma, Richard, Sylvia and Henry. "Markeya Montes, compared to all the other countries reporting the story, including Africa, China, Germany, the Soviet Union, Iran, Australia; well, too me, she has the best approach."

Evelyn stopped preparing lunch, "It's almost twelve o'clock. Let's pray with the rest of the world for God to return our children safe and sound."

Evelyn, Isaiah, Henry, Sylvia, Thelma and Richard joined hands, bowed their heads and closed their eyes as Evelyn prayed. "Dear God, your wonders never cease to amaze our lives. You've certainly opened our hearts to your Glory. You've opened our eyes to your Mighty Power. Father God, Thank You, for blessing our children…"

Tears watered Evelyn's eyes, and as she prayed, the kitchen clock stopped, and everyone was frozen between an earthly and spiritual reality. During this time, Michael suddenly appeared, and with him are four angels standing eight feet in height. Michael walked over and removed Evelyn and Henry's hands from Isaiah. Isaiah opened his eyes and stared at Michael.

"Michael, you're back. Everybody, Michael is here!"

Evelyn and rest of the group remained frozen in time.

"They can't hear you. Come with me, Pastor Hillman," Michael said.

"Where to? What about my wife…and everybody?"

"The angels will stay here and protect them."

Isaiah looked around the kitchen for the angels, but he didn't see them. "What angels?"

"You ever see angels before?"

"No, I don't think so…maybe!"

"Pastor Hillman, if you can't see them, then your eyes aren't fully opened." Michael said, as he reached out his hand to Isaiah. "Come with me. God will open the eyes of your spirit."

"Michael, what are you talking about? Am I coming back? What do you mean God will open the eyes of my spirit?"

"Take my hand and you'll see."

Isaiah hesitated, but remembering, he promised to answer Call on his life, he held out his hand to Michael, and then in a blink of an eye, Michael and Isaiah vanished from the kitchen and the clock began ticking again. Evelyn opened her eyes, and quickly realized something was amiss. Her voice, weak and full of sadness, cried out, "Isaiah is gone."

The Downings and Spencers opened their eyes and looked around the kitchen.

"Maybe he went outside. I'll check," Thelma said.

"No, Mom, he's gone. I'm feeling the same loss when Paula was taken. He's gone."

Evelyn sat down at the table and the others gathered around her.

Thelma used a napkin to wipe tears from her eyes, "Oh God, this is too much."

"It's the Rapture. God has returned for the adults and we're left here to suffer alone!"

"Sylvia, stop acting as if you know the truth. You don't," Henry said, but with loving kindness, he placed his arm around her shoulder.

"I agree," Richard said. "I want to continue our prayer. Our Father, we know how much you love all children,

113

and we love them, too. Our rebellion and ignorance has brought suffering into our hearts. We've closed our eyes to the poverty in the world, and we hid your truth in our lies. We know what's right, but we still go about destroying the perfect earth you gave us. We've polluted our air, our oceans, and our minds. We know our sinful flesh overcomes our godly spirit, so Father God, we pray for your loving grace to save us. Lord, forgive us! Dear God, we pray that your grace will deliver us in this time that you're preparing for the world. We pray to be a light in the world for you, and we know you've heard this all before, that we say one thing and do another, however, we truly believe our prayers today are true from our hearts, and we welcome your divine grace..."

Richard continued his prayer. Henry and Richard's eyes were closed, but Evelyn, Thelma and Sylvia kept their eyes open.

~

7

Amazement

**But as it is written, Eye hath
not seen, nor ear has heard,
neither have entered into the
heart of man, the things God
hath prepared for them that
love him.** 1 Corinthians 2:9 KJV

"What's God planning, Michael?" Isaiah asked, while they
walked through a city park.

Michael was hesitant, before answering, "I don't know."

Isaiah stared at Michael in puzzlement, "You don't know?
What are you telling me? All along you've led me to believe
the children were preparing the world for something new!"

"We are, but I don't know what God is planning. He
keeps that stuff to himself."

"Has God taken the Miracle Children out of the world
and for everyone else it's bad news?"

"Why do you always think of bad things? Pastor
Hillman, we're not out of the world, we're still here, and
we're preparing what God blessed us to do."

"So what are you preparing? What's the big mystery?"

"What you said about the prophets Elijah, Elisha, and the triple anointing was good for us to hear, and yes, we all have special gifts and talents to do great things with our lives, but we're still children, and we're not old enough to perform the great things you've talked about."

"I'm sure God knows that. Michael, you said all the Miracle Children agreed to prepare the world before you came here. Do you know where you came from?"

"From where everybody comes from, God! The Holy Spirit opened our hearts, and we remembered our spiritual promise to prepare the world for the New Day."

"What are you preparing?"

"You keep asking the same questions. You never believe anything, so why keep asking me stuff you know I'm not able to answer. The same day you had your dream, the Holy Spirit woke us up to what we promised to do, since then, every night when we go to bed, all the Miracle Children get together and we prepare for the New Day."

"You've been preparing in your dreams?" Isaiah questioned, amazed that there was so much he didn't know.

"We're not really dreaming, it's like we're Edgar Cayce. He could go into a trance and see a disease in a person's body and bring about a healing. His spirit had the ability to travel to places past, present, and future. He lived back in nineteen thirties or forties. The Holy Spirit teaches us all kinds of stuff like that. Anyway, we don't want to mess things up, so we want you to speak for us. Make us sound like the grownups we're going to be."

"Then there is a future?"

"Well, since God is still alive, I guess there's always a future...somewhere," Michael said, full of his usual playfulness.

"I'm glad you're enjoying this. Where are the children? Where's my daughter?"

"God has hidden us so we can prepare, and if you agree to speak for us, I'll take you to where they are. If not, then I'll have to speak for us, and hope I won't mess things up again."

"How can I speak for you when I'm in the dark about everything?"

"So are we, but we believe the Holy Spirit. We don't know how everything happens, but that doesn't stop it from being fun, and it should be fun for you, too."

"Is that why God chose children to prepare the world, because he knew it would be fun for you?"

"Probably, since believing isn't much fun for you, or other grownups."

"Yeah, fun for children, but an unknown fear for many men and women who don't have their lives in order. Michael, why did the Holy Spirit send you to get me, a grownup?"

"He didn't. The children agreed that you should speak for us. The Holy Spirit didn't stop me from coming, so I guess it's okay."

"I guess my leaving the church caused problems for everyone."

"No, I caused many problems for everyone," Michael said. His eyes filled up with tears. "I caused the Lottery Crash by making the lottery machines print the same numbers I gave my father."

"How could you do that?"

"My prayer gave life to my words. The first things we've learned, is that God blesses our words and they're very powerful. The Miracle Children have been blessed with powers the whole world will have in the New Day."

"That sounds amazing."

"Yes, it is."

"You made a mistake and God's grace protects you.

"When I used my power against my father, I was killed."

"Yes, words have power, but when Jesus brought you back to life it was an act that you're forgiven. God's true grace and righteousness, Christ Jesus will always save and protect you, and you have His word on that."

"I don't want to make another mistake. Please, speak for us."

"I'm honored that you think I could speak for you," Isaiah said, realizing that he's seen so many miracles since God anointed the Miracle Children, but, he still asked himself, why was he unable to take that step of faith the children have no problem doing. Why didn't God open up his ears to hear, like he did for the children, because if God did that, then, he'd be willing and able to answer God's Call on his life? When Michael said believing was fun for the children, he had to agree. The children loved it, and they all accepted God's Call on their lives without tears or fears. The Holy Spirit spoke, and didn't receive one rejection from the children. If their was a rejection, it wasn't made known, but he, Isaiah, as an adult, needed all the answers before he committed himself, and that, he realized wasn't walking in faith. Evelyn was right, he had to get married to Jesus and make their life together beautiful again.

"Pastor Hillman, you have to make a choice."

"I know...I know. I'll go with you," Isaiah said, though he really didn't want to go anywhere; he just wanted to bring the children back home.

"The Holy Spirit says your faith is weak and you're not being totally truthful. I'll take you back home," Michael said, in a wearisome tone.

"No, you brought me here, and I may be a little confused about everything, but I don't want to go home. I want you to take me to where Paula and the other children are. God, Jesus, and the Holy Spirit made me a part of this New Day, so I want to go forward, not backwards."

"Okay, take my hand."

"No, wait, I have to know how you're able...to...to do it? How were you able to bring me here?"

"We're still on earth, but we have new bodies. We're in an area something like dream-space, so that's how we're able to move to different places. Funny, huh?"

"Very...so what I'm seeing isn't real?"

"Some dreams take you to real places. We've learned how to see people, places and things, and then we're able to take ourselves there. Since we all have new bodies we're able to move through time and space at the speed of light. Adam and Eve were supposed to receive this gift in the Garden of Eden, but when they were kicked out, their separation from God stopped all the wonderful stuff their faith was going to achieve. The Holy Spirit says, when we stop loving, we stop living. God is love, and Adam and Eve broke the power of love when they followed Satan's lies and not God's truth."

"You've been taught so much. I want to learn the wisdom you're receiving from the Holy Spirit. I'm willing to go with you, but let's go back and get my wife, so Paula will be with her mother."

"The Holy Spirit says to remind you that you wanted to go forward, and if you go backwards, you'll stay there."

"I choose to go forward."

"Good, because I wasn't even sure you could travel out of time, but since you're here, you must have been blessed with a new body like us."

"I've had lucid dreams of flying before, but I've always been surrounded by people with no faces. I don't want to go there!"

"Okay, we won't go there, but you need to take my hand so you won't get lost."

"No...I want to test this and see for myself. In my dreams, I could jump off a building and fly, or I could run and take off," Isaiah said, and then he ran down a path in the park, and when he lifted up his arms, he rose above the ground and flew.

"It works, I'm flying," Isaiah shouted, but when he realized he was doing an impossible feat, fear took over, and he tumbled towards the ground.

"Wake up!" Michael said, as he shook Isaiah. Isaiah looked around and realized that he was back in his living room.

"What happened?"

"Your faith is still very weak, so like the apostle Peter when he walked on the water, fear took over you. (Matthew 14:30) We've been taught that many people panic in their dream-state, even though they have all the power to fight darkness."

"Michael, do it again. I want to travel to where the children are."

"I'm sorry, it's too dangerous for you to make the trip. Something frightened you. Did the people with no faces come after you?"

"I don't remember. Trust me, I don't care how dangerous it is; I have to go with you. I'll speak for you! I'll answer the Call!"

"Are you sure? You still don't know what God is planning."

"I'm sure! I have to bring everyone back home!"

"I don't think we're coming back. We heard on television that we've...we've been Raptured. You still want to go?"

"You watch too much television. Teach me how you do this, so I'll be able to bring everyone back home."

"Pastor Hillman, you're not in charge, you're our guest speaker."

"Yes, of course. Am I dreaming now?"

"No, we're back in time with the world. Close your eyes, so you won't get scared again," Michael said.

⁓

"Isaiah must be the only one taken. No other adults are reported missing," Richard said changing television channels.

Thelma nodded in agreement, "That's a good sign, Evelyn. God wants Isaiah to be with Paula and the other children."

"I'm hearing Isaiah talking to someone in the living room," Evelyn said, and ran out of the kitchen, however, when she rushed into the living room, Isaiah and Michael, are no longer there. Evelyn sat down on the sofa and cried, which caused Thelma and Sylvia to shed tears. Richard and Henry aren't immune to their wives sorrowful tears and soon teardrops filled their eyes.

Evelyn, realizing her crying was causing everyone to lose faith, spoke out, "No more crying...God has not given us the spirit of fear, but of power, and of love, and of a sound mind. (2 Timothy 1:7 KJV) No more crying! God is in charge!

Richard smiled, hugged Evelyn, which caused everybody to warmly embrace.

⁓

Isaiah arrived at the highest point of a grassy hillside overlooking a sea of one million, five hundred and fourteen thousand children of all sizes, cultures and races, who traveled out time to be with their fellow Miracle Children from many nations and countries around the world. The whole hillside was alive with their voices of many languages.

Isaiah listened for a moment, and smiled, "I've heard this sound before…I've heard it before!"

"The Holy Spirit says, when you listen closely, the sounds coming from everyone are the reverberation of one united force, which is the vibrating sound of the universe. **OOOOOOMMMM…**"

"It sounds so beautiful, Michael. I can hear it so clearly."

"The Holy Spirit says the universal sound are the thoughts of Father God sending ideas, thoughts, dreams and other kinds of information into our spirit. You're starting to hear in tongues, even though you still don't understand what you're hearing. It took me a long time to hear Susan and the twins, but now I can hear and see everybody."

Isaiah weakly smiled, but started to have a major anxiety attack, he wondered if he was having a lucid dream, or was he in the place he went to in his dreams, and then he wondered where was his physical body, where was reality, and when he acknowledged to himself that he was unconscious, or having some weird, Out of Body Experience, he became dizzy and sat down on the grass.

"Here, drink this," Michael said, and handed Isaiah a cup of rainbow liquid.

Isaiah peered at the rainbow liquid.

"Go ahead, drink it, it'll give you great powers."

Isaiah sipped the liquid, smiled, and then drank it all.

"I was kidding about the great powers, but you believed it."

"And your point was?"

Michael laughed, "The Holy Spirit says you have no trouble believing what you want. Come on, everyone wants to meet you."

Isaiah walked with Michael amongst the children and shook hands with everyone who crowded around him.

Seven year old, Lin Chui shook Isaiah's hand and spoke in Mandarin, "Hello, Pastor Hillman. I am Lin Chui."

"Hello, Lin Chui. I'm honored to meet you," Isaiah answered in Mandarin. "Michael, I just spoke in Chinese."

"You spoke in Mandarin, Pastor Hillman. I am Chinese, my language is Mandarin," Lin Chui said.

"Yes, of course. Thank you, Lin Chui. I'm just amazed I can understand and speak Chin...Mandarin," Isaiah said, causing Lin Chui and other children to laugh. Isaiah was further astonished when he realized that as Michael led him through the crowd, he spoke in Danish, Greek, German, Dutch and Swahili.

Finally they arrived at a stream of water where Michelle, Leon, Alonzo and Susan are sitting. Michelle handed Paula to Isaiah, and he sat down with her in his arms.

Isaiah opened his eyes at sunrise and Paula was no longer in his arms. He looked around at all the excitement coming from the children, and when he stood up, he saw men and women setting up microphones, cameras and satellite dishes.

"Good Morning, Pastor Hillman," Michael said, as he walked up and stood beside Isaiah. "I'm sure you're well rested, you've been sleeping for five days."

"Five days! Today is...?"

"The Fourth of January, 2013. Happy New Year, Pastor Hillman."

"Why didn't you wake me up?"

"The Holy Spirit said it was best you slept. Your anxiety would have disturbed everyone."

"I'm sure the Holy Spirit, has taken into consideration how disturbed the world is with over a million children missing for...for...how long has it been?"

"Twelve days."

"Twelve days! What's going on?"

"You play Chess? We hear God is waiting for Satan to make his best move."

"And what might that be?"

"What else? Knock off everyone who protects the King, and the King's Kingdom will fall!"

"Yes, of course," Isaiah said, and pointed at some grown men and women. "Who are they?"

"Angels, they brought us here, and now they're setting up everything for us. Since you can see the angels, your spiritual eyes must be opened, and now that you're awake it must be time for you to prepare what you're going to tell everybody. I hope you've dreamed up something good?"

Somewhat annoyed that he was with the children, and still didn't have the slightest clue as to what was going on, Isaiah answered, "The Holy Spirit woke me up, I'll leave it in His capable Spirit to bless me with the right words."

Michael laughed, and signaled thumbs up to the Sea of Children on the hillside. Suddenly, one million, five hundred and fourteen thousand Miracle Children stood, cheered, shouted and clapped their hands.

~

"I'll get it, Evelyn," Richard called out, as doorbell rang again and he opened the front door.

"Good Morning, I'm Jan Summers. I'd like to speak with Pastor Hillman."

"He's not here," Richard said.

"I've been so upset about Michael Spencer's appearance on my show...I had to get away...I want...I need to talk with Pastor Hillman about the missing children."

"He's not here."

"Where is he? Please, may I have his cell phone number?"

Evelyn called out from the living room, "Who is it, Daddy?"

"The television news lady."

"I've been away, and it's been twelve days now. Has Pastor Hillman heard anything from Michael? The children?"

"Ms. Summers, he's gone. They took him."

"Who took him?"

"We've told everybody, Pastor Hillman was on a sabbatical…we kept it a secret because we didn't want anybody to know. Isaiah has been taken away like the children."

Evelyn shouted from the living room, "Daddy!!! Come here…Come here!

Richard rushed off and Jan followed him into the living room. Evelyn and Thelma pointed at the television, as the Miracle Children waved at cameras sweeping over the grassy hillside.

"What channel is that?" Jan asked.

Evelyn picked up the remote, pressed a button, and an insert of Channel 2 appeared on the screen.

"Do you mind?" Jan asked, and used the remote to check out other channels. One after another, the same scene of the children appeared on all the other networks and channels. The children were wearing colorful, traditional clothes from their native countries…China, Africa, Brazil, Saudi Arabia, and all the other nations around the world. They were clothed in turbans, cowboy hats, sombreros, baseball caps, derbies and bonnets, as well as crowns of kings and queens. The children wore Scottish plaid skirts, Native Indian cloths from America, beautiful sarongs of the Pacific Islands, and capes, shawls, scarves, baby clothes and outfits. The array of styles and clothes are too numerous to mention.

As the cameras swept over the hillside, the children bowed their heads in prayer, however, all their voices together became one universal sound.

"OOOOOOOMMMMMMM…"

"It's so beautiful…Oh God, there's Isaiah," Evelyn hollered, and pointed at the television screen as Isaiah walked onto a stage clothed in a violet colored pastor's robe.

~

At the hillside, the children sat on the grass, stood, shouted, hollered and cheered as Isaiah bowed before them.

"Hello," Isaiah shouted in Spanish, Hawaiian, and many other languages. "Hello…Hello…Hello…I'm told, I'm speaking in tongues to the whole world and everyone will hear me in their own language. What's so amazing is that I'm hearing myself in English! Wow! Isn't that something?"

Isaiah yelled, and stretched out his arms as if to embrace all the children, and once again, the children shouted out their joy, and raised their hands in praise.

"Hallelujah! Hallelujah! Hallelujah!!!"

Isaiah yelled out again, "I'll say it again, WOW!"

Loud words of celebration came from the children, and then Isaiah held up his hands to quiet everyone, "I'm Isaiah Hillman, former pastor of Victory Union Church, and I'm sure everybody around the world is wondering what's going on? As everyone else, I'm sure my wife and my family are also concerned. Honey, Paula is fine, well cared for, and as you can see, so are all the children. Though, we see thousands of angels surrounding the hillside, I'm told they're invisible to the television cameras. We see them, you don't, but I just wanted to let you know, God sent thousands of angels here to help us start this New Day!"

Isaiah watched as the angels swept their television and movie cameras over the Sea of Beautiful Children.

"The Miracle Children brought me here to speak for them; they want me to make them sound like adults. I guess their reason is that they'll be taken more seriously as adults, so first, I'll say to the children, if God wanted adults, He would have anointed adults instead of the children to bring on this Great Event, this New Day!"

The Miracle Children gazed at Isaiah for a moment, and then at Michael who stood to the rear of the stage, but Michael shrugged his shoulders to acknowledge that he didn't know where Isaiah was going with his words.

"I know it's difficult for many people around the world to understand, or to wrap their minds around how God is able to take one million, five hundred, and fourteen thousand children out of the world, but I'll try to explain. First of all, we're not out of the world. We're still here. I know it's difficult for people to believe this, because it's still difficult for me, too. However, hear me, **it's never been difficult for the children to believe**," Isaiah said, as the children screamed and shouted in appreciation.

"Michael Spencer told me that it was fun for the Miracle Children to believe and trust God, but believing wasn't fun for adults. Michael's words still brings joyful chills through my body. Look at our beautiful children, and learn why Jesus called them the greatest in the Kingdom of Heaven,"(Matthew 18:4) Isaiah shouted, which elicited loud cheers from everyone.

"Okay, okay...I've thought about this, and if you know the Bible, you'll understand! The Prophet Elijah was taken up in a whirlwind to heaven, his body never buried in a tomb or grave. Michael Spencer told me about a man named Edgar Cayce, who went into a trance and was capable of traveling to places past, present, and future. Christ Jesus rose from the dead, left the tomb, and appeared to his disciples. Then Jesus led them to Bethany, and lifting his hands to heaven, he blessed them. (Luke 24:50 NLT) And while he was blessing them, he left them and was taken up to heaven. (51) So you shouldn't think this as being impossible. Astral Projection, Out of Body Experiences, Lucid Dreams, many of you have had such experiences, and probably like many of you, I didn't believe something like this could actually happen in reality, however, I'm here, and now I truly understand the prophetic word Michael Spencer spoke to the world…"Believe!"

The hillside, once again became a thunderous roar as the Miracle Children shouted in joy.

"Believe God. Believe God's Word, Christ Jesus. Believe God's Holy Spirit! And finally, believe God's Mighty Power! Michael Spencer told me about the exciting things God is preparing for the world in the New Day. Trust me, you'll be blessed to walk in it. However, I'll say to you again, the children brought me here to speak for them, and I'm here, and I still don't know what this is all about, and I'm shocked to find out that the children don't know either, but they made a promise to obey the Call on their lives, and not one of them has walked away from it. God Bless Them All!" Isaiah yelled, and caused more rousing cheers.

He picked up a glass of rainbow liquid juice, sipped the contents, and looked out at the children.

"The children tell me that they've prepared for this day, however, like the rest of the world, they don't know what the essence of God's mysterious plan for a New Day fully entails? I look out over this Sea of Beautiful Children, and I cry out, Lord, why am I here?…Why me?…Why am I here?" Isaiah asked, and somewhat upset, that the Miracle Children placed him in a situation he didn't know how to resolve. The hillside was so quiet; he could hear that elusive pin drop, and then Isaiah heard the Holy Spirit's voice in his spirit.

Tears in his eyes, Isaiah's voice became calm, "You know what? Just now, that still small voice spoke and gave me the answer as to why I'm here, and I have to confess, I've been selfish, thinking only about what I wanted to do with my life, well, the Holy Spirit told me what He wanted in two words, *Save Lives!* The Holy Spirit gave Michael Spencer one word, *Believe*, and now, those of you willing to put your life in God's hand, God is willing to save you. It's sounds so simple, but His words carry real power. Wow, two words…*Save Lives!* I recall the biblical history of the Israelites smearing the blood of a lamb on their doorposts, and the death angel passed over their house (Exodus 12:13), so let's pray together, and save your life by pleading the blood of Jesus over your life, your family, and your home. (Hebrews 13:20/21) Michael Spencer's father, Henry Spencer, believed he needed to get his life in order, and we prayed the 'Sinner's Prayer' together. I'm sure many of you need to do the same, otherwise, why would the Holy Spirit tell me to Save Lives? Don't get left behind! Those of you willing to believe in our Lord and Savior, Jesus Christ, repeat after me…no, wait, I first want to tell you about the Power of God opening your eyes today!"

Isaiah stared into a camera, "I know some of you may not want to take this walk of faith with Jesus, and you have the God given choice to refuse, but I was in the morgue with Michael's sister, Michelle, and Doctor Norman, who had pronounced Michael dead, and while we were praying over Michael's body, Michelle told us that Jesus was in the morgue, and he was bringing Michael back from the other side of life. I looked around, and though Michelle saw Jesus, the doctor and I didn't, however, what we did see was Michael's body being miraculously healed and brought back to life. The Word says we walk by faith, not by sight. (2 Corinthians 5:7 KJV) So again, you have the choice to make that walk with Jesus being offered today. The Holy Spirits says for me, to Save Lives, so everyone let's call on the name of Jesus Christ. In Acts 4:12, the scripture reads: neither is there salvation in any other: for there is none other name under heaven given among men, whereby we must be saved. Come, take that faith walk and repeat after me, "Dear God, I'm sorry for my sins..."

~

In Los Angeles, basketball players, coaches, fans, and vendors inside the Staples Center, who watched Isaiah on large monitors, stood and repeated the 'Sinner's Prayer' along with Isaiah, "I believe Christ died for me, and that his precious blood washes away all my sins..."

~

Tabriz, Iran. A Muslim family watched their television and prayed along with Isaiah when a bright light materialized in their living room. The light formed into the body of Christ Jesus, and everyone's spirit was filled with his words, "I am the way, the truth, and the life..." (John 14:6 KJV)

"By faith, I now receive..." Isaiah continued.

The Muslim family bowed in submission, and repeated Isaiah's words, "By faith, I now receive Jesus as my Lord and Savior. Trusting him for the salvation of my soul..."

"Thank you, Lord for saving my life," Isaiah prayed, and then raised his hands to give praise to God. "I truly believe in my heart, that today, the blood of Jesus has saved over a billion lives, and God's Loving Spirit welcomes you into the New Day. God Bless You! Amen!"

Isaiah completed the 'Sinners Prayer' and waved to everyone as Michael walked to center stage and stared out at everyone.

No one moved or said a word until, Miracle Child Akeem Wallace hollered out from the crowd, "Michael, Praise the Lord!"

The children once again cheered, shouted, and clapped their hands.

Michael laughed, "I was going to come here, and do what we've prepared, and then, watch and wait like everybody else to see what was going to happen today. After listening to Pastor Hillman's words, I believe in my heart God wants us all saved and brought into His Kingdom...God chose a few of us to open this day, however, I don't know...I mean we don't know how the day will end, so we hope you prayed along with our pastor, and that whatever else this day brings, you'll always remember that God loves you! Now, let's sing and **Bring On The New Day!!!**"

*Michael: **God has heard our cries***
*   **And listened to our lies***
*   **Now a bright light has come***
*   **To open up our eyes***
*   **He knows our fears***
*   **He knows you want to hide***
*   **But where can you go***
*   **That God will not see***
*   **God sees everybody***
*   **Through our eyes***
The Miracle Children:
*   **We've been blessed to see***
*   **Through God's eyes***
*   **Now look and see***
*   **And see what we see***
*   **Through God's eyes***
*Michael: **Run and get your Bibles***
*   **Read Jesus' words inside***
*   **Suffer not the children***
*   **Bring them all to me***
*   **Such is the Kingdom of God***
*   **Where truth is alive***
*   **Jesus wants to save you***

> *And bring you all inside*
> *Hear the words of Jesus*
> *Become like children again*
> *Hear the Holy Voice inside*
> *Become as children*
> *And see through God's eyes*

The Miracle Children:

> *You'll see all His Glory*
> *His Power and Majesty*
> *Knock, His door will open*
> *And you'll see inside*
> *You'll see the Kingdom of God*
> *Through God's eyes*
> *You'll see what God sees*
> *Through His All-Seeing eyes*
> *You'll see heaven*
> *In all your dreams*
> *You'll see your life renewed*
> *Through God's eyes*
> *Through God's eyes*
> *You'll see inside*
> *Through God's eyes...*

As Michael and the Miracle Children continue in song, television viewers around the world watch a video, while everyone on the hillside sang and watched giant television monitors of Baby Jesus, laid in a manger (Luke 2:7 KJV), who then metamorphoses into a child who receives gifts of gold, frankincense, and myrrh from the Wise Men (Matthew 2:11 KJV), then becoming a boy teaching in the temple (Luke 2:47), being baptized as the Spirit of God descends on him as a dove, and the voice of God thundered over the singing, **"This is my beloved Son, in whom I am well pleased."** (Matthew 3:16/17 KJV)

The Miracle Children:
> *Through God's eyes*
> *God's All-Seeing eyes*
> *You'll see inside*
> *Though God's eyes*
> *You'll see your life anew*
> *The Holy Spirit living in you*
> *You'll see and believe*
> *The New Day in you…*

The video then, reveals Jesus in the synagogue as he read from the Old Testament, **"The Spirit of the Lord is upon me, for he hath anointed me to preach the gospel to the poor; he hath sent me to heal the brokenhearted, to preach deliverance to the captives, and recovering of sight to the blind, to set at liberty them that are bruised, to preach the acceptable year of the Lord,"** (Luke 4:18-19 KJV) and as Jesus spoke, the video showed his miracle powers of thousands being healed, fed, delivered, and lifted up in their spirit. Jesus, as the Messiah, sat down with his disciples at 'The Last Supper' ceremonial worship of consuming the bread and wine, which symbolized His body and blood, (Mark 14:22-25 KJV) and finally, the video showed Jesus on Calvary's Cross, as thousands of angels sprinkle the blood of the lamb, on his wounded body, and he descended down into the pit of darkness, crying out in a loud voice, ***"Eloi, Eloi, lema sabachthani?"*** and everyone knew that Jesus had cried out, "My God, my God, why have you forsaken me?" (Mark 15:34 NLT) This was the moment when God had to separate from His Son, because His Holiness would not allow His Spirit, to look at the sins Jesus took upon himself to wash away the sins of mankind.

The Miracle Children sang on, as the world watched the video of Jesus, who took all the dark, ugly sins of mankind, past, present, and future into his Spirit, and he became a burning fire, that turned into a light so bright, that all darkness disappeared, and when he rose out of the ground, a field of beautiful lilies sprouted up, and Christ Jesus ascended up into heaven.

All the Miracle Children cheered as Michelle walked out onto the stage and waved to everyone, "I really, really love that video. Wasn't it awesome?" Michelle yelled, as everyone shouted with joy. "No matter how old you are, the Holy Spirit says, we are all Miracle Children, because when God breathed His Spirit into life, all life became a miracle, and no matter what your religion is, or what your age is, we are still one family, one blood, and we are all Children of God! Everyone in the world has been given special gifts and talents. Pastor Hillman says, we're going to grow up and become great scientists, doctors, adventurers, explorers, preachers, teachers, pastors and priests, so watch out, **Here We Come!**"

Michelle shouted, and then she sang a rousing, up-lifting song with lots of energy, which started, The Miracle Children's World Concert.

Isaiah is astounded, as he watched the children sing in Chinese, Spanish, Africana, and many other dialects from nations around the world. And while they sang, danced, and performed, they also did amazing flying and acrobatic skills. They flipped, somersaulted and leaped; they also played drums, bongos, tambourines, violins, flutes, guitars, horns, and thousands of other musical instruments from individual homelands.

"Wow!" Isaiah said in amazement, as he looked out at the colossal spectacle and celebration the Miracle Children joyfully shared with the world.

Michael, Michelle, Leon and Alonzo and Susan are all on stage, when Michael hollered out, "Hello World, we've been practicing for a while now, and we hope you enjoy this song we wrote together. It's called, 'Something Inside Is Grabbing Me'

The Miracle Children:
> *Something is happening*
> *God has set me free*
> *I feel good all over*
> *As voices call to me*
> *Something new is happening*
> *For all the world to see*
> *Something new is happening*
> *Something Inside Is Grabbing Me!*

Michelle yelled out, "Sing along with us. If you can't sing, hum!"

"If you can't hum, SHOUT," Leon and Alonzo sang.

"If you can't sing, can't hum, can't shout, *dance*!" Susan beamed and performed a spiritual dance as all the children urged her on with their musical accompaniment.

Susan's final dance move was to open a large floor hatch, and release a thousand white doves that flew out over everybody. She then signaled, for a group of children from Africa to do their spiritual dance, and to beat their drums loud and fast.

Miracle Children from Brazil, then sang...'Something Inside Is Grabbing Me' in Portuguese with a Samba beat, then one after another, children from other countries sang in their native tongues.

To bring the Miracle Children's Concert to its highest level of joy, an eight-year-old Israeli boy blew the song on his trumpet.

The Miracle Children's Concert was a perfect celebration, and something the whole world needed to see and enjoy.

~

8

Believers

Don't believe me unless I carry out my Father's work. But if I do his work, believe in what I have done, even if you don't believe me. Then you will realize that the Father is in me, and I am in the Father. John 10:37-38

Three fighter jets flew over the hillside. One of the pilots looked down at the Miracle Children from his cockpit and signaled, 'Thumbs Up' to the two other pilots, and then the jets kicked in their after burners, and broke the Sound Barrier as they accelerated and raced off.

At sundown, the three jets returned with a bomber that flew two hundred feet behind. When the bomber flew over the hillside, the bay door opened and millions of colorful confetti littered the sky, however, a large object was also dropped from the belly of the bomber and soared toward the hillside.

An angel immediately blew a ram's horn so loud, that it shook the hillside. Then another voice spoke, loud and clear, **"Be still, and know that I am God."** (Psalm 46:10)

All together, at the same time, Isaiah, the Miracle Children, and the angels lifted up their hands in Praise to God.

~

Billions of people around the world heard the ram's horn, and then the television screens and Internet monitors blacked out.

A second later, a news reporter came on a local television station and announced, "We've lost the signal from the Miracle Children's Concert..."

Evelyn, the Downings, and the Spencers stared as if frozen.

"What happen, Daddy?" Evelyn asked, excited, nervous, and afraid.

"The station lost the signal. Thelma, change the station." Richard said, quite nervous about the sight he saw of the jets and bomber flying over the hillside.

A News Host, on the next channel, announced, "We all saw a bomber fly over the hillside and drop confetti and something else...Ladies and gentlemen, I believe something horrible has happened..."

~

Back on the hillside, as a nuclear bomb **EXPLODED,** a gigantic mushroom cloud lifted up from the center of the explosion. Suddenly, a mighty wind was BLOWN over the hillside, and fire ignited trees, bushes and the grass. Television cameras and equipment melted in an instant, and the wooden stage was blown away in splinters. A dark cloud engulfed the hillside, and finally, the cloud covered the whole island in Black Smoke.

~

"It appears that a terrorist group has attacked the Miracle Children," Alison Hewitt reported from the National News Network. "Stay tuned, as we try to confirm the reports."

Evelyn let out a chilling scream, as the Downings and Spencers looked at one another in shock, fear and horror.

"Not again! No God, not again," Evelyn cried, as she stood, but becoming weak in her knees, she collapsed to the floor.

Thelma and Richard knelt down to help Evelyn.

"Not again? What did she mean?" Sylvia asked.

"Isaiah's parents were killed by a suicide bomber in Israel," Richard said, using a magazine to fan Evelyn.

"I'm sorry, I didn't know."

"He was three years old when it happened, so he doesn't really remember it," Thelma continued.

"He was there?"

"Twenty people were killed on the bus, but God protected Isaiah then, and God will protect the Miracle Children, now," Richard stated, changing the channel to a pastor in Houston, Texas.

"Let's pray and have faith. God knew this was coming! God knows everything," the pastor said, speaking to his congregation, but soon, he too is overcome by his inner emotions and his heart cried out, "Oh, God...My God...save us...save us from ourselves..."

The pastor knelt down as a young woman in the pew screamed out words of anger.

"Killing children isn't a new beginning of anything. It's the beginning of The End," the young woman yelled, which caused men and women to be overwhelmed with grief. Many fainted and fell to the floor, and an elderly gentleman experienced a major heart attack, and as the deacons and elders rushed about to help him, and the others who were overcome with grief, it didn't take long before the deacons and elders were also overtaken by the same sorrows as everyone else.

~

In Toronto, Ontario, Canada a news reporter was televising his report, "It's a madhouse here at the Sports Center, and now emergency crews have to remove the bodies of those who have been crushed and trampled by those fleeing the Center!"

~

Paris, France. Pierre Benoit reported from his News Desk, "Reports are coming in that our streets are full of rioters."

"Pierre, many businesses have been vandalized and burned. In protests against God, madmen have firebombed many churches. When the Nuclear Attack was confirmed, it seems inner hates, racism, and prejudices took over people's minds and they've ran into the streets committing crime, rapes, and murders as if there's no tomorrow."

"Denise, those who aren't out in the streets are locked behind closed doors in their homes with their curtains drawn…This is so horrible…"

~

Jan Summers, back in her television studio, reported, "In a matter of a few hours fires are burning throughout our nation, and people have taken the law into their own hands. Citizens are shooting anyone who approaches their homes and businesses. The President has issued Orders for the National Guard and Police Officers, to shoot and kill anyone on the street after six this evening."

"I'm tired, Daddy. Turn to something else, or turn off the television," Evelyn said, as Richard switched channels to a pastor.

"The Miracle Children tried to prepare us for the end of this life we cherished rightly and wrongly. Please forgive us our transgressions, Father God. We don't doubt your Mighty Power, and we know in our spirit that the children are in your hands, and that this day shall past. We believe in our hearts, minds, and spirits that Your Glory Will Shine forever and ever..."

~

At Jan's television studio, she spoke in a soft voice, "These satellite photos are from Star Island, in the Indian Ocean. The site still shows a black cloud hovering over the devastated island. The dim light shows a mournful view of the bombing's after effects, and reports are saying there's no sign of life, nothing to see, except the radioactive dust that the wind is spewing all around...why would a God allow this to happen? I don't understand a God who kills children…"

"Cut! Go to commercial!" the show's director yelled. "Jan, what are you doing? Just report the news!"

~

"Enough," Evelyn said, in anger she grabbed the remote control from Richard and turned off the television.

"Evelyn, you need to remember your husband's words."

"What?"

"How easy it is for you to forget what Isaiah said!"

"What did he say, Daddy? Tell me, what did he say! Do you think he knew this was going to happen and he hid it from us?"

"No, Evelyn, he told us he didn't know what the New Day was about, so how could he hide what he didn't know? Sweetheart, remember Isaiah's words when he said, thousands of angels were protecting them, so stop all your crying and show everyone here the faith you've been blessed with. You say you're married to Jesus, but it doesn't look like you totally understand your commitment to trust him in everything. Everything, means everything, Evelyn!"

Evelyn stares at Richard, but remains tearfully silent.

"Honey, God sent Isaiah and the Miracle Children to that island. And if God's Mighty Power took them there, He has the Power to take them away. Isaiah and the children are fine; it's our world that's going crazy. Now, give me back the remote and let me watch what's going on."

"Always listen to your father, Evelyn," Thelma said.

Evelyn stared at Thelma and Richard, it took a moment, but she wiped away her tears, smiled, and handed her father the remote, "Thanks Daddy, I'm glad you're here.

~

9

Paradise

Then as I looked, I saw a door standing open in heaven, and the same voice I had heard before spoke to me with the sound of a mighty trumpet blast. The voice said, "Come up here, and I will show you what must happen after these things." Revelation 4:1 NLT

Thousands of angels guided Michael, Michelle, Leon and Alonzo, Susan, Isaiah, and all the other Miracle Children to an area of two closed doors that are enormous and gigantic in size. They were equaled in length and width of the World Trade Center's Twin Towers that once stood at the area called, Ground Zero in New York City, the site that terrorists attacked on September 11th, 2001. The doors opened the way into Paradise, a beautiful memorial of remembrance, made of gold, copper, crystals, diamonds, silver, and so many other metals, minerals and jewels, that it was impossible to describe the mixture of colors and reflected lights, except as a pure rainbow from a heavenly paradise.

The Miracle Children stared in awe at the beautiful Memorial Doors, and as they marveled, the doors slowly opened to reveal a look inside Paradise, so perfectly bright, clear, and beautiful. Everyone's eyes sparkled with joy and excitement as a man walked out and greeted them.

"Welcome, I am, Father Abraham, and I'm honored to bring you into paradise, Our Father's place of rest for believers, an a perfect creation of God the Father, Jesus the Christ, and the Holy Spirit. You've all been given visions of paradise before in your dreams, now you're blessed to walk into the truth."

Abraham smiled, and then led Isaiah and the one million, five hundred and fourteen thousand Miracle Children into God's Paradise, and as they entered, their earthly clothing was turned into bright colorful robes of many colors. Each robe was individually and beautifully designed, honoring each child that was so privileged to wear an article of clothing just like Joseph's coat of many colors in the Bible. (Genesis 37:3)

On earth, at the Miracle Children's Concert, the children sang songs, danced, and played musical instruments for the world, but now, everyone in Paradise was singing, dancing, and playing musical instruments to greet them. Angels flew about and created rays of beautiful colors in their afterglow. Along with the singing, dancing, and music was the thunderous applauds of celebration for Isaiah and the Miracle Children.

Abraham led Isaiah and the Miracle Children, along streets lined with beautiful homes, trees, many colorful flowers, lakes and ponds. Many, many homes were adorned with stained glass windows, but none the same in design or colors. There were also movie theaters, playhouses, cathedrals, tennis courts, baseball fields, swimming pools and amusement parks. Whatever people enjoyed on earth, the same was available in Paradise, and much, much more. The only difference was that God blessed everyone and everything in Paradise, and the people never took it for granted. They enjoyed all their blessings with the true understanding of God's love for them.

As they walked with Father Abraham, many stars, celebrities, sports figures, scientists, doctors, preachers, teachers, pastors, priests, prophets, and evangelists stepped out from amongst the crowd of people and shook hands with Isaiah and the Miracle Children.

Isaiah looked around at his new surroundings and commented, "I believe we've been beamed up into the Kingdom."

"I think we're dreaming," Susan said.

Leon shook his head negatively, "No Susan, we're not dreaming."

"We're dead," Leon and Alonzo announced.

Susan asked, "Dreaming dead?"

"No. Dead dead!" Leon and Alonzo groaned.

"God killed us?"

Isaiah interceded, "Susan, Leon and Alonzo don't know what they're talking about. We're alive, and God has brought all of us into heaven."

"Dead people go to heaven, Pastor Hillman," Alonzo stated.

Leon groaned, "We're dead, dead, dead. One million, five hundred and fourteen thousand children, and one pastor, dead!"

A man and woman, with no visible faces approached Isaiah, which made him nervous like in his dream. As they came closer, their faces became visible, and Isaiah regonized his parents from childhood family photographs.

It became a very emotional moment for everyone as they hugged and kissed each other.

"How come I could never see your faces in my dreams?"

His father answered, "It was a horrible experience for you, Isaiah. You didn't want to remember our bodies being destroyed in the bombing, so you blocked it out of your mind. Look, we have new bodies here in paradise. Actually, you now have a better body than the one that took you to that island."

Isaiah's mother took Paula into her arms, "Hi, my beautiful granddaughter, I'm Leticia, and this is Arthur your grandfather. I'm so happy to finally hold you in my arms. You're so precious to us!" Leticia kissed Paula and handed her to Arthur

Everyone has tears in their eyes. Then, thousands of other relatives stepped forward and introduced themselves to Isaiah.

"Hi, I'm your, Uncle Samuel."

"Cousin Lucas Stern, I fought with General McArthur in the Philippines."

"Cousin Uko-Bendi, from Lagos, Nigeria," Uko-Bendi announced, and then, took Paula from Leticia's arms and kissed her three times, before passing Paula to the other relatives.

~

"We're very proud of you, Isaiah." Arthur said, after Isaiah had met and greeted thousands of his relatives.

"I feel over honored."

"There are celebrations like this everyday. When a family member crosses over, relatives bring them here to the Park of Beautiful Flowers. The name was chosen because the beauty of the flowers here cannot be found anywhere else! This park calms the heart of new arrivals upon entering Paradise. Of course, this special gathering created so many challenges to welcome you and all the children."

"Isaiah, can you imagine feeding thousands of ancestors for just one child? Jesus fed fish and bread only to five thousand. We have to do that, and we also have to serve desert," Leticia joked, which caused laughter from everyone.

Susan walked up and sat down next to Isaiah, "Hi!"

Isaiah smiled, "Everybody, this is Susan Faraday. A very special Miracle Child."

"Are we in heaven?" Susan asked, as she shook Arthur's hand.

"Susan, you're in a special place, called Paradise." Arthur said.

"Oh, we're not in heaven?" Susan said, surprised.

"No, you're in Paradise. God brought all of us here to rest and learn. Now the time has come, and we'll all return to the earth and start the New Day with you guys!"

"Arthur, I don't think you're right. The children tried to bring the New Day into the earth, but the people weren't ready to receive it, so I don't think we're going there anytime soon," Leticia said.

"God will bring paradise into the earth, Leticia."

"People will love living in Paradise. It's so beautiful," Susan said, looking around at the joyful celebration.

Arthur smiled, "Many people from earth don't get this far. Their spirits became so lost they're unable to pull themselves out of the hell they've created with their sins and disobedience. When you are born into the earth, you go to school and learn how to live in harmony with each other. Here, in Paradise, are schools for believers, because there are so many things to learn about the power of faith, that, not every spirit has yet experienced. You understand that?"

"God is not here?" Susan asked.

"Susan, what did Michael mean when he told the world to believe?"

"To believe in Jesus, and that heaven is a real place."

"Good, but many of us who are able to live in Paradise, believed what you just said, but we didn't learn everything, so we have to go to school. Some people start in Spiritual Kindergarten, and some start at a higher level, but everyone must go to school and learn how powerful believing is. All the doubts, that still live in your spirit, have to be recognized and replaced with truth. God sent His Holy Spirit to visit and live in everyone who believed, but not everyone is able to visit and live with God. Understand?"

"Michael told me God lives in heaven, and only special people live here."

"Susan, you're in Paradise. God lives in the Kingdom of God, the Holies of Holy."

"Is that where Jesus lives?"

"Yes, Jesus, the Holy Spirit, Father Abraham, many angels, prophets...and they're able to enter Paradise anytime they want, but only pure spirits are able to enter the Kingdom of God."

"I want to go there!"

Arthur smiled at Susan, "Sweetheart, many people have been in paradise a long, long time, and never been in the Kingdom of God. It's really that Special."

"I believe we're going there! I'll take you when we go," Susan announced.

"We?"

"The Miracle Children, we're going into the Kingdom of God."

"Who told you that?" Leticia questioned.

"Pastor Hillman taught us that it's written in the Bible: Let the children come to me. Don't stop them! For the

Kingdom of Heaven belongs to such as these." (Matthew 19:14 NLT)

"You have a spirit full of faith and confidence, Miss Susan Faraday," Arthur smiled, and hugged her. "No wonder God has chosen you."

"What's confidence?" Susan asked.

"Belief in the ability to accomplish the impossible," Isaiah answered.

"Pastor Hillman dreamed that the Miracle Children were blessed with a triple anointing. I believe his dream, and the Holy Spirit taught us how powerful believing is, and now, I believe God wants us to see his Kingdom. That's why we're here!" Susan said, with authority, and then walked off to visit with other Miracle Children and their families.

Arthur watched Susan for a moment, then turned and questioned Isaiah, "Is she always so sure of herself?"

"I've come to realize that the Miracle Children listen and walk in concert with the Holy Spirit. Susan seems to hear, see, makes a decision, and then, speaks."

"Ah, a prophet. I hope she decides wisely," Cousin Uko-Bendi commented.

"Do you see something else, Uko-Bendi?"

"Her seeing, hearing, and speaking are wise. Her decisions are young, Arthur."

"Yes, they are. Perhaps, that's why God chose children."

"Young decisions are more brass than gold."

"Richness of mind outshines all gold."

"A mind full of riches doesn't shine in the dark."

"You two, please, knock it off," Leticia said, and turned her attention to Isaiah. "We've been told about the New Day coming into the earth, but not much more than that. Arthur thinks our time here in Paradise is over, and we'll be sent back with you to start the Kingdom of Earth. What have you and the children been told?"

"Actually, absolutely nothing. I was hoping you had some answers," Isaiah replied, which caused everyone's spirit to wonder about God's plan for the New Day.

"Isaiah, there's absolutely everything, there's no absolutely nothing!" Uko-Bendi said.

"How about being absolutely wrong?" Arthur questioned.

"Wrong is something, not a nothing," Uko-Bendi smiled.

"God, please give these little boys some chores to do," Leticia prayed, which made Arthur and Uko-Bendi laugh.

~

10

Spirit

But seek ye first the Kingdom of God, and his righteousness; and all these things shall be added unto you. Matthew 6:33 KJV

"It's time to go," Michael said, when he walked up and spoke to Isaiah.

"Michael, Isaiah will stay at our home, and you will stay at one of your relative's home," Leticia said.

"No, that's not what I meant about going. Susan got us invited into the Kingdom of God. We're going there."

"Wow! Isaiah, that little girl must have…must have…I don't know what she has, but she must have it!" Arthur said, astonished.

"All the children were blessed, not just her," Isaiah answered.

"Michael said Susan got you all invited into the Kingdom of God, not the Miracle Children. Something about her is more powerful than the others."

"I thought God didn't have favorites?"

Leticia responded, "Son, many are favored, and some are highly favorite. Trust me, that little girl is special in God's eyes, you must protect her."

Isaiah nodded, taking his parents advice to watch over Susan, but was shocked when he saw family and friends disappearing in the park.

"What's happening?" Isaiah questioned.

"They're returning to their homes," Arthur explained. "Word has spread that God has granted Susan's prayer to visit the Kingdom of God. It's a wonderful experience, and when we go home, we're able to telepathically connect with the one entering the Kingdom. But millions of spirits attaching themselves to one spirit entering the Kingdom, well, you can imagine...how unsuccessful that would be? So the spirits that are unable to connect just relax, imagine, dream, and create in their mind and enjoy what they've heard about the Kingdom of God, and sometimes you're able to get in that way. However, those who are unable to enter God's Kingdom still love the experiences that they're able to create for themselves."

"On earth, you'll call it pleasure," Leticia blushed. "In Paradise, pleasure is holy, and since you, and over a million and a half, Miracle Children will be entering the Kingdom of God, there's every possibility many spirits will be able to connect and enjoy the Great Pleasures of God."

"I apologize, but it sounds so...sensual," Isaiah remarked, cautiously.

"God is pure delight and pure sensuality. Going into the Kingdom of God is like reliving the first day of your marriage. The Bible says: just as a young man cares for his bride; then God will rejoice over you as a bridegroom rejoices over his bride. (Isaiah 62:5) Son, besides pure delight and sensuality, another one of God's many attributes is Holy Passion, when He created Adam and Eve, they were to experience His Holy

Passion instead of, earthly, sexual passion; unfortunately, mankind has corrupted the real beauty of Holy Passion, which was God's plan in the beginning."

Arthur offered, "This experience you're about to receive is higher than anything you've ever experienced on earth, and from what I've heard, going into the Kingdom…well… Isaiah, you're going to experience the Super Abundance of God."

"Believe me, this experience is so powerful that men will turn off the latest sports event from earth!! Leticia said.

"You watch sports?"

"I don't, but your dad gets a thrill out of it. Once in a while, I'm able to drag him away, and we visit your dreams."

"I'm sure everyone is now waiting to attach their spirit to a Miracle Child…watch this, Isaiah…" Arthur smiled, as all the trash, food, bottles, etc…suddenly disappeared and only the pristine purity of the Park of Beautiful Flowers remained. "Paradise is something else, Isaiah. Something else."

"Where did everything go?"

"It just disappeared…Paradise is not like the earth, where people don't care about contaminating the environment, living here, Our God makes sure Paradise remains a Paradise," Leticia said.

Michelle walked up to Isaiah, "Take my hand, the Holy Spirit is opening the way for us now."

When Michelle joined hands with Isaiah and his parents, they all disappeared in the blink of an eye, and at the same instant, all the other Miracle Children in the Park of Beautiful Flowers also vanished.

~

Isaiah, the Miracle Children, and the guests are all in awe upon seeing **the Savior, Christ Jesus** walking amongst them. Voices sang out praises of, "Hosanna, Hosanna, Hosanna, to the Son of Our God!"

Isaiah and the children's reaction are indescribable and awesome as they clapped their hands in loud ovation with everyone else.

Jesus raised his hand in a grateful attitude, calling everybody to his attention. His smile is full of joy and kindness, while His eyes are full of genuine love, as a bright light glowed from His face.

"We welcome you, Pastor Isaiah Hillman, the Miracle Children, and all your love-ones," Lord Christ Jesus announced. His very calm voice was filled with Kingdom Authority and Majesty. "I'm very happy to see all of you, the true children of Our Father God. Your presence is truly a wonderful experience for me, and for everyone else living in Paradise and God's Kingdom. Everyone invited to enter Our Father's presence, has the ability to enlarge his or her vision, but you have to learn how to see beyond yourself first. To get into Paradise, you had to be separated from your body. To get into the Kingdom of God, you have to separate from your old thinking and see with the eyes of your spirit. Everybody close your eyes and be still...be still...be still... keep your eyes closed a little longer...okay, when you open your eyes, raise your hand to let me know if you've seen the Father with your spiritual eyes!"

The Miracle Children and visitors raised their hands.

"Leon and Alonzo Serna, what did you see in your vision?" Jesus asked, laying his hands on their heads.

"Rainbow Man," Leon and Alonzo, chimed.

Jesus laughed, "Leon and Alonzo, you see the beauty in mankind." He turned to Michael and asked, "What did you see?"

"A Powerful Hand," Michael said, with certain confidence.

"That's why you were chosen to be the leader of the Miracle Children. God has given you authority!!!" Jesus smiled, and hugged Michael. "Use your power to strengthen all your brothers and sisters."

"Yes, Lord," Michael answered, already feeling power strengthening his body.

"Michelle Spencer, how about you?"

"A heart full of true love, Lord." Michelle stated, her eyes and face beamed with love.

"You'll always have it," Jesus smiled, and kissed her on the forehead, as well as the left and right side of her face.

"My Dear, Susan Faraday, what was your vision?" Jesus asked.

"Fire." Susan announced.

"Hmmn…that's a very powerful vision, Susan," Jesus confirmed. "The world will test you."

"I know," Susan said, her voice filled with new confidence.

Jesus smiled, and then closed her eyes with his fingers. "Now what do you see?"

"A baby near some water."

"Do you know who the baby is?"

"Yes."

Tears of joy filled Jesus' eyes, as He moved on to the other Miracle Children, "What was your vision?"

"Bright Star!"

"Purple Cloud."

"Noisy Vibrations."

"Fourth of July Sparkles."

Jesus laughed, joked, and enjoyed all the visions the children saw, until he heard a little voice that stopped him.

"Marriage!"

"Who said that?" Jesus asked.

"Sonia Santiago, from Costa Rica, Lord." The Holy Spirit answered.

Jesus smiled, and then spoke, "Come forward, Sonia Santiago."

Sonia stepped out of the crowd and stood before Jesus.

Jesus, eyes filled with wonder, spoke to the little girl, "Sonia, when the dead rise, they neither marry…"

"Nor are they given in marriage; but are as the angels which are in heaven. Mark 12:25." Sonia said, and completed the scripture for Jesus.

Jesus laughed, "So beautiful. How old are you?"

"Eight years old. Father God has blessed me with a photographic memory."

"And your vision of God was marriage?"

"My vision was the wedding where you turned water into wine and performed your first miracle, John 2:1-11. The Bible also says in Revelation 19:9 - Blessed are those invited to the Wedding Feast of the Lamb."

"And what does that mean to you?" Jesus asked.

"God wants all his children to be married to the Lamb."

Jesus marveled at Sonia's Bible knowledge and wisdom, and then announced to everyone, "Today, I'm still more than amazed at the gifts Our Father has blessed His children with!" Jesus hugged and kissed Sonia, then took her little hand in his and led her over to Isaiah. Jesus placed his other hand on Isaiah's shoulder.

"Pastor Isaiah Hillman, what did you see?"

"Nothing," Isaiah said, disappointed.

"Close your eyes again. Count to three, and then reopen your eyes and tell everyone your vision."

Isaiah did as Jesus instructed him, and then reopened his eyes.

"I saw a vision of the Universe."

"Your hands will be full," Jesus remarked.

"I don't think that was God," Isaiah said.

"So true, and soon you'll be able to hear as well as you see," Jesus said, then he took Paula from Isaiah's arms. He looked into her eyes and said, "I can hear your spirit, Paula Hillman. What did you see?"

Paula looked at Jesus, their eyes connected, and her face glowed a special light of purity.

"That's a beautiful vision you saw, Paula. You'll always know the Kingdom of God belongs to you," (Matthew 19:14 NLT) Jesus smiled and kissed her. He then spoke to everyone else. "I'll explain what you've all experienced. Everybody, listen up. The first thing you've learned is that not everyone sees the same. You're from different countries, speak different languages, and have different life experiences, so you see differently. Okay, once again, listen up! Because, I asked you to raise your hand if you saw the Father, you've accepted that whatever you saw was the Father. Your visions were surely attributes of All Mighty God, however, from listening to your answers, I know what you really saw were visions of God's Holy Spirit. Pastor Hillman, your vision was close, but still far from the truth. Sonia Santiago's vision was closer to the truth, actually prophetic, because Our Father invited you all here for a very special, spiritual wedding planned just for you. Now, this time when you close your eyes, be still, and wait for God to open your spiritual eyes. Close your eyes...wait...wait...don't lose the moment, meditate, and stay in peace until Abba Father opens the eyes of your spirit. You'll know when it happens...stay in peace, you'll know when God opens your spiritual eyes...Good...Good, I see hundreds of spirits being lifted up...Once you achieve this you'll always have it...Wait for God to open your eyes... You're doing wonderful, I see thousands being lifted...over a million...three million..."

Jesus, held onto Sonia Santiago's hand, and when everyone was gone, He knelt down, anointed oil on her forehead, lips, and the palms of her hands. "Sonia, your spirit has been opened to the pure love of Father God. When the bridegroom truly loves his bride there's nothing greater. You have the power to teach the world about being married to the bridegroom. Now close your eyes, open your heart, and rejoice in the celebration that God has prepared for all of you."

In a flash, Sonia closed her eyes and vanished. Jesus smiled, lifted His hands in Praise to God, and then He, too, vanished.

~

"Oh Lord!" Isaiah cried out in amazement, when his spiritual eyes were opened, and he saw a Perfect Sky of blue, purple, and scarlet colors with gold beams of light separating each color. "Michael, it looks like the inside of a glorious cathedral, but we're outside."

"I see a waterfall of colors I've never seen before," Michael said. "What do you see, Michelle?"

"Beautiful birds."

"Those aren't birds, they're Angels," Leon said.

"Angels are bigger than birds."

"Not the one sitting on my hand," Alonzo answered, and showed everyone the angel, named Lovely sitting on the palm of his hand. Lovely rose to her feet, and stood about three inches in height, and then she flew from Alonzo's hand. As everybody watched in astonishment, she started growing and growing - up to a height of six feet, and then, she motioned for everyone to follow her.

Alonzo flew off first, however it didn't take long before everyone was flying behind Angel Lovely toward a huge orange/red mountain.

"It's so beautiful," Isaiah said, his heart filled with wonderment and excitement, and when he landed on the mountain, his eyes took in all the Glory of God's Kingdom, and what had to be millions of angels that flew about and created colorful auras with their spirits.

"Susan, what did you pray to get Father God to invite us into His Kingdom?"

Susan whispered, "I told God, when he invited us into His home, we wouldn't get it dirty!"

Susan's answer caused Isaiah's eyes to mist.

"Pastor Hillman, we're starting to glow like the angels," Michelle said, so excited upon seeing her actual aura forming around her body, which was a rainbow of beautiful colors.

"It's your body light, Michelle," Angel Gabriel said, as he landed next to her. "Eventually, scientists on earth will be able to see a problem in a person's aura and cure the bad DNA with special light particles. As you can see, God has blessed the Miracle Children with perfect, beautiful auras. You, too, Pastor Hillman."

"So there's no sickness in our spirits," Isaiah wondered aloud.

"None whatsoever," Angel Gabriel answered.

"Since we can see, will our eyes be like X-rays that will see sick people's bad aura?" Leon questioned.

"No, it's difficult to see a person's aura in the earth atmosphere. So you'll have to create machines with special lights, something like an X-ray, but the lights I'm talking about come from other planets in your universe. Like the rings found around the planet Saturn have these special light particles, and eventually mankind will learn how to capture these elements and work miracles on the human body."

"Saturn laser beams?"

Very good, Alonzo. However, they are also dangerous in the wrong hands, so Father God won't reveal how to beam the particles into the earth realm until the New Day."

"Welcome! Welcome! Welcome," the Holy Spirit spoke up, his voice recognized by everyone, which caused a hush in the Kingdom of God, and as everyone stared, His rainbow aura bloomed like a beautiful flower. The Holy Spirit's aura was a mixture of all colors, but those most prominent were violet, pink, red and gold. The light of His aura was so Pure, and so Magnificence, no one, after seeing the Holy Spirit, would ever doubt the Perfection of God's SPIRIT.

Like Christ Jesus before, the Holy Spirit's voice was full of Kingdom Authority and Majesty as He spoke, (Psalm 29:4) "You're on the Mountain of Life, from here all life is created. In other words, you're standing in the true Presence of Life. Christ Jesus, the Son of God, and myself, God's Holy Spirit were born on this Mountain of Life. Our Father spoke the Word, and we became the Holy Trinity, Father, Son, and Holy Ghost. All Praise to Father God!"

Everyone joyfully offered thunderous applauds, cheers and praise for the Power of God's Life Giving Force.

"Today, all the Miracle Children, and you, Pastor Hillman, have the honor of entering into a Marriage of True Empowerment with the **KING OF KINGS, AND LORD OF LORDS**. (Revelation 19:16 KJV) The energy of wisdom, ideas, dreams, understanding, inspirations, thoughts, knowledge, and power are so overwhelming that the human mind is only capable of realizing a small portion of God's empowerment. However, as a whole, you will bring a New Day into the Earth World. Here, on The Mountain of Life, is where I'm guided by God to speak to you through all the angels, preachers, teachers, ministers, prophets, pastors, priests, evangelists, apostles, singers, writers, poets, musicians, doctors, laborers, mothers, fathers, scientists..."

"I'm sure they understand, Holy Spirit," Jesus said.

The Holy Spirit bowed and laughed, "Thank you, Jesus, and I'll end by saying: Our Father speaks to everyone else who believes and put their life in His hands. God speaks, and all life forces that have God's Holy Spirit within them, will hear Me! So now, let your spirit experience this special Marriage of True Empowerment, that's overflowing with Life, Love, Beauty, Forgiveness, Passion, Patience, and a Humbled Heart. Receive the Wisdom, Understanding, and Strength of the Omnificent, Omnipotent, Omniscience, Omnipresent, and all the Power throughout heaven and on earth that was given to Christ Jesus after His Resurrection. (Matthew 28:18) The King of Kings, Lord of Lords loves to share his power with you, because He knows your hearts will bless the earth and bring on the New Day! Now, become One with Christ Jesus, and fill your spirits with all His Mighty Power that you're able to retain...As 2nd Timothy 1:7 states: For God hath not given us the spirit of fear; but of power, and of love, and of a sound mind." (KJV)

"All mankind has heard about the Presence of God," Christ Jesus voice echoed throughout the Kingdom of God, as He raised his hands in Praise. "Everybody wants to experience the Father first-hand, but few are chosen. It's impossible for one spirit to experience all of God's fullness through this Marriage of True Empowerment, however, all of you working together, will bring your experience into the earth, and the world will be reborn!"

All the angels, prophets and VIP's present on the Mountain of Life started singing words of worship to God, "Hallelujah, and All Praise to God, Abba Father."

As Isaiah, the Miracle Children, and the guests lifted their hands in Praise to God, they stared in awe as Christ Jesus appearance changed, and his clothing became dazzling white, far whiter than any earthly process could ever make it. (Mark 9:3), and He was transformed into the Bridegroom. His aura, beneath His white raiment, glowed a radiant light, so bright that it made the garment sparkle like a rainbow of iridescent colors.

"Everybody, give thanks and praise that Our Father, Jehovah-shalom has invited us into His Kingdom, and into this Marriage of True Empowerment," King David spoke with a voice that sang his words, and everyone responded in High Praise and Worship, until the voice of God spoke throughout His Kingdom.

"Pastor Isaiah Hillman, We say thank you. Michael, Michelle, and all our Miracle Children, We Thank You!"

The angels, prophets, special disciples and visitors offered thunderous applauds to Isaiah and the Miracle Children.

"The Enemy of Life, encouraged evil spirits in the world to drop a bomb on Our Holy Land and Our Chosen People. We could have stopped them with our many forces available here in the Kingdom; however, the world needed a sign that we are with them. That sign was you," God said with Great Jubilation.

The Holy Spirit then spoke, "El Roi, the God Who Sees, changed the minds of evil spirits by giving them a better target to destroy. That target was you, The Miracle Children, and as you can see, **they failed!** Father God blessed you beforehand with new heavenly bodies that will live forever."

(2 Corinthians 5:1-5)

Isaiah and the Miracle Children's spirits were filled with true happiness as the angels, prophets, and very, special spirits shouted out words of encouragement.

"Hallelujah!"

"El Elyon: The God Most High!!'

"Jehovah-mekoddishkem: The Lord Who Sanctifies You!!!"

"Pastor Isaiah Hillman, Michael David Spencer, Michelle Evon Spencer, Leon Jose Serna, Alonzo Dion Serna, Susan Marie Faraday, Akeem Wallace, Lin Chui…" Elohim, the Creator, spoke up, and announced the names of every Miracle Child, one million, five hundred and fourteen thousand children. It took a while, however, as God spoke, every eye became misty and filled with joy.

"Now that all of your names have been recorded and written in the Book of the New Day, join hands and receive the Marriage of True Empowerment!" God spoke, and the ceremony began.

The Holy Spirit smiled, "Your marriage with Christ Jesus will teach the Children of God, all over the earth that they will never be separated from Our Love!"

Pastor Hillman and the Miracle Children joined hands, and then, when Christ Jesus placed His hands on the heads of Michael and Susan, a Powerful Rainbow of Light flowed out of His Spirit and surrounded all the Miracle Children. The Rainbow Light bonded them individually, as well as together with Christ Jesus.

Some children joyfully cried, while others had a momentary blackout and fell into the arms of their brothers and sisters.

Isaiah also became weak in his knees when the powerful energy of Jesus' Rainbow Light overtook his body, and he had to be held up by two angels.

Millions of worshippers in the Kingdom of God, spoke in tongues, and sang joyously, and before long, all the Miracle Children were spiritually dancing and singing in celebration before the Lord.

~

Hours later, the Powerful Voice of God thundered throughout His Kingdom, **"My word in Isaiah 55:11-13 (NLT) says: I send it out, and it always produces fruit. It will accomplish all I want it to, and it will prosper everywhere I send it. You will live in joy and peace. The mountains and hills will burst into song, and the** trees of the field will clap their hands! Where once there were thorns, cypress trees will grow. Where briers grew, myrtles will sprout up. This miracle will bring great honor to the Lord's name; it will be an everlasting sign of his power and love...Pastor Hillman, and you, the Miracle Children have saved millions of lives in Jerusalem, Lebanon, Jordan, and many communities bordering the Holy Land. Thank you for believing and trusting the Holy Spirit. Tonight, many enemies will be destroyed. The door to salvation is closing; so, go back, and be a sign for the lost, by giving power back to the church! Those who listen, will hear. Those who hear, will see. Those who see, will do, and those who do, will be welcomed..."

End Part I – The Miracle Children

The Miracle Children - Part II

The Universe Answers

Hoping to breathe clean air
The Earth wonders aloud
Where forth comes this sin
That covers my land in a shroud
An answer isn't long in coming
As a voice speaks from afar

Oh Earth...sin comes from your Wind
Blowing deadly dust as it roars
Spreading viruses near and far
Poisoning new flowers
That are crying to breathe clean air
But your Powerful Wind
Is unable to stop
The spread of death and disease
That festers and breeds
In old and young seeds

Oh Earth...sin comes from your Water
Once fresh and beaming with life
Then factories flushed toxins into oceans
That trillions of sea creatures devour
And your Rushing Waters
Are unable to cleanse
The infections swimming in your bowels

Oh Earth…sin comes from your Fire
Burning earth enemies below
Hellfire's pitchforks stab and poke
As their screaming spirits are stoked
But the Blazing Fire is unable to defuse
The sins burning in their souls

Oh Earth…you've buried dead bones
Where food should grow
Hid metal coffins of radiation
For a future to sow
Vapors are erupting from your sand
Oil spills and litter
Deface your waters and lands
Garbage thrown out windows and doors
Your perfection once known is no more

Oh Earth…sin lives in you
No longer can you hide
All that you've let slide
If you want to survive
Something has to die
Something has to die

Oh Universe…cries the Earth
I will survive, I will not die!
Tomorrow my earth will quake
My Oceans will wash my lands and lakes
My Wind will blow all sin from the Earth
My Fire will burn evil from hell
And cause my earth to cry out loud
And when my seeds all die inside
I'll create new fruit and flowers to rise

Oh Earth...answers the Universe
Waiting for tomorrow
Delivered you into this sinful mess
Yesterday was the day
You should have stopped the hands
That destroyed your land
Now let your voice shout out
And pray your new seeds won't doubt...

11

Evangelists

*But now you belong to Christ Jesus.
Though you once were far away from
God, now you have been brought near
to him because of the blood of Christ.*
Ephesians 2:13 KJV

"I know in times to come our journey will be old history, old memories, and stories from a century no longer alive," Pastor Isaiah Hillman spoke into his digital camera, and continued recording his journey with the Miracle Children. "I was still twenty-five years old, when we were sent back to earth to bring the New Day into the world. We came home healthy, unharmed, and with our new, beautiful bodies. The world, that was so sorrowful about our disappearance, at first received us with open arms..."

~

Jan Summers pointed to an area on a map as she spoke to her television audience; "The terrorist bombing took place on Star Island in the Indian Ocean, forty degrees south of the Tropic of Capricorn. How the terrorists knew where the children were, is still unclear? The President has said that it'll take the Navy approximately ten hours to reach the island, but the Air Force, who sent a pilot to fly over the area, reported that the island is completely submerged in a radioactive dust cloud. The region is so deadly, that only one Navy Commando Officer, wearing special gear, will be permitted to go onto the island. At this time, many terrorists are reporting that the attack came from their group, and that many more deaths are imminent!"

~

Richard changed to the National News Network, and listened to news host, Alison Hewitt. "We all knew that the stockpiling of nuclear weapons, would someday get into the wrong hands, but it didn't stop governments from securing them to protect their borders. The call for nuclear disarmament has failed again and again..."

Richard changed to the Weather Channel, where a weatherman was pointing to a map of the Indian Ocean, "Luckily, the detonation fallout from Star Island, is moving southward toward Antarctica, so we couldn't ask for a better outcome!"

Richard yelled at the television, "Our children are gone, we could ask for a better outcome!"

~

"Conrad to Base, what happened?" Astronaut Conrad Parker yelled, as he looked at the earth from the space station. "Base, did you launch an attack?"

"No, you haven't finished transcribing the coordinates of the bomber. What's going on, Conrad?" Base Command asked.

"Command Base, it looks like a laser flash hit the exact coordinates we had for the base where the bomber landed... Oh My God, do you see what's happening?" Conrad shouted, as he stared out from the Space Station. "Command, I'm seeing thousands of what looks like laser beams striking and exploding everywhere!"

"Where are the attacks coming from, Conrad?"

"Everywhere, everywhere, go Red Alert. Go Red Alert, the earth is under attack!" Conrad screamed, as other astronauts rushed in, and looked on in terrified shock, as thousands of explosions happened all over the earth.

~

Richard watched as television anchorwoman, Alison Hewitt read a Breaking News story off a teleprompter, "Hundreds of explosions have been reported in the southern mountains of Afghanistan bordering Pakistan. Explosions are also being reported from Saudi Arabia, London, Chicago, Los Angeles, China, and here in Washington D.C. The attacks have killed thousands throughout the world and they haven't stopped. My God, what's happening...?"

~

The Prophet Elisha, and the company of soldiers, joined Elijah, as their spirits suddenly appeared on Star Island's hillside where the terrorists attacked Isaiah and the Miracle Children.

"Elohim, God Our Creator, your will be done," Elijah prayed, and offered praise to God as the Dawn of a New Morning began.

Everyone stared around at the desolate flatland of smoking dirt, ashes and steaming rocks from the nuclear detonation. Elijah, then cupped his hands over his mouth, and blew a howling wind over the devastation, and all the radioactive dust is blown off into space.

~

Space station astronaut, Conrad, and his fellow astronauts were still looking out at the earth, "Conrad to Base, thousands of lights are passing by the our station here."

"Base to Conrad, where are the lights coming from? Nothing is showing up on our radar screens. Is it another attack?"

"Conrad to Base, these lights are different...like...like, I don't know, infrared rainbows. Yeah, infrared rainbows from space, and they're heading toward the island where the nuclear attack took place."

"We don't know what's you're seeing, Conrad, but let us know if you see more attacks. We've stopped the Navy Commando from going onto Star Island. It's too deadly, so we'll have the Air Force do another fly over. Base Command, out!"

~

"Jehovah-jireh, our Provider, bring on the rain," Elijah prayed, as a sun shower replenished the earth and caused grass, flowers and trees to sprout up from the ground, which brought new life and a beautiful rainbow over Star Island, while at the same moment, one million, five hundred and fourteen thousand and one, flashes of rainbow lights raced from space and landed on the island.

"Father God, your Will be done, on earth as it is in heaven," Elisha said, as the miracle of bones, sinew and flesh were being reborn out of the rainbow of lights. "Jehovah-rapha, our Healer, Thank You! Thank you for birthing new life into the Miracle Children and Pastor Isaiah Hillman."

Elijah nodded as he looked out over the new lives, and then he, Elisha and the soldiers disappeared.

Isaiah and the Miracle Children looked up at the sky, as a bright light like a morning star, grew larger and more colorful as it hurled and soared toward the earth, and finally encircled everyone. Materializing out of the beautiful light was the Holy Spirit and numerous angels who hovered above everyone.

"The Lord God, Jehovah-shammah, is with you. Stay true as you go forth to complete the New Day." The Holy Spirit spoke, stretched out his arms, and prayed, "Thy Kingdom Come, El Elyon, God Most High."

Then suddenly, the Holy Spirit, Isaiah, the Miracle Children, and all the angels vanished from Star Island.

~

"Command Base, there's more activity of lights leaving Star Island, and traveling all over the earth. It's definitely some sort of alien attack," Conrad yelled, in fear for the planet.

"Base to Conrad, again, nothing is showing up on our radar screens!"

"It only lasted a few seconds. Space Shuttle out," Conrad said, as he watched a large rainbow of light disappearing into a black hole of space. Instead of commenting, he removed a flask from his jacket and poured himself a healthy drink.

~

In East Africa, a Miracle Child, walked into her village to the surprise of everyone. The villagers didn't see the angel who accompanied the girl, but the villagers sang, danced, and played drums to celebrate her return. The girl's father lifted her up onto his shoulders, and carried her through the village, and then placed her in his wife's arms. The mother cried tears of joy as she hugged and kissed her daughter.

Seeing the child safe in the arms of her mother, the angel disappeared.

~

In Singapore, a Miracle Child, walked out of his bedroom and into the kitchen where his mother was preparing breakfast. The mother screamed with delight and ran to her son.

The boy laughed, and then nodded his thanks to the angel that accompanied him. The angel disappeared.

~

"All the explosions were reported by scientists as a meteor breaking up upon entering the earth's atmosphere," Jan Summers reported, as scenes of devastation, destruction, and death were telecast to viewers. "Excuse me a moment, I've just received Breaking News that Miracle Children are returning to their homes."

Evelyn, Thelma, Richard, Sylvia and Henry stared wide-eyed as Michael, Michelle, and Isaiah, carrying Paula, entered the living room.

"We're back!" Michael announced, and caused Evelyn to cry out in joy as she rushed over and kissed Paula, while Isaiah acknowledged to their guiding angels that they were safe. The angels vanished from the living room.

~

Miracle Child, Hassan Ali, at a Black Tie Affair, walked on stage and began reciting his poem:

Hassan: *"Life comes from a moment in time*
　　　　Bringing hopes and dreams to all
　　　　Our guiding angels
　　　　So grand in their work
　　　　Freeing you to believe and trust
　　　　Your miracle working powers
　　　　A New Day is on the horizon
　　　　So beautiful you'll see
　　　　But please, be aware
　　　　As your journey begins
　　　　Of the many words
　　　　Filling your soul
　　　　Words that glow
　　　　Words that burn out
　　　　Words that love, but also hate
　　　　Words that sparkle today
　　　　But fade tomorrow
　　　　Words may bring you insight
　　　　And lift you on high
　　　　But always be watchful,
　　　　Words are also capable
　　　　Of bringing you
　　　　Down, down, down
　　　　So hear my voice
　　　　And share your words
　　　　As gifts from God
　　　　And always,
　　　　Always,
　　　　Release them with Love!"

Hassan bowed after he delivered his poetic words to an audience attended by Isaiah, Evelyn, and five thousand other parents and children. Everyone in the audience stood and clapped their hands as Hassan walked off the stage.

Hassan was followed by Hollywood actor, Kevin Mahogany, who walked onto the stage and quoted a Bible Scripture, "If my people, which are called by my name, shall humble themselves, and pray, and seek my face, and turn from their wicked ways, then will I hear from heaven, and will forgive their sin, and will heal their land. Second Chronicles 7:14. (KJV) Hi, I'm Kevin Mahogany."

Kevin bowed as everyone stood and applauded.

"Welcome to The Music Center. We're broadcasting this concert throughout the world, and we're graced tonight with the presence of a number of our Miracle Children," Kevin announced, motioning for the children to stand up and receive the rousing ovation from everyone, and when everyone sat back down, he smiled, "Oops, I've forgot that Pastor Isaiah Hillman, his wife, Evelyn Hillman, and their Miracle Daughter, Paula are also here with us."

Lifting Paula into his arms, Isaiah, Evelyn and Paula waved to everyone, and once again the audience stood and applauded, and when they were seated, Kevin laughed, "I didn't forget that they were here, I was just enjoying the power of making you stand over and over again."

Getting the laughter he hoped for, Kevin smiled, "I apologize in advance, please stand and welcome our special guests, Miracle Children, Michael and Michelle Spencer."

"Thank you. Thank you," Michael and Michelle yelled out in jubilation as they walked onto the stage and bowed to the standing ovation they received from the crowd.

"Thank you. Thank you," Michelle responded, as she waved to everyone. "We're so honored to be here. Thank you…Thank you…my brother, Michael has written a song titled, 'A New Rain,' and we hope his words will bring a new light into your spirit."

A small ensemble of Miracle Children played their musical instruments as Michael sang his song.

Michael: A great rain is coming
A new rain for everyone
It's full of living water
Sent from the Father's Son

Michelle: The heavens will deliver
The rain to everyone
Drink your hearts full
A New Day has begun

Both: A New Beginning from heaven
Sent from the Father and Son
The Holy Spirit will crown the earth
Bringing a new birth for everyone
Let your tongue taste the rain
And heal all your pain
Let your hearts smell the flowers
From this great rain shower
A great rain is coming
A great rain is coming
A great rain is coming
A New Day has begun

"Sing along with us," Michael said, as he motioned for everyone to join Michelle and him in song.

ALL: A great rain is coming
A new rain for everyone
It's full of living water
Sent from the Father and Son
The Holy Spirit
Will crown the earth
Bringing a new birth for everyone

~

"Michael, is this new rain really coming, or is it just some nice words you thought up?" Gossip reporter, Jean Claude questioned Michael after the concert.

"Words, music, songs, ideas, and dreams, travel throughout the Universe for us to grab hold of and share with the world. Those who open their ears will hear the words and write them down. The words for the New Rain came to me, while I was thinking about the New Day that's coming into the world."

Another reporter yelled out, "Michelle, what was heaven like?"

"Michael told the world to believe," Michelle answered. "If I told you what heaven's like, you wouldn't believe me. If I told you that Father God is zillions of times more powerful than what you could think or imagine, you still wouldn't believe me."

"What Michelle is saying, is that if you can't believe what the Holy Bible and Jesus says about heaven, you'll never believe us," Isaiah confirmed, and tried to walk away, but Jan Summers shoved a hand-mike in front of Isaiah.

"Pastor Hillman, was heaven a dream you all shared together?"

"I wouldn't call it a dream."

"Are you glad to be back home?" another reporter questioned.

"Home, yes. Though being back in this world only time will tell."

A shout came from someone in the crowd, "So Michael's song of a "Great Rain" doesn't excite you, Pastor Hillman?"

"I'm excited by Michael's ability to write such a beautiful song. I'm also thankful for the journey we've all experienced, but regarding this great rain, I know that, when God sends rain it falls on the just and the unjust. The rain fell on Noah and his Ark, and also on others who drowned. In essence, the rain may be a wonderful shower for some, but a disturbing storm to others. Thank you."

Isaiah walked off and joined Evelyn and her parents as Jean Claude whispered to Jan, "Why is he always so gloomy?"

"Some preachers only see gloom and doom. Peace on earth ruins their End of Days theology."

"Do you believe they went to heaven?"

"Jean Claude, if I thought that, then I would have to accept they were killed, turned into radioactive dust, and then, the zillions of dust particles were reborn into individual little people without one error! Come on, wake up…"

"Perhaps God knows something about DNA," Jean Claude surmised.

"Then why hasn't God brought back innocent children killed in other disasters? The so-called Miracle Children are back, but back from where, only they know? Also, why were thousands of people killed from all those explosions last week? Did some God do that, or did some government take the opportunity to terrorized the world?"

"I'm sure the government lied when it reported that the explosions came from a meteor shower. I've learned that the explosions came from a Space Station using laser beams to attack enemy targets."

"You got proof of that?"

"No, but word is going around that some terrorists are requesting billions of dollars, or they'll start attacking major cities next. We're headlining both stories tomorrow in The Searcher."

"So terrorists now have a Space Station?" Jan asked, knowing Jean Claude, and the gossip tabloid he worked for would promote any story.

"Your point is well taken, Jan. However, as far as The Searcher is concerned, the answer is, yes! Terrorists have built a Space Station!" Jean Claude laughed.

"I'm sure you'll sell millions of newspapers, Jean Claude," Jan smiled, with an air of sarcasm written on her face.

"Jan, if you come up with something hot, you can make a lot of money, and we don't care if you use an alias."

"I'm sure I will," Jan said, and walked away from Jean Claude.

~

"I've been asked to speak on my journey in heaven with the Miracle Children, and also about our visit with the Father, Son, and the Holy Spirit," Isaiah said, as he spoke to a large church congregation in Sedona, Arizona. "We were told that a nuclear attack was scheduled to hit the Holy Land, and millions of people would have been killed, or suffered the disastrous effect of radiation poisoning. Our Father gave the terrorists a better target, the Miracle Children, and as you've all found out, they failed. Many terrorists were killed, but there are still unbelievers living amongst us. Enough said, so now, I pray that you forgive me for changing my sermon regarding our time in heaven. Heaven is there, and we are here. Those of you wanting to know about God and heaven read your Bible, and it will reveal everything. Heaven is there, and it's real, but we are here, and our life here on earth is what we should be concerned about and changing. We need to be concerned about our existence here and now. Changes have to be made in this world! Terrorist cells have been destroyed, by what scientists are calling a large meteor coming into the earth's atmosphere and breaking up. Not true, scientists haven't answered how the meteors knew where to strike, and destroy thousands of terrorists, and their cells in the east, west, north and south.

The tabloid, 'The Searcher' claims the attacks came from a Space Station. Be careful about believing such stories to sell newspapers!"

A member of the congregation shouted, "What's the truth, Pastor Hillman?"

Others in the congregation also raised their voices; "The Space Station is the only answer if it wasn't a meteor!"

"The children were never killed. It was all a dream!"

Isaiah held up his hands to calm everyone down, "Yes, I heard all the stories, and 'The Searcher' still doesn't believe man walked on the moon, the earth isn't round, and six million Jews weren't killed in gas chambers. Why read that paper if you're seeking truth? Read the Bible! God told us before the attacks happened, that the Enemies of Life were going to be destroyed. However, we weren't told all evil will be destroyed, and there would be no more evil forces in the world. We all know new terrorists are born everyday! Terrorist abortion clinics are still in every town, city and state. Terrorists are writing dirty and filthy rap songs that our children are singing and dancing to. Terrorists sex clubs and prostitutes are still in plain sight for all to see. Terrorists burned my church to the ground, while gambling casinos, liquor stores, and drug houses are allowed to flourish near and far. Of course, I know many will be outraged that I've called many lawful things, Acts of Terrorism; I'm outraged, too, because our society enjoys many of these terrorist activities! To me, this is not a New Beginning, New Rain, or a New Day!"

Isaiah looked at the congregation staring at him in complete silence, "I guess this message isn't going over very well. Bishop Eubanks, your congregation isn't thrilled about my message. Is it because they want to believe without having to do anything? The word 'DO' is written one thousand, three hundred and sixty eight times throughout the Bible. The word 'Believe' and variations of the word, such as believing, believed, believers, etc. total one hundred and seventy-eight. Obviously, Father God, Christ Jesus, and the Holy Spirit believe people should do something with the time, talent and treasure they've been blessed to receive. Believe! Yes! But do something about your belief! Do something about crime! Do something about nuclear weapons! Do something about the songs being shoved into our children's minds! Do something about teenage pregnancies, abortions, perversions, greed, and lust. And do you know… what you should do…? ***Do you know what you should do?*** I'll tell you, so you'll never forget. ***Follow Jesus! Yes, you heard me, follow Jesus! You all know Jesus is the Word! So speak the WORD over you family, friends and love ones, and declare them blessed and highly favored. Speak the WORD over your body and declare yourself healed. Speak, and declare the WORD of God over Our World, and God will Save Us! Follow Jesus, and SPEAK! SPEAK!! SPEAK!!!…You have the power! God gave it to you!***

Bishop Eubanks, the church's pastor walked over, and put his arm around Isaiah's shoulder, "Thank you for a wonderful message, Pastor Hillman. Everyone, thank Pastor Hillman for coming today."

A few in the congregation clapped their hands.

Pastor Eubanks then scolded the congregation, "Come on, and show your appreciation."

Some members stood…and a few more clapped their hands.

"Thank you, and God Bless all of you!" Isaiah smiled, and picked up his Bible and left the church.

~

Preparing for bed, Evelyn stared at Isaiah in despair, "What were you thinking? They attend church on Sundays, but the rest of the week, believers and non-believers, indulge in what you labeled terrorist activities. Isaiah, for heaven to be realized on earth, there has to be a war. Is that what you want? A war! Armageddon!"

"I wasn't declaring war. I was hoping for people to start making changes in their lives and in the world."

"Honey, let's go back in time when you were leaving the ministry. Once again, I'm not sure you know what you're doing."

"Evelyn, I wasn't wrong!"

"I'm not saying you're wrong, Isaiah. They invited you there to talk about heaven, not to hear about the hell we still live in."

"Then what is this New Day all about? Isn't it supposed to be here on Earth? Honey, we asked God why bad things happened? God said, I will tell you why…I gave a High Angel in heaven, ninety-nine percent of My Power, and he used it for bad and became a devil. God told us man is like metal, and the devil is a magnet that pulls man into evil. God, then said, I'm also like a magnet that pulls man back to me, and I fight for you…with my one percent over the devil, I will win, and he knows his time is running out and his power will be ended. But mankind, by doing wrong, keeps the devil in power…Evelyn, evil has power because God shared his power, and He can't break His Word. Right now it's in the hands of the people to destroy the devil's power so he won't exist anymore…so the solution is in our hands!!! Honey, we don't need to ask God why! We are billions of people, and that means billions of powerful magnets. Satan is only one, we together have the power to destroy him, and bring this earth back into Paradise. Our world is giving eighty to ninety percent of our negative energy of unrighteous living to the devil. God knows that if this unrighteousness continues, His creation will fall. So my words at the church, was a warning that God won't let unbelievers control His creation forever. You have to face the truth like everybody else; God won't let people thank Him for a few days, and then go back to their same old sinful lives. He's getting tired of all our sins. Our world has become like the times of Noah, when people didn't want to listen to God. The same thing happened when God had to destroy Sodom and Gomorrah. They were full of corruption and disobedience…I could go on, but it'll only sound like preaching to you…I preach, and the Holy Spirit will teach and impart my words into your spirit!"

"You do want a war, don't you?"

"All I'm saying is we…"

"We, we. Stop it! They're children and little babies!"

"Evelyn, life is beautiful in heaven, God wants the same life here on earth."

"Did God tell you how to make that happen?"

"Why are you always against everything?"

"I'm not! But every time things calm down, you say something to make people mad all over again. I understand the experience left something wonderful in you, but it's inside you; so don't try to change the world, until you find how to get it out of yourself. You can't beat everybody over the head with your righteousness!"

"Why not, Evelyn? Why not?

"Because you're not the Savior King, and you're putting our family in danger!"

"Do you want the New Day, or not? You're either the problem or the solution. You have to make a choice!"

"Oh yes! It's so easy for you, isn't it?"

"You've been in church all your life, it should be easy for you, too."

"Well, it's not."

"Our daughter is a Miracle Child, I've been chosen to be their pastor, and a change is coming!"

"Yes, yes, yes, so what? Do you want the change today, this very second? Even God has given the world thousands of years to develop change. Slow down!"

"No! God has answered my prayers to help children outside the four walls of the church. You're my wife, I love you, but I won't slow down! I won't!"

Evelyn remained silent, but her eyes showed signs of fear, while her heart felt the pangs of loneliness. Isaiah was different, and his marriage with Jesus in heaven has made him so passionate, and now she wondered if she could pick up the Cross of Christ Jesus, like Isaiah so proudly did. She knew in her heart, she would lose him if she didn't, and scolded herself that she was the one who prayed for Isaiah to marry Jesus, and now that it has happened, she knew, deep down inside, she had to accept God's answer to her prayers. So she prayed a new prayer for God to produce good fruit from her, like He did for Isaiah and Paula.

"Are you all right?" Isaiah asked.

"Yes, I'm fine. I was just praying in spirit for God to bless my life like yours. Come to bed and hold me in your arms. The love you received in heaven will strengthen me."

~

Scott Perkins interviewed a church lady outside Bishop Eubanks' church in Sedona, Arizona, "So yesterday, Pastor Isaiah Hillman said he wanted to close abortion clinics?"

"That's not all he said! Along with the abortion clinics, he wants to close gambling casinos, stop the sale of pornographic movies, and close down Internet porn sites. He also wants to place heavy fines on the music industry that produces rap music, which I think is a good place to start, but wanting to close businesses that sell alcohol is a bit much. I mean, alcohol is still legal, isn't it?" the Church Lady said, seeking agreement.

185

"Yes it is. Anything else?"

"Believe me, he had a lot to say about prostitutes and drug dealers. He didn't even want to talk about heaven, and that's why our Bishop invited him to our church in the first place! And you know why he didn't want to talk about heaven?"

"No, tell everyone why?"

She whispered, "They were never really there. It was a dream."

"You're saying they all had the same dream?"

"That's what I read, and the children even said on television that it was a dream."

"I think a Miracle Child said it felt like a dream, not that it was. Thank you, Miss...?" Scott Perkins smiled, waiting for her response.

"I don't want to say my name on television."

"Why not?"

"That pastor, he has connections to God."

The reporter laughed.

"Yeah, you laugh. I hope you understand he's been somewhere and he's come back with marching orders from God," the Church Lady replied and walked away.

"The studio is giving me my marching orders. This is Scott Perkins, outside the Full Life Church in Sedona, Arizona.

~

"Hello," Isaiah said, answering his phone, then listened for a moment before he spoke, "Yes, I heard the news report. No, I don't care to comment. I'm sure my sermon was recorded at the church, so you can buy the DVD and hear what I actually said. Thank you."

Isaiah hung up the phone. A moment later, it rang again, but he didn't bother to answer.

"We all know new terrorists are born everyday! Terrorist abortion clinics are still in every town, city and state. Terrorists are writing dirty and filthy rap songs that our children are singing and dancing to. Terrorists sex clubs and prostitutes are still in plain sight for all to see. Terrorists burned my church to the ground, while gambling casinos, liquor stores, and drug houses are allowed to flourish near and far. Of course, I know many will be outraged that I've called many lawful things, Acts of Terrorism; I'm outraged, too, because our society enjoys many of these terrorist activities! To me, this is not a New Beginning, New Rain, or a New Day!"

Jan stopped the DVD of Isaiah's preaching at the Sedona, Arizona church, and turned to a Women's Right Activist, "Ms. Ruskin, Pastor Isaiah Hillman was quite outspoken in his strong opposition to abortion clinics yesterday. What are your feelings regarding his words?"

"I really don't like to involve myself with fanatics, but Mr. Hillman's comments need to be addressed. He resigned from his church, so he's no longer a pastor and has no right to speak for women. Listening to him, I hear him lumping everything into one pot. Evil forces, sex clubs, prostitutes, plan parenthood, and whatever else he doesn't like goes into one pot of boiling water. Jan, the man is a fanatic, but I'm unable to call him a religious fanatic, because he walked out of his church!"

"Jan, I may find fault with what he's saying, but he was speaking at a church, and preachers have been condemning those activities as long as I can remember," Senator Leaders said.

"I've heard that the congregation wasn't all that receptive to his views," Jan said.

Businessman Bernie Hudson spoke up, "People know where they want to spend their money. Yes, I own a number of businesses that sell beer, wine and liquor, but my markets also sell milk, cheese and bread. I agree with Ms. Ruskin, I don't like my markets being placed in the same mix as prostitutes and other illegal activities!"

~

A full moon lit up the midnight sky, as a black sedan traveled through the streets of a suburban neighborhood and stopped in front of the Hillman house. A man throws a hand-grenade at the house, and as the sedan sped away, a loud explosion ripped off the house front door.

The explosion snapped Isaiah and Evelyn awake, and the house smoke detectors began loudly beeping. Rushing out of the bedroom, they came in contact with flames that were racing up the staircase.

"Paula's bedroom, hurry," Isaiah yelled, as he ran down the smoke-filled hallway. Once inside Paula's bedroom, Isaiah closed the door, opened the window, and took Paula from Evelyn's arms.

"Climb out and drop to the ground,"

"Isaiah, I hear sirens coming. The firemen will help us out."

"How are they going to know we're in the back of the house? Don't think about it, just do it. I'll drop Paula down to you."

Evelyn climbed out of the window, hung down for a moment, and then dropped to the ground.

"You okay?"

"I'm fine. Go ahead, drop Paula down," Evelyn said, and looked up to the second floor window as Isaiah held Paula out, and dropped her down to Evelyn. Isaiah climbed out next, and like Evelyn, he held on for a moment, and then let go, and though he landed on his feet, when he tried to walk, he fell over and hollered out in pain from his twisted ankle.

~

As firemen fought the flames that burned the house, a paramedic wrapped Isaiah's sprained ankle.

"Do you have cell phone we can use?" Evelyn asked the paramedic.

"There's one inside the van on the front seat."

"Who are you going to call?" Isaiah asked.

"Mom and Dad! We need a place to stay."

"Honey, it's after one a.m. You can call them in the morning. When we're allowed back in the house, I'll pack some clothes, get my wallet, and we'll move into a hotel."

"You can't even walk. The stairs were on fire, so how are you going to get up to the second floor?" Evelyn argued, which caused Isaiah to frown.

The paramedic spoke up, "You can ask the firemen to get some things for you. They do it all the time."

"Thank you, we'll do that," Evelyn said, as she hugged Paula.

~

"Isaiah, you quit the ministry! Why would you go preaching at that church?" Thelma asked, as she sat in the motel room with Richard, Sylvia, Henry, Michael and Michelle.

"I made a mistake, and we lost our home because I wanted to point out some things that people needed to change. I'm sorry."

"You spoke the truth. You don't have to be sorry for that, Pastor Hillman," Henry said.

Evelyn became upset, "Stop calling him that. He's not a pastor anymore!"

"Evelyn..."

"Isaiah, stop. They threw a bomb into our home because of what you said in that church. They're trying to kill you!"

"Mrs. Hillman, I'm a new person because of your husband. As a pastor, he saved my life. In appreciation, I'm forming a group to find those who destroyed your home and bring them to justice. The 'Warriors Of God' will Fight Back!" Henry said with authority, as the adults stared at him with puzzlement. "I'm serious, and Michael and Michelle are joining me."

"Are you crazy? You want to involve your children in your power trip," Evelyn said, not wanting to believe what she just heard.

"My two and all the other Miracle Children!" Henry smiled, but this time only, Evelyn and Thelma, looked at him as if he's lost his mind. Isaiah, Sylvia, Richard, Michael and Michelle smiled along with Henry.

"Warriors Of God! Sounds good to me, Henry," Richard said, and patted Henry on the back.

"It sounds foolish, Richard. Besides, you lost your warrior status when you started collecting Social Security," Thelma smirked, and turned her attention to Evelyn. "You ready, this tiny motel room is making everybody nutty."

Evelyn, preparing to leave, looked at Isaiah, "Let's go, Isaiah. Daddy, help him up. Michael, get his crutches."

"No, that's all right. I'm not going up to the house today. I want to rest up," Isaiah said.

"What are you saying, Isaiah? Are you breaking up your family again?" Thelma asked.

"I'm not in the mood to hide out in your home."

"My home is not a hide out," Thelma said, with her usual air of self-righteousness.

"You know what I mean. I don't want to be run out of town. I'll stay here in the Nutty Motel."

"Isaiah, Mom, stop with the jokes!"

"Evelyn, you can stay at our place," Sylvia said.

"Sylvia, you have two bedrooms. My parents have five."

"Everybody, listen up. God knows what we're up against, and we need to trust Him. I'm staying here at the motel. Evelyn and Paula will stay here, too. That's it! End of Conversation," Isaiah said, laying down his law.

"Cool," Michael whispered to Michelle.

~

"You made the right decision, dear," Thelma said, in her effort to show support for Evelyn, who sat in the back of the car.

"Leave her alone, Thelma. You don't know what the right decision is," Richard said.

"So you want your daughter and granddaughter fighting all the evil in the world?"

"Thelma, Evelyn can't keep walking out on Isaiah every time life doesn't go her way. You keep throwing boomerangs and eventually it'll knock you out of the box!"

Thelma stared at Richard, "You are crazy, aren't you? When you come back to your right mind, I hope you realize that Evelyn and Paula don't want to live their lives in, on, or near anybody's soapbox!"

Richard and Thelma's laughter caused Evelyn to weep.

"See what you've done, Mr. Wise!"

"Thelma, if you left home in anger, do you think I'll be waiting around for you to return?"

"Where would you go?"

"I've got options."

"Options? Where would you go, Richard? To that tramp cheerleader you left to marry me?"

Richard and Thelma laughed again, but this time Evelyn laughed along with them, "Thanks, Mom, Dad, you guys have been married thirty-five years and you still enjoy each other. I want the same relationship with Isaiah. We used to laugh and enjoy each other's company, but things got so messed up. You're right, Daddy, I can't keep walking out on Isaiah every time he does or says something that I don't agree with."

"You want to go back to the Nutty Motel?"

"Yeah, before some tramp knocks on his door," Evelyn joked.

"Honey, do you want Paula to stay with us?"

"No, that's all right, she will stay with her father, me, and the rest of the Miracle Children."

Richard smiled. Thelma groaned.

~

"Good Morning, everybody," Jan smiled, as she hosted her television show. "Today, Sunday, January 27th, 2013, 'Talking With Jan' is broadcasting throughout the nation, the world, and over the Internet. Please welcome my guests to the show. To my left is Mr. Isaiah Hillman, and along with him, are the Miracle Children, Michael and Michelle Spencer, the twins, Leon and Alonzo Serna, and finally, five-year old, Susan Faraday. I'll start with you, Mr. Hillman. Are you still a pastor?"

"I see you're going right for the jugular."

"Why waste time!"

"Currently, I'm not a pastor of a church."

"How could you die, go to heaven, and come back unpastorized?" Jan asked, and created lots of laughter from her studio audience.

"My house was bombed, so I guess some people think my words are still pastorized."

"Are you aware that Channel 11 News was delivered a letter this morning and it reads: We are the Earth Soldiers, and we're the ones who threw the hand-grenade into Isaiah Hillman's house. Stop your devil talk, or next time we'll make sure your family will burn in the fire! Care to comment."

"The Earth Soldiers sound like Earth Devils," Isaiah answered.

"Michael, your pastor's home was bombed, and he had to escape this terror with his family. Do you have more than one word to say about that?"

"The whole world heard that one word, and since I've told everyone to believe, we were missing for over two weeks, spent those days in Paradise, and also spent time with God, and now that we're back. Are people still thinking they can kill us? Duh!"

Leon, Alonzo and Susan laugh, but Michelle motions for them to be serious, before she commented, "Our purpose is to prepare the world for the New Day. God hasn't changed His plan, and neither have we. Earth Devils won't be able to stop us, so try to understand, we're protected by God!"

"You can't be killed...no, forget that...are you going to prepare the world with singing?" Jan asked.

"We will become doctors, scientists..." Leon said, as Alonzo added his thoughts along with Leon, "Preachers, teachers, writers, actors, singers, dancers, businessmen, and lawyers...well, honest lawyers!"

Everyone laughed at Leon and Alonzo's joke.

Jan smiled at Susan, "Susan, did you see God in heaven?"

"We saw Jesus and the Holy Spirit. We heard God's Beautiful Voice!"

"Is God invisible?"

"Pastor Hillman says God is Spirit. (John 4:24 KJV) He's not skin and bones like us, but His Kingdom is so beautiful."

"Hmmn, that's interesting. Okay, what did the Kingdom look like to you?

Susan hunched her shoulders, "Like a big dream."

"Many Miracle Children have said that. So were you all just dreaming?"

"No, it just felt like that."

"I understand. If there's a New Day coming into the world, then there must a future. Susan did you see yourself grown up in the New Day?"

"Yes."

"And what will you be?"

"I'll be me," Susan said, which elicited more laughter.

"Very funny…but tell me, what work will Susan Faraday be doing at twenty-one years old?"

"I'll be doing property."

"Property? Are you going to sell land? Real estate?

"No. I can see."

"You can see land!"

"She means, she can see. Susan is a prophet," Michael said.

"Oh, you'll be doing prophecy? That's so wonderful. Prophesized something you see coming."

"Now or when I'm twenty-one?"

"Let's go with now."

Susan contemplated for a moment, and then answered, "God says we must love each other, and those who don't want to love must be destroyed."

"How will they be destroyed, Susan?"

"By fire."

"I guess, Pastor Hillman read that to you from the Bible."

"No, I can see fire. People will be burned up like that tree over there. I'll show you what I see!"

"That tree isn't real, plus it's protected with a fire retardant substance. It can't burn!"

Susan stared at the tree, and then it burst into flames. A stagehand ran and grabbed a fire extinguisher, but before he's able to spray the tree, it's burnt to a mound of cinders.

"God can burn anything!" Susan said.

Jan, and her studio audience showed real signs of fear as they stared at Isaiah, Susan, and the four other Miracle Children.

~

"Susan, did The Holy Spirit tell you to cause that fire?" Isaiah asked, as they walked toward the church van.

"No, I can do stuff like that."

"We can do all kinds of cool things with our new spirit," Leon informed Isaiah.

"Like what?" Isaiah asked.

Leon and Alonzo answered, "We can fly."

"We all were blessed by God to prepare the world for the New Day. Don't you remember that?" Michelle confronted Isaiah.

"Okay, I remember that. But what's this flying and setting things on fire about?" Isaiah said, as he sat down with the children on a grassy knoll near the van.

"We all have gifts and talents. Susan can see fire. She said that in heaven. Don't you remember that?" Michael asked.

"Seeing fire and burning stuff up isn't the same," Isaiah said.

"We've been learning how to do all kinds of new stuff," Alonzo said, full of excitement.

"Our bodies are the same as everyone in heaven. We can travel out of time whenever we want," Leon whispered. "We just have to keep it secret."

"How come you know all this stuff and I don't?" Isaiah asked.

"You still can't hear," Michelle said.

"No, I guess not, but now you're saying we can actually fly here on the earth?"

"You'll learn how to fly when you learn how to step out of time," Michelle said softly, as if talking to a doll she's playing with.

"It's like going into dream-space, so you'll have to learn how to hear," Leon giggled.

"I guess I have to hear the Holy Spirit."

"Yes, you have to hear the sound of the Holy Spirit. It's like a mighty wind rushing into your spirit," Susan said.

"So, hear the wind, then you'll be able to go into dream-space with your new body," Leon offered. "You understand?"

"Hear the wind…" Isaiah whispered.

"Yeah, the mighty windstorm of the Holy Spirit, and then you'll be able to fly, but only people with new bodies will be able to see you," Alonzo stated.

"A dog saw me flying," Leon joked.

"I scared a bird," Alonzo said, one upping Leon.

"I raced an eagle," Leon scoffed.

"I bet you lost!"

"Only the first time!" Leon said, making everyone laugh.

"When do you have time to do all these things?" Isaiah asked.

"We told you, when we hear the wind. Don't you remember anything?" Leon said.

"Do you know your name?" Alonzo joked.

Isaiah laughed again, enjoying the humorous spirits of Leon, Alonzo, and the others, but he soon, wondered why he was always kept in the dark about everything. He heard the Holy Spirit, when he was told to Save Lives, but that's about all he's heard in his spirit, and now he had to hear a wind inside himself…Once again, he felt like an outsider compared to what all the children were learning about themselves and each other, "So, do you hear this wind when you're sleeping, dreaming, or while you're awake?"

"Whenever we pray, we're able to connect with the Holy Spirit" Michael answered.

A reporter walked up and spoke to Susan, "That was some performance, Susan, why did you do it?"

"To teach people not to harm God's children," Michael answered.

"Fire will burn up everything Pastor Hillman wants to change," Michelle explained.

"We want everyone to know that the Earth Devils will be defeated. The 'Warriors Of God' are coming," Alonzo said.

"But you won't see us," Leon yelled.

"That's enough for today. Excuse us, please," Isaiah said, as he ushered the children into the van.

~

"WOG, also known as 'Warriors Of God' are protesting outside the Family Life Clinic in Desert Springs, California. The father of the two Miracle Children, Michael and Michelle Spencer, is leading the group," Connie Santos reported, as she stood with Henry. "Mr. Spencer, Family Life Clinic offers legal services. Why are you protesting this site?"

"They do abortions in there, so don't try to dress it up with pretty words. Pastor Hillman announced to all of

America that abortions kill babies. We have to stop this ugly, terrorist practice!"

"Henry has found his calling," Isaiah said, as he watched the interview on his motel room television.

"He's got Sylvia, Michael, Michelle and three other people protesting with him. I don't think it'll start a revolution," Evelyn said, as she changed the channel.

"A group calling themselves 'Warriors of God' has formed outside the Golden Crystal Casino. The Miracle Children already have shut down lotteries around the world, and now Reverend Billy Smalls and his WOG's are hoping to close Las Vegas."

"You agree with this, Isaiah?"

"I agree with you, it won't start a revolution. None of the other children are involved, so it'll die down," Isaiah replied, taking the remote from Evelyn and changing the television channel.

"Mayor Wagner in San Francisco has outlawed all sex outside the bedroom, and television commercials with sexual overtones will be banned, forever. Police are already arresting prostitutes, lap-dancers, pimps, Madams, rappers of dirty lyrics, and owners of Adult Sex Clubs and Internet Porn Sites," Alison Hewitt reported, as the National News Network showed a video of angry citizens shouting and exchanging angry words with politicians and police.

~

"Brandon, I'm on my way," Alison Hewitt spoke on her cell phone, as she stepped off the National News Network Super Jet in Los Angeles. "I hear you, Brandon, but Jan Summers doesn't own the children. She's had a free ride with the story, but now I'm out here with my crew, and the children agreed to do the show. I've lined up some community and business leaders...I'm getting into the limousine, right now. We should be there within an hour."

An hour later, Alison walked into the television studio, "Thank you all for coming. I'm Alison Hewitt, and I'm out here in Los Angeles to bring you this important discussion with the Miracle Children, Michelle and Michael Spencer, Leon and Alonzo Serna, Susan Faraday, and the Miracle Children's pastor, Isaiah Hillman. There are no opening statements, so the floor is open for questions, but realize that the show is being televised over the National News Network, so lets be cordial and respectful that we have children present and viewing. The gentleman at the mike, please state your name, your business, and then your question for our guests."

"Manny Powers, owner of Powers Electronics. My question is to the children's pastor. Sir, though I agree with your moral principles, I'd like to hear your take on the disastrous results of your stance."

"Mr. Powers, you sell televisions, computers, cameras, cell phones and other electronic equipment, but I wouldn't accuse you of the disastrous results coming from the products you sell unknowingly to child molesters and pedophiles, even though you know they use your electronic equipment."

Mr. Powers smiled, but his annoyance was noticeable as he sat down.

"Thank you, Mr. Manny Powers. Okay, the next gentleman at the mike. Be careful, Pastor Hillman throws hardballs," Alison said.

"My name is James Stanley, Mayor of Redwood, Arizona. You must understand that it takes time to develop a plan that will take into consideration everyone's Rights? We're a country of Law and Order, and people have the right to vote on new laws, rules and regulations. Do you understand that the problems we're facing can't be changed overnight?

"Why not?" Susan asked, somewhat puzzled.

"Susan, what I'm saying is that laws...let me say it in a way you'll understand. Love must be expressed for those who do wrong. In doing that, people who do wrong can see that God still loves them, and that all the Miracle Children loves them, too. Knowing they are loved will help them change their lives. Laws are acts of love, understand?"

"You believe that?" Susan asked.

"With all my heart," Mayor Stanley smiled, with enough sincerity to make even a heathen agree.

"Pastor Hillman, do you believe him?"

"Susan, laws mirror our sins. When you look in a mirror you can see good or bad, but a mirror can't erase what you see. Jesus' death on the cross, wiped our sins from God's eyes. Believers now live under God's grace, and God's grace is the true act of love."

Susan pondered for a moment, and then nodded that she understood, "I'm only five years old. Pastor Hillman is our teacher, and I love him. We'll give you five years to make love."

Much laughter came from audience members.

"Susan, why don't you explain what you mean," Alison said, getting her audience to quiet down. "Are you saying this because tomorrow is Valentine's Day?"

"Tomorrow is my birthday, I'll be six."

"Happy Birthday, Susan..." Alison started singing and the audience joined her in the song. After the singing, Alison knelt down in front of Susan and smiled, "Susan, I'm starting to feel that you're not joking about making love. What happens if we don't make love?"

"You will go into the fire," Susan smiled, sweet and innocent, however her words carried enough power to place more fear in many hearts.

"And if you're not, Shadrach, Meshach, or what's his name…Abednego, you don't want to go into the fire!" Leon yelled out.

"Susan's prophecy is in your hands, and it's time for you to believe that God is unhappy!" Alonzo said, as he walked out the studio with Michael, Michelle, Leon and Susan following.

"Your children sure know how to create news, Pastor Hillman," Alison smiled, who really felt true enjoyment in her heart from the Miracle Children's theatrics.

"They hear a Higher Power," Isaiah smiled, weakly.

"Well, Susan Faraday, our Little Prophet, gave us five years to make love, so we best start making our beds," Alison laughed, shaking Isaiah's hand. "Thank you, Pastor Hillman, and also extend thanks to my missing Miracle Guests. Stand by, after the commercial break, I'll be back with some very special guests."

~

"What happened back there?" Isaiah asked, as he drove the children home. "Susan, did the Holy Spirit tell you to give the world five years?"

Susan remained silent.

"Who told you to say that, Susan?"

"Pastor Hillman, you know she does stuff on her own. Now we're all on our own!" Michelle concluded.

"What are we going to do?" Leon asked, questioning Isaiah.

"Why ask me? You guys are the ones who hear the Holy Spirit."

"We're doomed," Alonzo announced.

"Stop it! We're not doomed!"

"We are, and if we are, so are you!" Leon said.

"Leon, Alonzo, I'm warning you, stop it! Susan, who told you to say what you said?"

"Me."

"We're really, really, REALLY DOOMED," Leon and Alonzo shouted out in fear.

"We're not doomed, and when you walked out together it was a prophecy to the world that you were all in agreement," Isaiah said.

"We agreed then, not now," Alonzo answered.

"We're had the Holy Spirit then," Michael said.

"We don't anymore," Michelle informed Isaiah.

"I'm not understanding. What do you mean?"

"Gone," Leon said.

"POOF," Alonzo and Leon deduced, together.

"Gone where?"

"No wonder you can't hear," Leon groaned.

"You can't even hear us," Alonzo also groaned.

"We've lost communication with the Holy Spirit, FOREVER!" Leon and Alonzo shouted.

"If you two keep it up, I'm going to send you back to heaven!"

"Besides killing the twins, what do you suggest, Pastor Hillman?" Michael asked.

"Michael, you still have your special gifts, don't you?"

"Maybe," Michael answered, with no confidence.

"Maybe? What's happened to you? Susan said, the world had to learn how to love, you all agreed with her, and then now, here in the van you've lost the power to believe. No wonder the Holy Spirit left you!"

Silence.

"Susan doesn't seem bothered by her prophecy, and neither am I, and if it doesn't cause me to panic, then you children have no reason to think all is lost. Okay, let's say this together, God gave us the power to prepare the world."

"Prepare the world for what?" Michael asked.

"Michael, silence is God's peace. He knows you're ready. He's given you the power, so whatever we have to prepare, Miss Susan Faraday gave us five years to do it. Let's say these words together, God gave us the power!"

"God gave us the power."

"No, No, No, say it out loud and with power. *God gave us the power to prepare the world for the New Day!*"

"God Gave Us The Power To Prepare The World For The New Day!!!"

"Excellent, now communicate those words to all the other Miracle Children throughout the world."

~

12

Silence

If the people of the village won't receive your message when you enter it, shake off its dust from your feet as you leave. It is a sign that you have abandoned that village to its fate. Luke 9:5 NLT

"The Holy Spirit is no longer guiding the children?" Evelyn whispered to Isaiah in a crowded restaurant.

"From what I understand, when Susan prophesied that we must learn to love one another or be destroyed, her prophecy became a warning to the world, and in the meantime heaven has closed its doors. We're on our own until February 12th, 2018."

"That's terrible!!!" Evelyn said, as people sitting near, turned and looked at her. She smiled politely, "Sorry."

"Evelyn, did I ever tell you that you have such a lovely way to express yourself." Isaiah smiled, and then whispered, "Try to understand, the children losing contact with the Holy Spirit creates many problems for the next five years.

The miracles from heaven will be cut-off, healings will stop, and angels that once protected believers from disastrous accidents will be absent. Inspirations, discoveries, and all the wisdom sent every day from heaven would be placed on hold. The world has taken all the favors, gifts, and blessings from God for granted far too long."

"Isaiah, you have to let the world know this."

"I don't think that's a good idea."

Evelyn lowers her whisper, "Are you serious? God closes heaven and you want to keep it a secret."

"Sweetheart, try to imagine the outcome of this news. You saw how the world reacted when Michael made that television appearance and said one word. God's closing off the heaven will make suicides hourly activities. I'm telling you, people will lose their minds. Crime, rapes, murder..."

"Okay, enough. I get it! Why did Susan do it?"

"She spoke what was in her heart, but she also stopped the New Day from coming into the world. The other children had tears in their eyes realizing they no longer heard the voice of the Holy Spirit, but Susan hasn't shed a tear, and when she burned that tree, we were all taken by surprise."

"**They can't do it!!!**"

Customers stared at Evelyn again.

"Sorry, another surprise. We'll be leaving soon," Evelyn announced to the customers, and then lowered her voice again. "Isaiah, the other children can't do what she does?"

"I don't think so. They knew she could see things, but causing fire, and that her prophetic words would close heaven, well, I hope God is in agreement with her."

"Did you talk to Susan about her prophecy?"

"I'm not sure what to say to her. She's different from the others kids. They all heard the Holy Spirit in common, and they looked to Michael for leadership, since he was the oldest. I believe Susan acts according to her own thoughts."

"No, Isaiah, not to her own thoughts, but God's inspired will. She's special in God's eyes, you must protect her."

"My mother told me the same thing. I asked Susan if she was going to help people change their lives. She said no, that people must change their own lives, or she'll burn up the ones who didn't."

"Is she serious?"

"Evelyn, Susan is a little, six-year old terror...A real life goddess of fire," Isaiah stated. Evelyn laughed and Paula giggled.

"I see Paula and you aren't broken up about this."

"Honey, I'm sure God knows you'll be there to guide the little firecracker."

"Jesus told me my hands would be full," Isaiah confirmed, and wondered why Michael told everyone to believe, and the Holy Spirit plainly told him to save lives, and then why would heaven closed its doors? It doesn't make sense! His faith tells him to believe, trust God, and protect Susan, but he knew in his heart that guiding a child who sees fire everywhere, and then acts in accordance with God's Will, or perhaps, acts independently of God, the Holy Spirit, and all the other children, well...that surely would be a step of faith on his part, especially since he didn't see fire, but he could see trouble.

~

"Has everybody seen today's headline?" Ivan Stone questioned, as he held up a newspaper and spoke to the Earth Soldiers at their remote cabin in West Virginia Hills. They're all wearing camouflage army fatigues, and Ivan had a 357 Magnum holstered on his hip. The newspaper headline reads, **'Susan Faraday Prophesies Heaven or Hell!'**

Ivan continued, "I know we all feel the same about this headline and this little girl. As businessmen of questionable enterprises, you're already feeling the wrath she has placed in the minds of religious fanatics. Believe me, your liquor stores, sex-houses, and gambling casinos will feel it too, and it may sound unbelievable to you now, but once the public comes out in support of her menacing declaration, I guarantee you'll be on the losing end. The government is already creating laws to stop abortions throughout the United States. The same laws will spread into Mexico, Canada, and the rest of the world. I know three of you, and myself, privately own many of these clinics. We'll be the first hit, and then, what's coming under fire next, is free speech, freedom of religion, and your right to fight back."

Kenny Cash, who operates over a hundred money-lending businesses on the West Coast, spoke up, "I can see that 'Cash Flow Now' may come under attack, but people will still need cash."

"I'm all for you, Kenny. Your profits off the poor is certainly greed at its best, but you know nobody in this room would ever borrow a dime from you," Ivan said, with enough sarcastic venom, to create agreements from the other ten men and women.

"I'll adjust," Kenny said.

"Good for you. The rest of us will like to adjust as well, but I don't see life getting better for us."

"What's the solution?" Jensen questioned.

Ivan sighed, "Jensen, your corporation owns over thirty sex-clubs. You already know you're in trouble, so the only thing to do is to stop her prophecy, and to do that she must be killed!"

Everybody's mouths drop open in shock.

"You look at me like I'm crazy, but her death will stop this foolishness, and it will stop the other children from trying to rule the world!"

"Mr. Stone, I agree she has to be stopped, but killing her will only get God to bring her back to life. He's done it with that Michael Spencer boy, and he's done it for all these so-called Miracle Children."

"That was a lie, they were never dead. You all know many people have been brought back from the dead, so there was nothing extraordinary about that kid. As for the children, their physical bodies were hidden from our sight, but they were actually dreaming in their beds. Today, whether they were dead or alive doesn't matter anymore, the children are now on their own since heaven has closed its doors," Ivan offered, as he looked around at his soldiers' grim faces. "We kill her, and her words die with her!"

"How do you know heaven is closed and the children are on their own?" Kenny Cash questioned.

"I've been told that all vibrations and energies coming from heaven have stopped, and my source has inside information. Trust me."

Kenny Cash stood up, "I'm not in this. I may have some business practices that raise eyebrows, but they're legal, and I'm not going to hell for killing a child. I'm out."

Ivan yelled out in anger, "Kenny!"

Kenny, walking toward the door, turned and stared at Ivan, "What?"

"Let us know if heaven opens its doors for you?" Ivan snarled, and then shot Kenny in the forehead. Kenny falls to the floor and nobody present said anything.

"I know the rest of you are with me, but I needed to show you how serious this is," Ivan commented, shoving his weapon back into its holster.

~

"Hello," Isaiah said, opening his motel room door.

"I have a delivery for you, sir. You have to sign for it," the mailman said, and handed Isaiah his handheld computer pad to sign.

"What's the delivery?" Isaiah asked, not seeing a package.

"I'll get the bags from my truck," the mailman smiled, and then walked off to his truck and returned with two large canvas bags full of letters. "There are five more bags, mostly from children judging by the handwritings on the envelopes. A lot of them are addressed to Pastor Hillman, America. I guess they're from your Miracle Children."

"Isaiah, what happened," Evelyn said, upon returning to the motel room with Paula and seeing Sylvia, Michael, Michelle, Leon, Alonzo and Susan reading letters and stacking American dollars, Japanese yen, Euro dollars, and other currencies from around the world.

"Michael had the Miracle Children send an offering to buy you a new home," Alonzo said.

"The money we counted is over a million dollars and we've only opened three bags," Leon joyfully raised his fist in a Victory Salute.

"Dear Pastor Hillman, I am from Tehran. Thank you for saving lives," Michelle smiled, reading one of the letters.

"I got one from Argentina, but I think it's written in Spanish," Michael said.

"Give it to the twins to read," Isaiah said, as he opened another letter.

Later that day Isaiah returned to the motel room.

"How much was it?" Evelyn asked.

"The bank gave me a receipt for two million and fifty-six thousand dollars so far. They had to close, so they allowed me to place the uncounted bills in the vault and we'll finish the count tomorrow. We can buy a new home...what's wrong, why are you crying about this?"

"It won't stop, Isaiah. They've been showing this horrible video all evening," Evelyn cried, wiping tears from her eyes. She changed the channel from a Variety Show to the National News Network.

"This is from a group calling themselves Warriors of God. We've viewed the DVD, but we must warn you that the graphic material isn't suitable for younger family members," Alison Hewitt confirmed, as Isaiah watched her news report of three men wearing black uniforms, hats, and shoes, plus their headwear covered their faces, to reveal only their eyes as they stood behind a propped up Kenny Cash in a chair.

Though he's dead, the Earth Soldiers have wrapped a black bandana over his eyes and the bullet hole that Ivan shot into his forehead. The man standing in the middle, calmly spoke, "We, Warriors of God, are sorry that we have to go to this extreme. Mr. Kenneth Cash wanted to protect his very profitable business enterprises, and when word came to us, that he paid an assassin one million dollars to kill Susan Faraday and destroy her prophecy, we knew we had to act. Any last words, Mr. Cash?"

Silence.

"I didn't think so!"

The man pointed a gun at the back of Kenny's head and shot him, which caused Kenny's dead body to tumble out of the chair and onto the floor.

"The assassin is still out there!" the shooter shouted, and then the DVD stopped, and the television screen went black.

"I'm sorry about that. Let's break for a commercial," Alison sighed, as she sat back and read a News Brief.

~

"In our studio is Mr. Henry Spencer, the leader of WOG, the Warriors of God, and the father of Miracle Children, Michael and Michelle Spencer," Jan Summer announced, as Isaiah and Evelyn watched the television show from their motel room.

"Mr. Spencer, you've denied any associations with the murder of Mr. Kenny Cash."

"Absolutely!" Henry stated, as strongly as possible.

"We've received an audio disc from a group calling themselves, Earth Angels."

"I'm sure those behind the shooting are lying about who they are. We, the Warriors of God, don't hide our faces."

"Why don't you listen, Mr. Spencer? You can comment after hearing this," Jan said, as she signaled her engineer to run the audio.

"The Earth Angels have been chosen by God to bring the world back to its right mind. We know it looks like Susan Faraday is a little angel, but now she has become possessed by the devil. Now that she can spit fire, we must stop her devilish prophecy for the world. Her words must be put to death. Heaven was with her in the beginning, but now heaven has closed its doors because of her powerful ability to spit fire. Only a demon spirit can spit fire. I know this shocks you that heaven has abandoned these children, but because of her, your prayers won't be answered, the sick won't be healed, and the dead won't rise," the voice on the audio announced and warned the world what was upcoming.

"Is this true, Mr. Spencer? I've watched the shooting of Mr. Kenneth Cash, and listened to this audio disc a few times, and I still shudder at the horror. Joe, let's go to a commercial, while Mr. Spencer gathers his thoughts," Jan said, knowing Henry didn't have an answer, but she'd give him time to think one up.

The telephone rang in Isaiah's room.

"Hello."

"That little demon is dead," the caller said, and then hung up.

"Who was that, Isaiah?" Evelyn asked.

"Wrong number," Isaiah answered, going into the bathroom and shutting the door. Getting down on his knees, he whispered, "Father God, how do they know your Holy Spirit isn't with the children anymore? How do they know you've closed heaven? Father God, is there a Judas child amongst us? My God, how do they know? How do they know?"

Silence.

Isaiah continued with his prayer, "Father God, I've told the children that your silence is your peace. It's your way of letting the Miracle Children and myself know we have the power within us. Father God, Your silence is now my peace…our peace. Thank you for giving us your Mighty Power of Peace!"

~

"God gave the Miracle Children, and everyone on earth the power to subdue this world," Isaiah stated, as a guest speaker on 'Talking With Jan' television show. "Susan sees fire, she doesn't spit fire out of her mouth. Jesus didn't have a problem with her gift, why should we? We all have gifts and powers to walk on scorpions. (Luke 10:19) I've said it before, the Earth Soldiers, Earth Angels, or whatever they want to call themselves, sound like Earth Devils. They've probably buried Mr. Kenneth Cash's body, so we'll never know the truth until these devils are brought to justice. I believe they are the scorpions the Bible talks about. Listen, prophecy doesn't stop with Susan Faraday's death. Terrorists tried to stop God's New Day with a bomb, and they failed! Her prophecy comes to its conclusion in five years, and the changes we make on this planet will determine what happens after that time period."

"Pastor Hillman, you didn't answer my question. Have the children lost all contact with heaven? Are the Earth Angels telling the truth?"

Isaiah took a moment before answering, and when he spoke, his voice was gentle and calm, "I've answered your question, God has given believers all the power they need to stop the devils of the earth, and if it's by burning them in the fires of hell, so be it!"

"You've become more radical, less the Man of God."

"Susan Faraday said she will be herself when she grows up. I've become me."

"Funny. Do you actually believe that child's words will come true?" Jan asked.

"Yes, and the evil forces wanting to kill her, also believe her words were spoken as a prophetic warning against them! Now, we can do nothing and see what tomorrow brings, or we can make changes to our world. The choice is ours. I've mentioned this before, but its time to remind the world that in Deuteronomy 30:19, God states, "Today I have set before you life and death, blessing and cursing; therefore choose life that both you and your seed may live." (KJV)

"I'm not sure, but isn't Deuteronomy from the Old Testament? Are those words still relevant today?"

"Ms. Summers, God said make a choice. Your viewers shouldn't wait until the last minute to change their lives."

"Pastor, politician, and spokesperson, answer me one more question. The Earth Angels announced that heaven closed its doors. If their statement is true…tell me, why is God hiding?"

"God is not hiding. If people can't see the light shining from His Miracle Children, or from His preachers, teachers, and prophets, then, they are the ones who are hiding. Ms. Summers, I've come here to let the world know, that the door to salvation is closing. Susan Faraday isn't afraid that a death threat has been placed on her life, she's seen heaven, and now she wants you to see it here on Earth."

"Thank you, Pastor Isaiah Hillman, your words have caused hearts and minds around the world to take time to listen. You've been watching a Special 'Talking With Jan' News Report. I'm Jan Summers."

~

"Susan, come in here. Susan, where are you?" Catherine Faraday yelled, while packing a suitcase. "Susan!"

"I'm here," Susan said, running into the bedroom, she looked at her mother packing a suitcase. "Are we going away?"

"We're going to Grandma and Grandpa's house. Go get some things you want to take with you."

"I need to see Michael."

"Why?"

"I have to tell him something."

"You don't have to see him to communicate. Go get your stuff."

"I have to show him something."

John Faraday stopped packing his suitcase, "What do you have to show Michael?"

"A secret."

"Pumpkin, there are bad people who want to stop you and the children. I'll bring Michael up to the house and you can show and tell him your secret up there, okay."

"Okay," Susan agreed, as she walked out of the room.

"That girl has no fear. You think she's still hearing the Holy Spirit?"

"She says she doesn't. She wouldn't lie about it."

"Then where did she get this secret from?"

"I don't know, John," Catherine said, as tears formed in her eyes, thinking about what they were facing.

John took her into his arms, "Don't worry, even if she's not hearing anymore, God will protect her."

Catherine nodded in agreement, but as John carried suitcases out of the house, he still wondered where his daughter got her secret?

Catherine came out of the house holding Susan's hand, but before getting into their car, three unmarked cars drove up. Men and women wearing black suits stepped out of the cars.

"Hello, I'm Tanya Russell."

"Want me to destroy them, Poppy? I can burn them up!"

"No, Pumpkin, if they were bad guys they would have killed us already," John said, and then spoke to Tanya. "How can I help you?"

"We're from the White House," Tanya answered, showing everyone her Secret Service Badge. "President Morrison is concern for your safety and he's sent Air Force One to fly you to a safe house."

"What's a safe house?" Susan asked.

"It's a special house where no bad people will be able to get inside." John smiled, and then looked at Tanya and the others for a moment, before adding, "If the president thinks our daughter's life is at risk, I'd think the other Miracle Children in her church would also be at risk. Will a safe house be made available for them?"

"We'll make your request known," Tanya offered.

"What do you think, Catherine?"

"Sounds like you're enjoying this," Catherine said.

"I need to see Michael," Susan informed her dad again.

"Yes Susan, I know, I'm taking care of it. Any other demands, Queen Faraday?"

"Get Michelle, Leon and Alonzo to come to the house, too!"

"It must be a very important secret, Pumpkin."

"It is," Susan responded, as Secret Service Agents escorted the Faradays to a car.

Three houses down the street from the Faraday's home, was a white Ford sedan, with two men inside, watching the Faradays being driven away from their home.

"I don't think it is, Ivan," an Earth Soldier proclaimed, while talking on a cell phone with a semi-automatic weapon resting on his lap. Turning off the cell, he looked at the driver, "Ivan said the car is bullet proof, but I don't think it is!"

The driver frowned, "If Ivan said the car is bullet proof, then he must have gotten the info from his contact."

"So we can still put some fear in them!"

"I'm not in this to scare people. We'll follow, and when they get out of the car, kill her!"

The driver drove off, but when the Secret Service cars drove through a security gate at Burbank Airport, he frowned and drove off in the opposite direction.

~

"Can I help you?" Isaiah asked, standing to defend Evelyn and Paula when two men approached their dining table.

"We come in peace," Carlos Silva smiled, holding out his hand for Isaiah and Evelyn to shake."

"We've been sent by the president to offer you a safe house," Anthony Anders said.

"The president of what?" Evelyn said, wanting clarification.

"I'm Anthony Anders," the taller Secret Agent said. "This is my partner, Carlos Silva. May we join you?"

"The president of what?" Evelyn questioned, again.

"The United States, Mrs. Hillman," Anthony smiled, showing her his Secret Service ID, as he, and Carlos sat down. "President Morrison is concerned about your safety. He's going to implement some new laws and there's a possibility that there will be some repercussions against your family."

"The threat on Susan Faraday has caused grave concern at the White House, especially since a new group calling themselves, 'The New World Order' have offered a five million dollar contract for her death," Carlos noted, calmly informing them of the new death threats, as if it's a daily walk in the park. "The President thinks there are a lot of people who wouldn't mine collecting that money."

"Then shouldn't you be protecting her life?" Isaiah said, in frustration.

"Susan and her parents are already in protective custody," Anthony said.

"How do I know you're telling the truth?" Isaiah said, becoming as suspicious as Evelyn, who nodded in agreement with Isaiah.

Carlos took out his cell phone, "You can talk to Susan and her parents if you like. President Morrison has made Air Force One available for their trip to Washington."

"We want to go where they are. We also want Michael Spencer and his family there, too!" Isaiah demanded.

"Accommodations are being arranged, Pastor Hillman," Anthony said.

"And where will that be?" Evelyn asked.

"Let me find out for you," Carlos answered, as he touched numbers on his cell phone. He listened for a moment, and then spoke, "Agent one, nine, seven, seven calling in. I'm with the Hillman's, they want to know where the Faraday safe house is located, and can they stay there with Michael Spencer and his family? Okay…they've put me on hold."

They all sat in silence awaiting the information.

"Hello, yes, I understand. Thanks." Carlos turned off the cell phone. "The safe house location isn't big enough to accommodate the Spencers and yourselves. President Morrison is sending Air Force Two for you. He'll provide a Safe House for all of you at the White House."

"That sounds great, but I want to talk to Susan and her parents to make sure they're safe."

"Of course," Anthony said, pressing numbers on his cell phone.

~

Anthony Anders and Carlos Silva escorted Isaiah, Evelyn, Paula, Michael, Michelle, Sylvia and Henry Spencer, aboard Air Force Two, the Vice-President's Boeing 757, while Air Policemen, wearing dress uniforms, and having their M1 Carbines at Arm's Rest, stood watch. At the front and back of the 757, are weapons carriers with machineguns mounted on them, and standing alert behind the weapons, were Air Force Security Police ready to fire.

Inside, everyone marveled at the plush interior of the Vice-President's 757, and the television monitors, that were screening Classic Animation Movies.

When Leon and Alonzo, and their parents, Mario and Diana Serna came on board, the twins sang out a cheer.

Leon/Alonzo: ***"We're back to attack!***
         The White House got our back
         God is moving us to the top
         And we won't be stopped!"

Everybody laughed and clapped their hands as Leon and Alonzo joyfully dance down the aisle.

"The Captain is ready to take-off. Everybody take your seats as we prepare for flight," an Air Policewoman announced, as the 757 began to taxi, and Isaiah stood and motioned for everyone's attention.

Isaiah: "*I know you're all excited*
　　　　About this trip, I am, too!
　　　　However, I must warn you
　　　　Don't get caught up
　　　　With life in the White House
　　　　Watch your attack
　　　　The President may not have your back
　　　　So open your ears to hear
　　　　And listen very clear
　　　　Don't lose your way up in there
　　　　Don't lose your mind up in there!"

13

Atonement

There are six things the Lord hates-no, seven things he detests: haughty eyes, a lying tongue, hands that kill the innocent, a heart that plots evil, feet that race to do wrong, a false witness who pours out lies, a person who sows discord among brothers.
Proverbs 6:16-19 NLT

"Welcome to the White House," President Aaron Morrison smiled, greeting everyone at the Executive Mansion in Washington, D.C. "First Lady Jennifer Morrison, our daughter, Samantha, and the White House Staff, have all promised to be here for you. This room, the White House's Diplomatic Reception Room is the former site of President Franklin D. Roosevelt's Fireside Chats with America. The rug's border on the floor has emblems of the 50 states and the wallpaper has 32 views of North America. Such as: Niagara Falls, New York Bay, West Point, and the Boston Harbor."

The Hillmans, Spencers and Serna family looked around the Reception Room with eyes of wonder.

"This is where we greet very special guests from around the world," First Lady Morrison commented, as the President, Samantha, and herself shook hands with everyone.

"Pastor Isaiah Hillman, I'm honored to meet you. Too me, you'll always be a pastor."

"Thank you, Mr. President. I'm honored to meet you and your family," Isaiah grinned, as he shook the hands of the President and his family.

The President, the First Lady and Samantha greeted Evelyn, Paula, Leon, Alonzo, the Serna family, and the Spencers. Coming to Michael and Michelle, the president went beyond shaking hands to giving them both warm hugs, "Thank you, Michael and Michelle, your beautiful singing touched many hearts around the world."

"Do you believe in the New Day?" Michael questioned, wanting to know if they were on good ground and whether the president had their back, or not.

Henry whispered, "Son, be respectful."

"No, it's a fair question, Mr. Spencer," President Morrison answered. "The New Day, isn't that a song you wrote, something about a 'New Rain' coming from heaven? Michael, songs are wonderful, but as president my actions will help or ruin America. So no, I don't believe in this new birth, new rain, or this new beginning you sing about. I'm more in agreement with your pastor, when he said that evil forces are still in the world, and to him and myself, this is not a sign of a new anything. I'm sure God has something more wonderful for the world than children singing songs about a New Day! And we have five years to find out what it is, right?"

"How come you've never said anything about us on television or in the newspapers?" Michelle questioned.

Jennifer Morrison spoke up, "We weren't in the White House when this all started, so when the President came into office, he decided to watch, wait, and see what was going on. The world was already stirred up about you kids..."

"We're the Miracle Children!" Leon exclaimed.

"God blessed us to bring a New Day into the world," Alonzo announced.

"We won't be stopped!" Leon and Alonzo yelled out.

The President held up his hands to calm them down, "We surely recognized your special blessing, and we should have said something. We're sorry, please forgive us."

"Do you believe in God?" Alonzo questioned.

"A horrible, nuclear nightmare happened on Star Island. That's a fact! Now whether the Miracle Children were there or someplace else, isn't known. I'm sure something magical happened on that day."

"It wasn't magic," Alonzo insisted.

"Of course it wasn't magic for you, but you have to admit that stories about your bodies being melted down to liquid particles, and then blown away by a destructive wind, seems unbelievable."

The First Lady smiled, "We're looking forward to hearing everything about you, and our daughter Samantha is especially interested learning more about heaven."

"Yes, let's get to know all about each other, and hopefully our actions here at the White House will be another wonderful experience for you," President Morrison offered, happy to end the Official Greeting to his White House guests. "Now, my staff will show you to the rooms made available for you while you're staying in the White House."

The First Lady spoke up: "Samantha will also take you on a tour of the White House. There are a hundred and thirty-two rooms, thirty-five bathrooms, six levels, four hundred and twelve doors, one hundred and forty-seven windows, twenty-eight fireplaces..."

Michael interrupted the First Lady, "Ma'am, where's Susan?"

"Yes, I guess that's more important to you. Susan and her parents are staying in the Lincoln Room. They'll join you for dinner at four, three hours from now."

"Samantha, make our guests feel at home, and don't get everyone lost on your Grand Tour."

"Dad, you're the one who gets lost in here."

"Shush, sweetheart, Presidents don't get lost."

The adults laughed, but the children remained silent as the president waved goodbye to his guests and escorted the First Lady out of the room. In the White House corridor, President Morrison sheepishly smiled at the First Lady, as he woefully spoke, "What did we get ourselves into?"

"Trouble. Lots of trouble," First Lady Morrison groaned.

~

"They look nice together, don't they?" Evelyn commented, as she laid the sleeping Paula on a bed.

"Who?"

"You know who I'm talking about, the President and the First Lady. Samantha is seven years old, and growing up in the White House. Why don't you run for president so Paula will have this nice life?"

"Why don't you? President Evelyn Rene Hillman sounds good!"

"I just may do that!"

Isaiah looked around their elegantly furnished bedroom. "It's nice of them to invite us here knowing how dangerous it is."

"Dangerous how, Isaiah? You think the Earth Devils will try to bomb the White House?"

"I meant dangerous, politically.

"He's an Independent who's been in office for ten months, so nobody likes him."

"Evelyn, be careful what you say, the rooms may be bugged!" Isaiah warned, causing Evelyn to do a double take, before realizing he was joking.

"They come from wealthy families in New Orleans. Democrats and Republicans will jump for joy when the country votes him out of office."

"They have a lot of money, and money people will keep him in power."

"You think they have secret cameras spying on us?" Evelyn grinned.

"Probably."

"I'm going to take a bath in that beautiful tub. Want to join me?"

"Cameras are in there, too!"

"I'll turn out the lights," Evelyn laughed.

"Infrared cameras," Isaiah joked, making them both laugh as they undressed, and entered the pink marbled bathroom.

~

"Susan, are you happy to have your special brothers and sister here with you?" Jennifer asked, as an informal dinner is served in the State Dining Room.

"Yes, I'm happy. Are we going to live here for five years?"

"I'll let the president answer that question."

"Susan, as long as these Earth Devils threaten your safety, you'll be our guest here at the White House, or until I'm kicked out of office and the next president is an old fart," President Morrison answered, creating lots of laughter.

"You're much different than what we expected. How come you met with the Earth Soldiers?" Michael said, pushing the president into another corner, and turning the laughter and gaiety in the opposite direction.

"Michael, I think they called themselves, Earth Angels," Michelle commented. "Not Earth Soldiers."

"Is that true? Are you meeting with people who want to kill Susan?" Samantha questioned.

"Of course it's not true, Samantha," President Morrison remarked, but somewhat shaken by Michael's unexpected attack. "Michael, you need to be a little more diplomatic with your accusations. You know, like kick the president after dessert."

No one laughed.

"I guess joking won't resolve this issue. Michael, who told you something so silly?"

"The Holy Spirit warned us in heaven who to watch out for."

"If you think we're the bad guys why did you come and live here?"

"To let you know we're not afraid of powerful people," Michelle stated, causing a dead silence throughout the dining room.

Isaiah, finding himself in an uncomfortable position for the thousandth time, spoke, "Mr. President, I was in heaven with the children, and I don't recall such a conversation."

"Pastor Hillman doesn't hear what we hear in the spirit," Michael said, acknowledging Isaiah's lack of spiritual hearing. "We are one million, five-hundred and fourteen thousand children, and we can talk to each other in spirit. Pastor Hillman doesn't see what the children here in Washington see!"

"I don't believe this! You think I want to harm you! That the United States government wants to...wants to harm Susan?" President stated, astonished.

"We wouldn't say something that's not true," Michelle said.

"Michael and Michelle, stop it!" Isaiah admonished, most sternly.

"My children are special!" Sylvia exclaimed, ignoring Isaiah's outburst. "They've been sent by God to bring a New Day into the world, and if someone here in the White House is guilty of conspiring with evil forces, than be warned, they're not afraid! We're not afraid! Let's go, Michael, Michelle. Henry, are you coming?"

Sylvia, Michael, Michelle, and Henry stood up from the dining table, followed by Susan, Leon and Alonzo.

President Morrison stood and raised his voice, "Hold on, you just hold on! You accuse us of doing something so evil, and then you want to walk out like you do on some television show? Oh no, you don't get off that easy. Do you have some evidence or names? Bring it out in the open. I don't have anything to hide, and I'll fire anybody on my staff meeting with earth soldiers, evil devils, dark angels, and anyone else out to harm you!"

President Morrison turned and looked at the waiters and staff members in the room. "Staff, waiters, please leave the dining room, I want to speak with the children alone. What you've heard in here is not to leave this room with you! Do you understand?"

The staff and waiters nodded their understanding as they left the dining room.

"Who met with the Earth Angels, Michael? Do you have a name?" Isaiah questioned.

"Someone called the Secretary of Defense," Michael affirmed.

Shock and dismay covered the president's stunned face, as well as the faces of Isaiah, Evelyn, and the Faradays.

Henry and Sylvia smile the smile of, 'Gotcha.'

"You have proof of this, Michael?" President Morrison questioned. "That's a very serious charge against the Secretary!"

"Question him, not me," Michael answered defensively, and once again dead silence filled the dining room.

"My God, I hope you're wrong," President Morrison groaned.

"God is not wrong," Susan stated.

"No Susan, I didn't mean God is wrong," President Morrison apologized, saying to his wife as he was leaving, "Jennifer, explain to Susan what I meant, while I have a talk with the Secretary. Thank you, enjoy your dessert."

~

"How was your dinner, Mr. President?" Phillip Hunter, Secretary of Defense said, upon entering the White House Oval Office.

"Interesting."

"Good. You wanted to see me?"

"Yes, have a seat, Phillip."

"Must be serious, since you're calling me Phillip."

"It is serious, Phil. Some allegations have been made, and I'd like to know the truth. Have you been meeting with members of the Earth Soldiers or Earth Angels?"

"The Earth Angels contacted me, and I met with them. They wanted you and the people of the United States to know that it wasn't them who sent that audio and DVD to Channel Eleven News."

"What are the names of the people you met with?"

"I don't know, they didn't offer up their names, and well, they hid their identities."

"You met with people who hid their faces?"

"I didn't know beforehand that would be the outcome."

"When did this take place?"

"Last night. I was going to tell you after the dinner with your guests. I guess somebody there beat me to the punch."

The president rubbed his brow, and then looked directly into the Secretary's eyes, "Phil, you know what this will look like in the press. Even if they aren't the ones who staged that killing of Mr. Kenneth Cash, or they didn't offer a reward for Susan Faraday's death, it'll appear to everyone that they were involved."

"Not the ones I met with. It seems there are many groups calling themselves Earth Soldiers, Earth Angels, WOG, New World Order, and Defenders of Liberty...Mr. President, those are just a few groups the F.B.I. is tracking. The real Earth Soldiers and Angels are afraid for their businesses, which I must say are of questionable taste."

"So you do know who they are?"

The Secretary groaned, "No, I misspoke, I don't know who they are. I'm assuming they want to protect their questionable business enterprises."

"Who went with you to this meeting?"

"I was alone. I'm sorry, I guess it turns out to be a bad decision on my part."

"Very bad."

"I'll talk to the children and relieve their suspicions."

"Why do you think the children are aware of your secret meeting?"

"I'm just talking off the top of my head. You had dinner with them. They seem to be aware of things we don't know."

"Like what?"

"I don't have anything concrete, but they have put a lot of fear in the good people I met with...Mr. President, what can we do to resolve this situation?"

"I don't think that's possible. I'm scheduled to do a State of the Union Address tomorrow evening. I want you to write up a Leave of Absence and have it on my desk in the morning."

"Excuse me. Are you serious?"

"Yes, Phil, I'm serious. And, I want you to know, it'll be a permanent leave on your part if you're not telling me everything you know about this group. I don't know what you were thinking, but you've placed the White House, the presidency, and the nation under serious scrutiny. Maybe you can sort out the good angels from the bad angels, or people who hide their identity, but I'm unable to. Neither will anyone else. I'll keep our conversation private. I suggest you do the same."

"You're firing me because I tried to bring some understanding to some powerful businessmen."

"Phillip, are they personal friends and you're trying to protect them?"

"I don't know who they are."

"Why would you go alone to speak with them?"

"Mr. President, if you think it's best I take leave, that we can't appease the children, then I'll respect your decision."

"Forget about the children! You haven't said anything to appeased my suspicions. Phillip, don't you understand why it was brought to my attention?"

"I understand. I'm sorry, Mr. President. I'll get your request on your desk, and hopefully we'll be able to work this out as soon as possible," Secretary Hunter offered, and shaking the President's hand, he walked out of the Oval Office.

~

"So you believed him?" Michael asked, in a meeting in the Oval Office with the children, parents, and President Morrison.

"You guys have raised my concerns for your safety. That my Secretary of Defense was foolish enough to meet with some unknown businessmen, soldiers or angels, whether they were responsible for the murder of Mr. Cash, or not, I wonder who else is signing up with them. Michael, who told you about the Secretary?"

"I don't think Michael should answer that," Isaiah answered, now suspicious of everyone.

"I haven't earned your trust, Pastor Hillman?"

"Mr. President, the Secretary came out of your White House!"

President Morrison nodded his head in agreement, "True. Okay, no names. Michael, I need to put a stop to these fanatics before they recruit more people wanting to cause harm to the Miracle Children, and I'll tell you now, after my State of the Union Address tomorrow evening, a lot more people will be upset. If you guys know, Mr. Hunter met with this group of people, then you also must know who they are, and where they held this meeting."

"We don't know," Michelle answered.

"It was a dream," Alonzo announced.

"A dream!" President Morrison said, exasperated.

Leon continued, "A Miracle Child here in Washington had a dream of a man coming out of the White House and getting into a tank with some soldiers."

"And from this child's dream you make the man out to be the Secretary of Defense!"

"No, she didn't know who the man in the dream was, so I told her to go onto the Internet and look at pictures of White House men," Michael smiled, pleased with his investigation.

"She picked out the Secretary of Defense," Michelle confirmed, also pleased.

"Tank Man!" Leon and Alonzo chimed together.

"Yes, I guess he ended up being Tank Man," President Morrison acknowledged. "Let's move on. Susan, you gave us five years to change our world into a loving society. I can only make changes here in America, however, I hope the influence of the White House will encourage other nations to follow our lead. Is there anything else you want?"

"I want a Bible."

"You can read the Bible?"

"No, but Michael can read."

"Okay, Susan, I'll get you a Holy Bible. Is there anything special you want me to tell everyone tomorrow?"

"We made up some stuff for you to tell everybody," Susan answered, as Michael removed an envelope from his pocket and handed it to the president.

"We will like you to make these changes in the world," Michael announced.

"I'm able to speak to America, my influence may not reach the whole world."

"Read our words and the whole world will hear you," Michael said.

"Before announcing your words to the world, I'll have to read them first to make sure we're in agreement with each other. Now, let's all go down to the White House Bowling Room and have some fun."

~

Walking down the White House corridor, Isaiah questioned Susan, "Is there something special you want to learn from the Bible?"

"Secrets!" Susan whispered in Isaiah's ear.

He whispered back to her, "You want to know Bible secrets?"

"You said we got power, and Jesus got power. We need to learn Jesus' power."

"Yes, that's a good idea," Isaiah smiled, but wondered, who was this little girl?

"I'm me."

"Susan, I don't think it's right for you to read my thoughts?"

"I can't read yet, but I can hear your voice."

"How come I can't hear you?"

"We don't know, but we can listen to you."

"I'd rather you didn't."

"Are you afraid of us?"

"No, I'm not afraid, but since I'm not able to hear your thoughts, I think it's wrong for you to listen to mine.

"Why?"

"Susan, I don't know why, it just doesn't feel good."

"God thinks it's good."

"Honey, you're a very intelligent little girl. Would you like the bad people to know what you're thinking?"

"They wouldn't like what I think."

Isaiah sighed, and knew he was unable to win his way, "What other powers do you have?"

"I don't know them all right now?"

"You do know the Earth Devils want to...want to send you back to heaven, don't you?"

"Yeah, they don't like me."

"And you're still not afraid?"

"No, I like heaven, but the Holy Spirit wants us here."

"You're still hearing the Holy Spirit?"

"No."

"Then how do you know what the Holy Spirit wants?"

"Because I saw the secret of the New Day in heaven."

"You saw fire, and a baby near some water, you didn't say you saw the New Day."

Susan whispered, "I know, and the New Day won't come if we mess up?"

"Susan, what's the…?"

"Pastor Hillman, it's a secret. I can't tell you!"

"This secret, do all the Miracle Children know it?"

"No, they didn't see the baby near the water."

Isaiah started to wonder who was the baby she saw, but since he knew some of her gifts, he decided to keep his inner voice silent.

Susan realized Isaiah was hiding his thoughts. She took his hand and led him into the bowling alley.

"I'll pray that you learn to hear, so you won't be scared."

Isaiah smiled, however Susan noticed this smile was nice, but his face was troubled.

~

President Aaron Morrison, sat at the side of a fireplace, where the soft glow and burning ambers set a mood of warmth and coziness, as the television director yelled out, "Five, four, three, two..."

"Good evening, my State of the Union Address will be broadcast around the world to discuss the serious state of affairs we're facing today. The nuclear bomb attack on Star Island opened our eyes to what evil forces are willing to do to have their way. My Secretary of Defense, Phillip Hunter has experienced serious heart problems since the attack, and has taken a 'Leave of Absence.' His leave saddens me, especially at this day and hour, however it has been a difficult time for him and his family. Due to the threats against Susan Faraday's life, and possible harm coming to a number of other Miracle Children, they have been moved here, into the White House for protective custody. If we can't protect them here, we won't be able to protect them anywhere. The people who put a death sentence on a little girl in an effort to stop her prophesy is an ugly evil that has manifested itself into our world. How do we stop this evil force? How do we make evil look at itself in a mirror? Personally, I don't believe evil will ever look at itself, as it would rather charm you into sharing its desires, and once evil forces pull you into the dark, you'll lose the light that was shining in your life. So, we as a people, as a human race of people, we must expose evil to the light. Susan Faraday stated that we must love one another, or be destroyed. Love or die in our hatreds, prejudices, and bitterness."

President Morrison stopped his address when Samantha carried a tray over to him. On the tray is a cup of hot chocolate.

"Thank you, Samantha."

"You're welcome, Mr. President."

The president smiled as he watched his daughter leave the room.

"Yes, I'm sure the First Lady staged that for the world to see that we also have a young daughter. Many of you also have sons, daughters, nieces and nephews that you love and adore. Susan Faraday's prophecy is for all of us to change the world. We can ignore it, take it lightly to please her and the other Miracle Children, or…we can become serious about making changes. I'm of the latter solution, and my term in office for the next three years renders me the opportunity to make a few changes. As President of the United States of America, I'm issuing some Executive Orders. I'm distraught and angered that ugly voices are raised to kill someone, just because she wants the world to be a better place to live in. Have we, as a nation become so immoral? Have we lost our common sense? I'm reminded of Pastor Isaiah Hillman's comment when he appeared on Jan Summers' television show. His statement sent a cold chill through my heart when he said we kill people everyday with Capital Punishment, mercy killings, war, murder, and most offensive of all, we kill our future.

The children are the future and we kill our future by voting against free health care for everyone. We kill our future with poor nutrition, poorly paid teachers, and doctrines fifty years old. Today, this country, and hopefully our world, will come together and fight for the New Day the Miracle Children have been sent to prepare us for. Today, as President of the United States, I'll start the fight against what I feel is destroying our future. First is the homelessness and hunger that destroys the hopes and dreams of many of our citizens. Second are the diseases that destroy our bodies. Third, and the most offensive, is abortion. Abortions destroy our future scientists, geniuses, doctors, and so many other promising lives!"

President Morrison paused for a moment, then continued his address, "Tomorrow morning, all abortion clinics and abortionists operating in the United States of America will be shut down!"

~

The once murmuring voices in the White House Press Room exploded.

"Is he crazy?" a news reporter shouted.

"There are laws. Congress! The Supreme Court!" another reporter yelled.

"Shut up, so we can hear what he's saying," a third reporter hollered over the loud clamor, as the television monitors showed President Morrison, as he sipped his hot chocolate before he spoke into the camera.

"Let's Move On. We face an uncertain wrath in five years, or we can lessen that wrath if we change our ways..."

In the White House Theatre, the Miracle Children and their parents applauded as they watched and listened to the president's address on a wide-screen television.

"The government will issue Federal Vouchers for all citizens to get free healthcare, medicines and vaccines.

Vouchers will be issued to our brothers and sisters living in Third World countries, so that they can get free or low-cost medicines and vaccines. Pharmaceutical companies have been stockpiling drugs, vaccines, and medical supplies in warehouses for years, and many of these drugs, medicines and vaccines expire over time and have to be thrown out. Then tax breaks are granted to these same companies to accommodate their loss. Of course, some of these unscrupulous businesses will re-label and sell these over-priced, expired medical cures to an unsuspecting public overseas. That day is over! A company caught selling expired products will be fined twenty times the amount of their monetary gain. Let's move on...Home and Food Vouchers will be issued to all homeless persons. The vouchers are good for all Class C hotels, motels and rooming houses. All American corporations operating in the United States, and in foreign lands will pay an extra ten percent surcharge to help 'Build A Better Future.' When I said every corporation, it means every single one! The recipients of the American vouchers will be put to work and will receive a decent wage. Anyone refusing to honor my Executive Orders has the right to close their businesses, and set up somewhere else in the world, however, you'll face stiff tariffs when you try to market your products back here in the United States. The Miracle Children's New Day will come to America!"

~

Once again, voices raged and shouted their discontent in the Press Room.

"My God, our country is being destroyed by an Independent Socialist Communist President!"

"There goes his presidency. He's out of there for sure!"

"He's trying to save the country!"

"He's pushed thousands of businesses and jobs into Canada, Mexico and China," A reporter joked, which caused laughter from others.

~

"Americans, friends and neighbors around the world," President Morrison continued his Fireside Address. "I know this all sounds unbelievable to you, but we also know that we should have done this a long, long time ago. Now, I'll read the Miracle Children's Declaration. One: Their declaration states that all persons without work will be given jobs. Jobs will be created to clean up cities, towns, and communities. Jobs to paint and repair all that's broken. By doing this, the children state heaven will come to the Earth. Two: Private and Public Businesses must sweep and wash down the exterior of their property. Fines will be issued to anyone not keeping a clean and safe environment. Second offense will be a thousand dollar fine. Third offense your place of business will be confiscated and sold at auctions. Yes, these children state what's on their mind. I've found that out first hand. Let's move on..."

~

Mayor Margaret Bell, of Valley Springs, California, spoke as she sat on a panel at Jan Summers' Town Hall Meeting, "I'm not one to throw stones, however, I know stones will be thrown, because President Morrison has clearly overreached his authority."

"In what way, Mayor Bell?" Jan asked, enjoying the firestorm President Morrison created.

"The banning of saggy pants. That has to be a stretch!"

"That wasn't an Executive Order. That came from the children," Jan commented.

"I have to agree with the children. Saggy pants are acts of rebellion against our country, our flag, and our God," Pastor Magee confirmed, as loud disgruntled "Boos" came from the saggy pants audience members. "Yeah, you're offended, but the self-image you show of yourself is an ugly, ungodly inner spirit, so you better pull up your pants now, or you'll surely pull them up in prison!"

Some muffled laughter came from the audience; even from some of the saggy pants wearers for they knew that was where saggy pants originated.

"Pastor Magee, I guess you would agree with the hundred thousand dollar fine against music producers, singers, and writers if they continue to produce music that is foul, abusive, and of questionable taste," Jan questioned.

"Yes, of course. They need to clean up the filth they deliver to our children's eyes and ears. How many support that?"

Ninety percent of the audience members raised their hands to support the pastor's views.

Pastor Magee openly smiled, and gave a thumb's up to the audience.

"We have a question for the panel from an audience member," Jan said, and held a mike out to a man. "Please, state your name, and whether you own a business under attack by President Morrison's Executive Orders."

"My name is Ivan Stone, and yes, I own a number of business enterprises under attack, and I'll be bankrupt in the next thirty days! Does anybody on the panel have an answer for me?"

"What are your business enterprises, Mr. Stone?" Mayor Bell asked.

"Women Rights Clinics!"

Pastor Magee smirked, "Don't you mean abortion clinics?"

"Yes, they've been called that," Ivan answered, which caused a momentary silence amongst everyone, until angry shouts were railed against Ivan Stone.

"You kill babies."

"You are a murderer."

"You're a profiteer of death!"

"The devil kills our children!"

A woman shouted out her support for Ivan, "Woman's Rights Clinics are legal!"

"Not anymore!" a man answered.

"Ivan, join the Earth Soldiers. They love people like you!" another woman hollered in anger.

"Perhaps I will. At least they have answers," Ivan hollered back, and when he saw ten angry citizens walking out of the meeting, he whispered to his companion, Teri Crimson, "I think we've opened the door for new recruits to join the Earth Soldiers, and we probably picked up some people who watched the meeting on television. Great idea to come here, Teri."

"Glad you liked it, Sir," Teri answered, as she walked out with Ivan.

~

14

Caring

***Come unto me, all ye that labor
and are heavy laden, and I will
give you rest.*** Matthew 11:28 KJV

"President Morrison, in an effort to feed the hungry in America, and Third World countries, has opened government warehouses stockpiling food. Here at home, the can and dry foods will be distributed to homeless shelters, churches, and charities, while the Red Cross will distribute food supplies around the world. Everyone in the nation agreed that it was a good thing," Alison Hewitt announced for the National News Network.

~

"Two months after President Morrison State of the Union Address, Federal Vouchers have been issued to pharmaceutical companies to make a profit, while freely distributing drugs, vaccines, and the medical supplies to hospitals and clinics serving poor communities. The companies were stockpiling their supplies knowing they could make more profits in a better market. The Federal Vouchers will enable senior citizens, children, and the poor to get free health care. There were lots of complaints from medical insurance corporations and drug companies, however, realizing the good they were creating in the world, many have done even more than what the Executive Orders demanded, and finally everyone agreed it was a good thing," Alison Hewitt reported.

~

"It's a good thing," Susan Faraday said on her guest appearance on 'Talking With Jan.' She's wearing a cute pink outfit, with a violet broach pinned to the top.

"I agree, Susan. The New Day Cleanup Campaign has created a respect for the earth. Garbage is swept up from beaches, streets, and storefronts, and the good thing is that instead of dumping garbage and cigarette butts out of car windows, people are stopping at trash receptacles to empty their stuff, and it's all because of you."

"God likes people now," Susan smiled.

"God didn't like people before?"

"God loves people, but He didn't liked what they did to his creation."

"Did the Holy Spirit tell you that?"

"No, Pastor Hillman told me that."

"What else did Pastor Hillman tell you?"

"God lets your television show go everywhere, even though you don't...believe!"

"I see," Jan weakly smiled, knowing she best be careful with her questions, because Susan Faraday was very strong with her honesty. "Susan, if someone doesn't believe, will God let them into heaven, or will he send them into the fire?"

"You should read the Bible, my pastor says all the answers are in there," Susan answered, and waved to her Mom and Dad who sat off camera.

"I believe when you die, life is over."

"It wasn't over in paradise. We saw many people who died, and they were still alive, so it's not over!"

"You're a very interesting little girl, but do you understand that many people think all acts are random, not caused by a God or a devil, but even I must admit, unbelievers are really lost for answers about the Miracle Children! Yes, it's a fact that Star Island was blown up, but were you really there?"

"The angels took us somewhere and told us when the planes flew over it was time to leave."

"So you left before the bomb hit Star Island?"

"Why don't you believe?"

"As a news host, my personal belief isn't what my audience wants to hear. They are more interested in your answers, and it seems to me that you don't know anything about the bomb."

"I know terrorists bombed the island, not God."

"Good answer."

"You want another good answer. We're still alive, and all the terrorists are dead!"

Jan smiled, "Yes, that's a good answer. Let's change the subject; fifty-dollar fines were issued to people who violated the Clean Up Law. One thousand dollars for a second offense, and now, instead of confiscating their business it's closed for thirty days while the owner sits in jail. Do you think that's fair?"

"Yes!"

"Honey, if a business is closed for thirty days, the people who worked there will be out of work, and they won't get paid. That's not fair."

Susan took a moment before she responded, "The people who worked there didn't do their chores. They didn't clean up their trash. If I don't do my chores, I don't get my allowance. If they don't do their chores, I think God will have to do it for them, and God will get mad, and take back the money he gave them."

"Pastor Hillman, tell you that?"

"No, I told me that. The same thing has to be for grown ups and kids. If old people wear saggy pants, then kids can wear saggy pants. I think that's fair."

"The people who make the saggy pants couldn't make them anymore, so now they're making clear, See-Thru pants."

"My mother told me the story of the King who had pants made out of invisible thread, and he didn't know he was naked until a little boy laughed at him. We should laugh at the people who wear See-Thru pants," Susan laughed, really enjoying the spotlight.

"What do you think the story means?"

"A king can't fool children who can see."

"I'm sure you know your intelligence is much wiser than most seven-year olds. Do you still see fire?"

"Yes."

"Do you have a new prophetic prediction for me?"

"I see you waking up and praying."

Jan, unable to contain herself, laughed out loud, "Thank you for this special interview, Susan Faraday. I also want to thank the President, First Lady Morrison, and the White House Staff for allowing 'Talking With Jan' into the White House for this wonderful experience with the little prophet who's changing the world. This is 'Talking With Jan,' I'm Jan Summers. Goodnight."

~

"Sunday's show with Jan Summers and that little girl is what I'd call, Pink Fluff," Ivan Stone stated, while being interviewed by Alison Hewitt. "She said Jan Summers is going to wake up and pray…that isn't something prophetic. Alison, these days, everybody wakes up and prays."

"Not everybody prays, Mr. Stone!"

Well, I pray my 'Woman Rights Clinics' will be looked upon as solving problems, not creating them. We've waged the biggest fight against the government and lost. The President wouldn't resend his Executive Order and vetoed many Bills from the House and Senate. I'm out of business."

"Police have arrested a number of your former employees for operating clinics underground. Were you sponsoring those illegal clinics?"

"Of course not," Ivan openly denied, and glared at Alison. "I've sponsored the Bills that the president wouldn't sign. That was a legal action!"

"And it failed. Abortions are priced too high for women wanting the procedure, and too risky for doctors to perform. In the last six months, women have become more selective with whom they shared their bed, and now social diseases, infections, viruses, and Aids have experience major decreases. Everybody has agreed that it's a good thing!"

"Everybody except the Earth Soldiers! I'm hearing they are building up their underground forces to fight back."

"I've heard the same thing, but President Morrison's Executive Orders are working and the Earth Soldiers' anger isn't."

"Anger boils over when you make too many presidential decisions against personal freedom. Alison, I'm afraid that 'Building A Better America' is adding more fuel to the fire raging inside people, and they will react differently in the future."

"Perhaps you're right, Mr. Stone, but I'm praying the world will run with Susan Faraday's Love Fest, instead."

"Time will tell, Alison." Ivan Stone commented. "I'm out of business for now, but there'll come a time when women will fight back regarding negative decisions made about their body, their rights, and the freedom to choose for themselves!"

~

"I have to say, who would have thought in one year, President Morrison's Executives Orders have gained such a strong following. Polls show ninety-five percent of Americans agree that the Orders are a good thing. Do you think it's because of Susan Faraday's prophecy facing us, or has it become a fact that people 'Follow the Leader' like sheep?" Jan questioned Pastor Magee.

"Sheep listen to the voice of the shepherd, so sheep followed Abraham, Moses, Jesus, Gandhi, Martin Luther King, Malcolm X, Kings, Queens, Presidents, Despots, Hitler, Manson...as Pastor Hillman says, I can go on, but it'll only sound like preaching to you," Pastor Magee said, and elicited some laughter from the studio audience. "No question about it, we're followers even to the life or death of our souls."

"Exactly, people wanting to kill a little girl because she said something they didn't like is stupid," David Loca, a clothing manufacturer said. "I believe President Morrison was able to close all the abortion clinics because he made us wake up and see we were killing our future."

"Mr. Loca, you've created a very lucrative business venture with your See-Thru Pants."

"Miss Summers, we also created colorful underwear for children, teenagers, and adults to wear under our pants. In six months, we have manufacturers in Brazil, Canada and France. Today, we're developing See-Thru Shoes, and designing many beautiful socks to wear in our shoes. People love our See-Thru products..."

"You're creating child pornography!" an audience member yelled out, and caused rude speculations from others.

"Children are wearing the filthy images on your underwear to school!"

"Excuse me! Colorful animation characters are filthy images?"

"Your clothing comes from the devil!"

Jan smiled, but her producers didn't want an 'On Air' riot, so she changed the subject, "Mayor Bell, what do you like about the President's Executive Orders?"

"Well…America can now be truly called, 'America the Beautiful.' The Global World once again appreciates the benevolence of the United States of America."

"I'm surprised corporations have played ball in deference to their relentless pursuit of profits."

"Corporate profits were three hundred percent at the lowest. The president's surcharge is a ten percent tax. Do the math! Profits, at minimum, are still holding at two ninety."

"Mr. Loca has the ten percent surcharge hurt your business enterprises?" Jan asked.

"Let's not speculate!" Mr. Loca answered, and once again audience members shouted and yelled out their rude speculations.

Jan inwardly smiled, enjoying the success of her 'Talking With Jan' television show.

~

"Pastor Hillman, how are things in America?" Karl Kitchens, host of London, England's 'After Breakfast Show' questioned Isaiah. The audience was full of Miracle Children and their parents.

"Great, we're no longer living at the White House. The President has moved Susan and her parents to a safe house. Michael and Michelle Spencer are living with their parents, and I've moved my family back to California as well. We have a new home, Praise God, and I have some more good news, Michael and Michelle completed a musical sensation with some of the greatest gospel singers in the world, and they've sent CDs here for everyone."

The Miracle Children in the audience scream with excitement as men and women strolled through the audience and handed out CDs.

After the show is over, Isaiah warmly hugged, shook hands, and shared lots of laughs with the children. During the wonderful experience, a young girl tugged at Isaiah's jacket, and he crouched down and spoke to her, "Hi, what's your name?"

"Christian Sparrow."

"Such a beautiful name. How old are you Ms. Christian Sparrow?"

"Seven."

"Christian, what gifts did God bless you with?"

Christian took Isaiah's hand, led him away from the grown ups, and whispered, "I see dreams."

"Are you a prophet like Susan?"

"No, she sees fire. I see dreams."

"Christian, everybody sees dreams, not knowing what they mean is the big problem. Do you know what they mean?"

"Not yet."

"So what's so important about your dreams?"

"My father says I have the Gift of Daniel. I can see the dreams of other people."

"Wow, that's a very special gift. Have you looked at my dreams?"

"I can't see your dreams!"

"Christian, I'm sorry, but I'm not understanding what you're trying to tell me."

Christian whispered, "I only see the Miracle Children's dreams. Susan doesn't talk about it, but she's having bad dreams. Real bad."

"What is she dreaming about?" Isaiah questioned, now concerned for Susan.

"She sees people destroying the world. You have to stop them!"

"Me?"

"Yes, you're in charge," Christian answered, and walked away.

Isaiah glanced at the other children that smiled for the adults, but when they looked at him, a strange chill flowed through his body. Then he sensed in his spirit, that all the children heard what Christian said about Susan's bad dreams, and once he sensed that, the strange chill came over him again, and it felt as wonderful as when he entered the Kingdom of God. Knowing the children had the power to communicate amongst themselves, he wondered if he had traveled to that same dimension in his spirit. Reviving the wonderful feeling that overtook him, he spoke in his spirit, 'Christian, tell me why I'm in charge?'

The Miracle Children in the television studio, turned and looked at Isaiah as Christian spoke, 'Because, you're our pastor.'

In spirit, Isaiah answered, 'I got that.'

A split-second later, Isaiah heard the spiritual voices of one million, five hundred and fourteen thousand Miracle Children, and at first it sounded like a strong wind that raced through his mind, but the difference was that he was able to conjugate all the voices together, which sounded like the children were speaking in tongues, however, within seconds, Isaiah interpreted the spiritual gibberish down in his spirit, until the hum of the universe broke through and filled his mind, ***OOOOMMMMMMM***...the same sound he heard when all the children were on the hillside, but now, and to his astonishment, he was able to hear one spiritual voice, loud and clear.

'Hello, Pastor Hillman, we welcome you into our special communion of voices,' Michelle cheerfully greeted Isaiah.

'Hi, Pastor Hillman, you've finally found your way,' Michael also greeted Isaiah in spirit. 'Are you okay?'

Isaiah, eyes closed, sat down, and spoke again in spirit, 'Yes, I'm feeling wonderful.'

'Scientists hear the sound of our voices, and though we're six times louder than usual radio waves, they just think something weird is happening in the universe. Funny, huh?'

'Michael, it feels like I'm wired to everybody.'

'Can you hear me, Pastor Hillman,' Christian questioned.

'Yes, Christian, and I'll check on what you've told me.'

The television host, Karl Kitchens touched Isaiah on the shoulder, "Pastor Hillman, are you okay?"

Isaiah looked up at Karl, and then at the Miracle Children, who have individual auras surrounding their bodies, and when he stared at his own arm and body, he saw the same spiritual light glowing around him, but he didn't see the aura of Mr. Kitchens, or the other adults.

"I'm fine, Karl, I just needed a little time to meditate in spirit."

"Yes, we all need to do that once in a while," Karl smiled.

"So true, there's knowledge in the universe we all need to learn about," Isaiah said, and then spoke in spirit. 'I don't see the spiritual aura of adults!"

Michael answered, 'We'll see everybody's aura in the New Day.'

'Wow, thank you, Father God, Christ Jesus, Holy Spirit, thank you for opening my ears to hear and my eyes to see,' Isaiah prayed, as he walked over and hugged Christian, "Christian, I'm able to see and hear now."

"I know. Now you'll learn why it's so wonderful to be us?"

"So will everybody when the New Day comes into the world," Isaiah laughed, as he leaned down and kissed her on the cheek. "Can you see my dreams now?"

"You're not dreaming."

"No, I guess I'm not," Isaiah laughed again, as Christian led him over to meet her parents.

15

Wisdom

*There are three things that will
endure-faith, hope, and love-and
the greatest of these is love.*
1 Corinthians 13:13 NLT

Cairo, Egypt: Isaiah and Evelyn, vacationing with the
Downings, Spencers, and the Serna family, visited the
three pyramids: The Great Sphinx, Khafre, and Khufu-
The Great Pyramid. Riding on camels, they wore white
Egyptian Royal Robes, and Michelle wore a Queen Nefertiti
hat, while Paula had on a beaded Cleopatra headpiece that
covered her head and face, and the twins, Leon and Alonzo,
wore King Tut headpieces.

There were crowds of tourists, and many Egyptian
citizens, men, women and children, who followed the
families wherever they went, and while Isaiah and the
families photographed one of Seven Wonders of the World,
many cameras were photographing them. They also shook
lots of hands and signed many autographs. When they
stopped for a rest break, and sat on the stones of the Great
Pyramid, the families were approached by a group of ten

Saudi Arabian men. The men wore thobes, which was a long white shirt, and on their head they wore a red and white scarf called a Ghuta. A black headband was worn around the Ghuta.

A teenager stepped out from amongst the Saudi men, but the men kept a close watch as the youth bowed, and held out his hand to Michael, "May I shake your hand, please?"

Michael stood, bowed politely, and shook the teenager's hand, "Nice to meet you, Sir."

"I am sorry. I am, Ali bin Abdul Aziz-Al Sa'ud. I am new Miracle Children."

"A new Miracle Children?" Michael questioned, in puzzlement.

"I am sorry. I see you, your sisters and brothers on television. I become a new Miracle Children."

"Michael, I think, Ali bin Abdul Aziz-Al Sa'ud is trying to tell you he's saved," Isaiah said.

"Yes, yes, I am saved. I like your God, He gives powerful life."

Michelle looked at Ali's entourage, "Looks like you have a powerful life."

Ali smiled, "Yes, you are Michelle?"

"Yes, Michelle Evon Spencer."

"Yes, Michelle Evon Spencer, I have powerful life as Crown Prince of Saudi Arabia, and they are Saudi Arabian Security Police. I am well protected from enemies of my father. I saw on television the terrorists drop bomb on you, and you live again. You have more powerful life. I am vacation here. You come to my home, I dinner you."

Everybody laughed.

"I say wrong. I am still learning your language."

"It's okay. We understand," Michael said.

"We would love to come and be dinner," Leon joked.

Alonzo poked Leon in the side, and then bowed to Ali, "We thank you for inviting us to dinner, but we must travel on to Israel."

"Ah, my father must also be there. When you come back to my country, please find me," Ali smiled, as he took a moment to perform the traditional kisses on the cheeks of Michelle, and the others, and then bowed and walked off with his entourage of security police.

Michelle yelled out, "Ali bin Abdul Aziz-Al Sa'ud, come be our guest in Israel."

"I am sorry, Michelle Evon Spencer, King and Crown Prince cannot be in Israel at the same time. There is still trouble, but thank you for invite. Allah be with you."

Michael and others watched as Ali waved, and then became hidden amongst his entourage of security police.

"Michelle Evon Spencer, I see a vision of you being married to Crown Prince of Saudi Arabia," Alonzo said, while Michelle blushed.

"No, I see the same vision, and Michelle is the bride of King Ali bin Abdul Aziz-Al Sa'ud," Leon said.

"And you two will be my Court Jesters," Michelle answered, and walked off with the Royal flair of a Queen.

~

Jerusalem, Israel: Isaiah, Evelyn, Paula and other family members walked down the Via Dolorosa; the stretch of road Jesus struggled with the cross on the road to Golgotha. They also visited Jesus' Garden Tomb, and the site of his Crucifixion, before they traveled on to the Knesset, Israel's Parliament.

Security police stood guard at the Knesset, as a long line of bulletproof black limousines drove up, and passengers stepped out and entered the Parliament.

The King of Oman was in the first limousine, then from another limo was the King of Saudi Arabia, then President Morrison's limo arrived, with him and the Secretary of State. The fourth limo's passengers were Isaiah, Michael, Michelle, Leon and Alonzo. From the fifth limo, two Secret Agents exited first, and then Susan Faraday, stepped out and waved to the crowd of onlookers. She's grown three inches taller, and holding her new doll close to her heart as the Agents rushed her into the building.

~

"Welcome World, I am, Susan Faraday. Today, Valentine Day, February 14, 2015, I'm eight years old," Susan acknowledged, and received a loud ovation and birthday cheers, while she stood on a footstool behind a podium with many microphones attached.

"Thank you...Thank you...NuNuTu is the name of my new doll. In Paradise, there's a Park of Beautiful Flowers. The colors of the flowers are so awesome; and like little children, the flowers need to be watered, fed, and given time to grow. In the New Day, the Park of Beautiful Flowers will bloom in everyone's spirit, so to remind you and me of that day, I've painted NuNuTu with every color of God's Kingdom. Isn't she beautiful?"

Susan held up NuNuTu, the doll's colors are very, very similar to the Holy Spirit's aura, and like Him, the doll's colors that are most prominent are violet, pink, red and gold.

Susan waited for all the applauds to stop, before she spoke, "Thank you, again...NuNuTu and I are honored to open this wonderful day in the Knesset with First Corinthians, 13:1-7 from the Holy Bible: (NLT)

Susan: *"If I could speak in any language*
In heaven or on earth
But didn't love others,
I would only be making
Meaningless noise
Like a gong
Or a clanging cymbal
(2) If I had the gift of prophesy,
And if I knew all the mysteries
Of the future
And knew everything about everything,
But didn't love others,
What good would I be?
And if I had the gift of faith
So that I could speak to a mountain
And make it move,
Without love
I would be no good to anybody
(3) If I gave everything I have
To the poor
And even sacrificed my body,
I could boast about it,
But if I didn't love others,
I would be of no value whatsoever
(4) Love is patient and kind
Love is not jealous
Or boastful
Or proud
(5) Or rude
Love does not demand its own way
Love is not irritable,
And keeps no record of when
It has been wronged

> (6) ***It is never glad about injustice***
> ***But rejoices whenever the truth wins out***
> (7) ***Love never gives up,***
> ***Never loses faith***
> ***Is always hopeful***
> ***And endures through every circumstance."***

Susan's recitation was received with loud applauds and continuous cheers, until she held up her hands to silence the crowd. "Thank you. Thank you. A New Day will come to all who want to have a relationship with God. Finally, there are three things that will endure. **Faith, hope and love. And the greatest of these is Love.** (1 Corinthians 13:13 NLT) **Amen. Love you, bye, bye."**

Susan waved to everyone, and received an ovation that thundered throughout the Knesset. Isaiah lovingly hugged Susan as she walked off the stage, "That was excellent, Susan. You found the right words to say today."

"Love...is Jesus' secret power."

"Yes it is, and He used that power better than anybody."

"You know why you're able to hear us now?"

"Because I listened."

"Yes, before you always questioned, and that's not belief. And also because you didn't quit God."

"I'm sure you're right," Isaiah smiled, hugged Susan again, and then stepped up to the podium.

"The great songwriter, Stevie Wonder wrote the words: Isn't She Lovely, and Susan Faraday is just that, Lovely!" Isaiah announced, which created more handclapping and cheers from everyone.

"Now let me add on to what Susan Faraday has said about love. In First John 4:9-10 (NLT) it's written, God showed how much he loved us by sending his only Son into the world so that we might have eternal life through him. This is real love. It is not that we loved God, but that he loved us and sent his Son as a sacrifice to take away our sins. I understand there are many who have different beliefs, but all our nations gathered together today is a testament to the New Day coming into the world. It is my honor to be invited here, and though nothing in our world compares with the Kingdom of God, we do see a future of heaven here on earth, however, we have to build now for that Earthly Kingdom of Love. To present the next step toward the New Day, help me welcome the President of the United States of America, Aaron Morrison."

President Morrison walked over and stood behind the podium. He waited until the applause subsided before he spoke.

"Thank you. Thank you. Pastor Isaiah Hillman wasn't told of the changes I've made, however, I think it's more appropriate to honor the ones who created this wonderful, Great Project for the world. Please welcome, the Miracle Twins, Leon and Alonzo Serna."

Leon and Alonzo, outfitted in black tuxedos, white shirts, and white ties walked onto the stage. They spoke in unison, "As representatives of the Miracle Children, we are honored to be invited here to tell you about the dream we had."

"Pastor Hillman heard our dream first," Leon started.

"And being such a wise man in our affairs," Alonzo continued, and then he and Leon spoke in unison again. "And getting the okay from all the Miracle Children in the World, Pastor Hillman flew, ran, and walked across the mighty Potomac River. He fought off fifty Secret Agents disguised as alligators/crocodiles..."

"Alligators, Alonzo."

"Leon, I like crocodiles!"

Leon whispered in Alonzo's ear as they waited for the audience's laughter to stop.

"Pastor Hillman fought off fifty Secret Agent men disguised as Austin Powers...Yeah Baby."

Leon and Alonzo once again waited for everyone's laughter to quiet down before they continued, "And then our fearless pastor fought off one hundred White House West Wingers, and after many words...Words we cannot mentioned here, Pastor Isaiah Hillman was able to burst through the doors of the White House Oval Office and scared President Morrison, three shades of colorful red."

Leon and Alonzo laughed along with all the Kings, Queens, Presidents, Great Rulers, and Leaders in the World, then they bowed to the crowd, to one another, and last they bowed to President Morrison "Please welcome back to the podium, President Aaron Morrison."

A loud ovation of cheers echoed throughout the Parliament as the twins walked off and President Morrison returned.

"I'm glad those little rascals didn't talk about my having to change my See-Thru-Pants," President Morrison joked, creating much laughter from all the gathered guests.

"Once again, thank you...Pastor Hillman did come to the White House with the Miracle Children's proposal, for an Educational City to teach Arts and Sciences to the world. This Educational City will teach law, medicine, farming, environment, architecture, government, banking, spirituality, and International Love for all nations. What's amazing about the project is that the first Educational City will be built between Israel and Palestine. The campus will house one million, five hundred and fourteen thousand students. It'll house the world's greatest and gifted educators. Christians, Jews, Moslems, and other faiths will study and learn together. Youths of different thoughts, ideas and opinions will come together, learn together, and share their experiences together. The same day, that Educational City breaks ground here in New Jerusalem, additional Educational Cities will break ground in Africa, Asia, America and Australia. Instead of building walls to separate people, we're going to build Educational Cities to bring them together. Yes, a New Day is coming into the world!"

Everyone in the Knesset shouted and cheered in appreciation.

~

"It'll never happen, Ms. Summers!" Mr. Kelton said, while he shook his head in disbelief.

"Why do you say that, Mr. Kelton?" Jan questioned, while conducting another 'Talking With Jan' Town Hall Meeting.

"There are always problems with things that are right and good."

"So you like the Educational Cities, even though you see problems?"

"They'll need ten thousand U.N. Peacekeepers in every city, twenty-four seven, three hundred and sixty-five days a year, plus they'll need to do this until Kingdom Come. The cost of such grandiose, high-minded ideas will be over and above astronomical."

"Yes, I'm sure it'll cost a lot of money, but many countries have agreed to their initial expenditures. Thank you, Mr. Kelton."

An elderly woman stepped up to the mike next. Her voice was weak and strained, "Whatever the cost it's one step toward tomorrow and a giant leap for the future!"

Some people laughed, many applauded the woman.

"Do you have a question for the panel, Ma'am?"

"Nah, I just wanted to say that. Thank you," the woman announced, and trudged back to her seat.

Up next at the mike was another senior citizen. "How much will it cost to live in these Special Cities, or is only for rich kids, and uppity folks?"

"Uppity, haven't heard that in a long time," Jan responded.

"Uppity folks, they still out there. There's a few of them in here, too!" the senior confirmed, as the audience laughed to acknowledged his truthfulness.

"It's a good thing. Instead of building war machines, we'll be building some of the world's greatest minds," Mayor Bell smiled, pleased with announcement of the Educational Cities. "Students will be issued vouchers from the country they represent. Of course, most students will come from the wealthiest nations, however, President Morrison has stated that one third of all students will be from low-income families and Third World Countries."

Another senior citizen motioned with his finger as a cautionary protest, "I hear that by the time these cities are completed, the Miracle Children will be old enough to live there, and they will be given a free pass. Now, once they are all educated, I'm thinking they plan to take over the world. Mark my words, they may be godly children now, but we all know peoples outgrow their godliness and enjoy sinful lives a whole lot more. I'm not going to be here much longer, so you younger folks best guard your future!"

"Thank you, sir," Jan said. "That's something we all should keep in mind. We have time for one more question."

"My question is for anyone on the panel," a young woman addressed everyone, as she read from a handwritten note. "If heaven has closed its doors, and the children no longer hear the voice of the Holy Spirit, and groups of Earth Soldiers, Devils, Angels, and WOG's are growing larger everyday, why are we creating Educational Cities where these groups can come together and recruit more members into their destructive ideas and beliefs?"

"Pastor Munroe, would you like to answer that question?" Jan asked.

"Young lady, your question has many answers and none of them will be agreeable to everyone. The New Day that God has given onto the Miracle Children to prepare our world for wasn't separated by race, religion, or nation. Groups, pro and con, will continue their fight, but we, as parents, teachers, and preachers must fight for our children's education everywhere. We are all God's children, and the inconvenient truth we all must face is that America is no longer a world to itself. We live in a New World, that's reaching for Global Opportunities, so I believe, a child born somewhere else in the world who receives a great education will be an asset to us all."

"Thank you, Pastor Munroe. In our days of many changes, I agree education should be ever widening. You've been watching 'Talking With Jan.' I'm Jan Summers."

~

"Paula, slow down before you fall and hurt yourself," Evelyn shouted, as Paula ran up the walkway to their new home, and Isaiah and the cab driver busied themselves removing luggage and bags out of the trunk.

"It's been a pleasure to drive you home, Pastor Hillman. I can't wait to tell my wife," the driver said, as Isaiah pulled out his wallet to pay the cab fare. "Put that away. My wife would make me sleep in this taxi if I charged you!"

"Tell your wife, thanks. God bless you and your family.

"Thank you, Pastor Hillman. Coming from you, I know my wife will jump with joy. God bless you and your family forever."

"Amen! Thank you, and in accepting your free ride, how about your family joining us for dinner after we get settled in from our trip abroad?"

"If I didn't accept, my wife would...would, I have no idea what she'll do!"

"It's accepted then. Your wife can pick a restaurant she loves," Isaiah smiled, as they carried the luggage into the house.

"It's President Morrison," Evelyn informed Isaiah, and handed him the telephone.

"Hello, Mr. President...Thank you, sir. Yes, I'll call you right back after speaking with Evelyn and Paula," Isaiah said, as he sat down on his new sofa and hung up the phone. "How would guys like to fly to Washington D.C. tonight? It's just for two days, and President Morrison has requested our presence."

"Your presence. Miracle Girl, you want to go to Washington and see President Morrison?"

Paula began to cry, "No."

Paula's tears troubled Isaiah and Evelyn.

"Okay, honey, we'll stay home and let Daddy go see the Big Bad Wolf by himself," Evelyn joked, and used a tissue to wipe away the tears that flowed down Paula's cheeks.

"Stay home, Daddy, bad people," Paula cried, and wrapped her arms around his neck.

"Do you see Daddy getting hurt, Paula?" Evelyn asked, in fear for Isaiah.

"No, not Daddy."

"Who do you see getting hurt?"

"Susan has bad dreams."

"Isaiah, maybe you better tell President Morrison that Paula sees bad people in Washington."

"Paula, there are bad people everywhere," Isaiah said, and kissed Paula to ease her fear, though inwardly, her tears really troubled him. She was a Miracle Child, and if she saw bad people, then he better alert the president. "God will protect us. Don't worry."

"Alonzo say God closed his windows and doors."

Isaiah smiled, "Alonzo and his brother say a lot of things. Listen to what your mom and me tell you, okay?"

"Okay."

Isaiah looked at Evelyn. She frowned, but remained silent, because Paula said Isaiah wouldn't be hurt, and the death threat on Susan kept her well protected. Isaiah told her about what the little girl in London saw in Susan's dreams… and…well, she agreed with Isaiah, God would protect His Miracle Children. God did it on Star Island, and He would do it at the White House, however, she reached out and took Isaiah's hand. "Paula, let's pray for everyone to have a wonderful time in Washington."

"I already did…but bad people still there."

Evelyn shuddered at Paula's words, squeezed Isaiah's hand, and then took Paula into her arms.

"I'll alert President Morrison," Isaiah said, and picked up the phone.

~

"Our World is not heaven, however ninety-three percent of homelessness has been erased, illegal drug use is no longer a major problem in our nation, and abortions have been stopped, one hundred percent!" President Morrison stated as he addressed a large group gathered in the White House Rose Garden. "The Educational Cities that the Miracle Children, Leon and Alonzo Serna dreamed about are already on the desks of developers, with a new one added in South America. In essence, America is blessed, the world is blessed, and we owe it all to our gifted and talented children."

The President turned and looked at Michael, Michelle, Leon, Alonzo, Susan, and Isaiah as they stood behind him. He clapped his hands in appreciation and everyone joined in.

President Morrison continued his speech, "Today, in great appreciation for Pastor Isaiah Hillman, and the one million, five-hundred and fourteen thousand Miracle Children throughout the United States of America, Canada, South America, and so many other countries, too numerous to mention, I have the honor of presenting, The Special International Medal of Honor to Pastor Hillman, and to all the Miracle Children throughout the world."

Loud applause and cheers echoed throughout the Rose Garden as President Morrison pinned, the Special International Medal of Honor on Michael, Michelle, Leon and Alonzo. When President Morrison stepped in front of Isaiah and Susan, the cheers and applauds became even louder, so loud that the silencer gunshots that blasted holes in the President's back and Susan's chest are unheard, but everyone reacted in horror when President Morrison and Susan Faraday fell to the ground, and the blood on the two victims, including Susan's doll, NuNuTu immediately registered, and pandemonium broke out as the crowd scattered, and people ran madly in fear for their lives.

FBI and Secret Agents pulled out there guns, but having no idea from where the gunshots originated, they put their lives in harm's way and stood guard over the bodies lying on the ground.

~

Evelyn, who saw the horror that was televised for the whole world, lost all sense of reality and screamed, cried, hollered and shouted, "Oh my God, Jesus, why, why, why? Oh, God, why?"

Richard and Thelma do their best to comfort their daughter, but Evelyn was so out of control Richard wrestled her to the floor and pinned her down, as Paula cried out, "Mommy...Mommy...Mommy..."

～

The terrifying event also filled the Spencer's home with shock and horror, as Sylvia cried out in pain and sorrow. Henry did his best to comfort her, as he prayed, "Our Lord, God...protect us...forgive us..."

～

Tears gushed from Diana and Mario Serna, as they hugged each other and stared in horror as they watched the scene of the shooting on television. They both knelt down on their knees and prayed as a news reporter spoke as loud as he could over the horrible clamor that came from the Rose Garden.

"Miracle Child, Prophet Susan Faraday, and the President of the United States, Aaron Morrison have been shot...it hasn't been confirmed yet, but I'm hearing that they were both instantly killed. We're confined thirty feet away from the shooting, and with everybody surrounding the victims it's impossible to get a clear view of the bodies...Wait, wait, I'm seeing Secret Service Agents lifting and carrying Susan Faraday off into the White House. What's going on? Has God brought her back to life?"

～

A Secret Service Agent ran down the White House corridor with Susan's bloodied body in his arms. The Faradays ran behind him, and from the opposite direction, two paramedics ran up.

"Put her down. Put her down!" a paramedic yelled, as the agent responded by laying Susan's body on the floor and the paramedics immediately rendered emergency CPR, while Susan's parents fell to their knees, weeping in prayer.

~

During the fear and panic, Secret Agent, Martin Canaby yelled out over and over again, "Code Red, Code Red! Surround everyone. The media, parents, visitors, everyone will be held for questioning. Code Red!"

"Mommy, hurry up," Samantha Morrison cried, as First Lady Jennifer Morrison stared, as if in a trance, while her husband, President Morrison was placed onto a stretcher, and lifted into the rear of the ambulance. Samantha climbed into the back of the ambulance and took her father's hand, and yelled again to her mother, "Mommy, hurry up. Come on!"

First Lady Morrison, in paralytic shock, was lost to reality.

Samantha yelled out a third time, "Mommy, please!"

Isaiah took the First Lady's hand and tried to usher her toward the ambulance, but she didn't budge, but cried out, "Isaiah...Michael...Michelle...save him! Heal his body. Save the President."

"Do something!" Isaiah commanded Michael and Michelle.

Michelle whispered to Isaiah, so the First Lady wouldn't hear. "What can we do? Healings come from heaven!"

"Heaven is silent as a test to see what you children are going to do," Isaiah said.

"You think we can?" Michael questioned.

"God gave you Jesus' power! Do something!" Isaiah demanded, as he grabbed a paramedic. "Put these children in the ambulance with President Morrison."

"Yes sir, Pastor Hillman," the paramedic said, as he helped Michael and Michelle into the back of the ambulance.

Isaiah hurried over to the First Lady, "Come on, and let's get you to the hospital."

The First Lady still didn't move.

"She's in shock, help!"

Isaiah lifted the First Lady up into his arms, and carried her off as three Secret Agents hurried over and offered assistance. The ambulance that carried President Morrison, Samantha, Michael and Michelle raced off, as the emergency red lights flashed and siren wailed.

Meanwhile, Martin Canaby yelled out as the ambulance sped off, "Did anybody see anything?"

A lady raised her hand.

"Yes, ma'am?'

"I saw someone."

"You're first!" Canaby hollered. "Take her inside. Anybody else see the shooter?"

"I think..."

"Take this gentleman inside."

Two Secret Service Agents ushered the lady and man into the White House.

"Everyone else, hand over your cameras, cell phones, and recorders to the agents. Thank you for your calm, unquestioned cooperation," Canaby stated, and then rushed off into the White House to a makeshift interrogation room where an agent is with the lady.

"Hi, what's your name?"

"Mrs. Ellen Stanton. Are you in charge?"

"I'm Martin Canaby, Mrs. Stanton, and yes, I'm in charge. Two shots were fired, did you see who fired the gun?"

"I think...the woman standing next to me...did," Mrs. Stanton answered, not sure of herself.

"You think you saw a woman fire a gun?"

"It happened so fast." Mrs. Stanton cried, "She, she shoved...her pocketbook into my side."

"Thank you, that's great information. Joe, take Mrs. Stanton into the monitoring room. Mrs. Stanton, you're going to look at some videos and photographs of the ceremony to see if you can point her out. It's going to be all right. You want some coffee, tea..."

"A shot of cognac would help," Mrs. Stanton tearfully, requested.

"I'm sure it will. Joe, please take Mrs. Ellen Stanton into the monitoring room and get her something to calm her nerves," Canaby said, shook her hand, and hurried out of the room.

"I want some good cognac!" Mrs. Stanton demanded.

The agent nodded and escorted her out the room.

~

"Are you sure it was a man, Mr. Hickman?" Canaby asked, as he questioned the gentleman that sat in another White House room.

"Yes, sir. I saw him with his gun out."

"Did you see him shoot the president or the little girl?"

"No, I didn't see that. I just saw he had a gun in his hand."

"He had a gun in his hand and the Secret Agents didn't tackle him!"

"No, but some agents talked to him. They knew him."

"Was he an agent?"

"He must have been. He had a gun out and the other agents didn't shoot him!"

Martin Canaby groaned, "Harry take Mr. Hickman over to the monitoring room."

An agent entered the room, "Martin, you need to see this."

Canaby followed the agent out of the room, "What do you have, Barbara?"

"One of our own, Martin," Barbara offered, as she opened the door into the monitoring room where a number of Agents and FBI men are standing in front of a monitor. They stepped aside to allow Canaby to view the monitor.

"Okay, run it," Barbara said.

A technician pressed a button and a DVD disc of the White House Rose Garden proceeding came on a monitor. Speeding up the disc, the technician stopped it a second before a woman in the crowd shot the president in the back. Replaying the disc in slow motion, the woman was acting as if she was fumbling in her pocketbook for something, then the disc revealed a bullet being fired from inside her pocketbook.

"Get me a close up of her face," Canaby groaned to the tech.

"It's Karen Watson, sir," Barbara said.

"I know its Karen, and I'm sure she's gone by now! Get me a damn close up!" Canaby shouted, as the tech moved the disc along until he got Karen's face on the monitor. "Print that, please. Barbara, get her picture out to the media, the police..."

"There's more," Barbara said.

"Excuse me!"

"There's more. Carlin, put in that other disc," Barbara said, as the technician removed one disc and inserted another. Pressing play, the disc showed a man shooting a gun.

"God, what's going on here?" Canaby groaned, and flopped down in a chair. "Karen Watson and Earl Sisco. Two of our own. I brought them over here from the Phillip Hunter's detail when he took sick leave. Print Sisco's picture. Check them both out. Their backgrounds, where they've been, who they called, and how the hell they became Secret Agents!"

~

"Thank you. I hear they're alive because of you," First Lady Jennifer Morrison said, entering a hospital Waiting Room and hugged Michael and Michelle, but they looked solemn and defeated. "What? Say something! Aren't they still alive?"

"We think so…the President was alive in the ambulance, I think the doctors are operating on him, but they made us wait in here," Michelle answered.

"What about Susan?" Isaiah questioned.

"The same. Doctors are operating on her, too,' Michael said.

"The Holy Spirit?" Isaiah asked.

"No word," Michael sadly remarked, as he sat back down.

Jennifer looked from Michael to Isaiah, "What?"

"It's nothing," Isaiah replied.

"No tell me. If my husband's…No, if the President of the United States needs something, tell me. I'll get it for you!"

"I don't think it's something anybody is able to do."

"Why not?"

Isaiah ushered Jennifer over to a sofa, "What those earth devils said on their audio tape is true. Since Susan Faraday's prophesy, the Miracle Children haven't heard from heaven."

"Why not? Didn't she get her prophecy from God?"

"Susan said she hasn't heard from the Holy Spirit, so we believe she prophesized out of her own spirit."

Tears filled Jennifer's eyes, "What else do you know? Tell me everything, then I'll know how to help."

"One of the Miracle Children who sees dreams said the Death Angel was visiting Susan's dreams. I guess she foretold the truth."

270

Jennifer was quiet for a moment, and then wiped her tears away, "Get that child here. We need to know more about Susan's dreams. Also, get that boy here from Philadelphia, you know the one who healed those people at the bank robbery."

Isaiah closed his eyes and spoke in spirit, 'Akeem Wallace, Philadelphia, and Christian Sparrow, London, England, we need you here. Come to where we are.'

A moment later, Christian walked into the waiting room.

"Little girl, your parents are not in here. Go to the other waiting room down the hallway," Jennifer said, and escorted Christian to the door.

"Pastor Hillman called me here," Christian stated. "I'm Christian Sparrow."

"First Lady, meet Christian Sparrow who flew in from London," Isaiah said, as he embraced Christian.

"Is it really you?" Jennifer questioned, as she touched Christian's face, shoulders and arms.

"It's me. I can travel fast."

"I see. And Akeem, can he travel fast, too?"

"His mother wanted to come with him, but she's unable to travel like us," Christian said.

"I see. I think I see. Isaiah, come help me set up travel plans for Akeem and his mother," Jennifer said, as she led him out of the waiting room.

~

An hour later a helicopter landed on the ground of the Washington D.C. Medical Center. The propellers stopped, a door opened, and Akeem and his mother are helped out as Jennifer and Isaiah hurried over to welcome them.

~

16

Trials

*But if you don't even believe me
when I tell you about things that
happen here on earth, how can
you possibly believe if I tell you
what is going on in heaven.*
John 3:12 NLT

"Inside News has uncovered this breaking news story. Two Secret Service Agents, Karen Watson and Earl Sisco, are being sought for possible involvement in this morning's shooting at the White House," Paul Hudson reported, as he stood outside the White House gates, while the television news camera filmed his broadcast. "The two agents were members of the Secretary of Defense, Phillip Hunter's team. Anna Kosmento is at that location. What have you found out, Anna?"

"Paul, Secret Service Agents were already inside the home of Secretary of Defense, Phillip Hunter when we arrived. The secretary isn't home, but we've learned that the two agents, Karen Watson and Earl Sisco were in charge of the secretary's special security, and they've been spotted leaving here with Mr. Hunter, so we're not sure if the secretary left willingly, or under duress. The White House needs to answer questions about the secretary's involvement with Earth Soldiers. Word has leaked out that the president was aware of Mr. Hunter's secret meetings with the alleged shooters and was told to take a sick leave. I'm Anna Kosmento, Channel 13 Inside News!"

~

"I'm sorry, Evelyn," Isaiah sighed, while he paced the floor in the hospital Waiting Room. "Honey, it's been crazy here. No, they're not dead. Michael and Michelle prayed over them, so there's hope that Akeem Wallace will be able to heal them. Yes, I'll be here for a while. Sure, if that's what you want to do. Leave Paula with your parents, and I'll... Evelyn...Okay, I'll make arrangements for everybody. Love you, I'll call you back in an hour."

"It's going to be all right," Jennifer offered, and sat down with Isaiah. "I'll get the President Pro-Tem to send Air Force Two for your family. I'm sure he's using Air Force One, right now."

"You're some powerhouse of action!" Isaiah exclaimed.

"I was lost for a moment, but I'm a little more clear-headed now. Tell me more about this traveling the Miracle Children are capable of doing. Can you do it?"

"I've journeyed to heaven and back. It has something to do with hearing the wind inside your spirit."

"Can you do it?"

"No! I don't know, maybe. Why?"

"I need to know who can do what? I need you to learn how to do this traveling thing. I need..."

"Please, First Lady Morrison, slow down."

"No, time is running, not slowing down. You need to find out how they're able travel...why they can do it, and why you can't? I need to know everything!"

Akeem entered the room.

"What's the good news, Akeem?" Jennifer queried.

"The doctors say they are on life support systems. We have power from God to heal, so I think something is stopping us."

"What do you think is stopping you?" Isaiah asked.

"I don't know, something really dark, and my spiritual light of healing is unable to get passed it. I'll keep trying to get through."

"That's not good enough," Jennifer argued. She stared at Michael, Michelle, Christian and Akeem. "Pastor Hillman hasn't learned how to do this traveling thing. So, can you guys take me somewhere?"

"Where do you want to go?" Christian asked.

"Take me to heaven. I want to talk to God!" Jennifer insisted.

Isaiah, Michael, Michelle, Christian, Akeem and Ms. Wallace stared at Jennifer as if she's completely out of her mind.

"Your human body can't pass through. You have to have a new body like ours," Michael explained.

"Why? Pastor Hillman didn't have a body like you and you took him to the hillside concert on Star Island!

"He must have had the triple blessing, otherwise he wouldn't have been able to travel like us. Anyway, God used His angels to take us to heaven, we don't know where it is!"

"In the New Day, the whole world will shift and everyone will learn how to move faster than time, but that's in the future, not now," Christian stated.

"Beside, traveling to Star Island isn't the same as going on a trip to heaven," Michelle said.

"What's the difference?"

"We had to die to go to heaven. You want to die?" Michael said, his voice bleak with misery.

"Michael, you didn't die, you already had new bodies and you vanished from the Island before the bomb exploded. Now, I want to talk to God. If God has left you children on your own, I want some answers. I want to know why?"

"Lady Morrison, the Holy Spirit isn't talking to us anymore."

"Why isn't the Holy Spirit talking to you, Michael? What did you do wrong?"

"We don't know," Michelle cried, tears streaming down her cheeks, which caused tears to water Jennifer's eyes, but Jennifer brushed hers aside.

"Christian, when Pastor Hillman told you to come here to Washington, how did you know where it was?"

"I didn't know. I came to him."

"If you can come to him, you can take me to where God's Spirit lives," Jennifer demanded, with a voice of authority. "Let's go, Christian, I don't have a new body like you, but I don't mind dying to speak to God!"

"How do you know we left the Island before the bomb exploded?" Christian questioned.

"Because my God would never harm a hair on a child's head!" Jennifer answered, and taking Christian's hand, she closed her eyes, but before they were able to travel, a bright, white cloud of smoke covered them. The Prophets, Elijah and Elisha materialized in the cloud with a contingent of heaven's soldiers.

Elijah spoke first, "The Earth Realm is under attack."

"Stop the attack here. Don't open a pathway into heaven for evil forces to enter," Elisha warned, and then... SWOOSH was the sound heard in the room as the prophets, soldiers, and the bright, white cloud disappeared back into eternity.

Jennifer opened her eyes and looked around, "What happened? Why are we still here?"

"We've found out why heaven is closed," Christian answered, clearly startled by the news.

~

"They didn't say anything else?" Henry said, his heart wanted to fight the evil forces, but he didn't know how to destroy an invisible force. He looked around the White House private conference room for answers, but Isaiah, Evelyn, the Spencers, and Downings were silent.

Christian calmly spoke up, "That's all they said, Mr. Spencer. We're in charge!"

Sylvia, unhappy and dismayed by the turn of events, questioned, "Why close off heaven? Why doesn't heaven join forces with us and destroy the evil force."

"They did. Christian said we're in charge. Heaven is using their forces, the Miracle Children here on the earth to stop this evil attack," Isaiah said, but his answer didn't excite anybody.

"Is this in the Bible, Pastor Hillman?"

"Henry, this isn't the first time heaven has become silent. Over four hundreds years, from Malachi to the New Testament of Christ Jesus, mankind didn't hear from God. In Malachi 4:1, the Lord Almighty said, the Day of Judgment is coming, burning like a furnace. The arrogant and the wicked will be burned up like straw..." (NLT)

"Isaiah, you're not helping!" Thelma angrily retorted. "God's closing heaven and expecting little children to fight a war against evil is, too me, stupid, dumb, outrageous, and anything else I can't think of right now."

"Grandma Downing, obviously the children are the best weapons here on earth. They don't seem disturbed by what they've heard, they still believe and trust God, and they aren't looking for a way to escape. We've all seen what the world is like with adult men and women running things. Remember, God told us to take dominion and subdue the earth. (Genesis1:28) I guess we didn't accept the responsibility."

"You don't have to be so sarcastic, Isaiah. I was just stating my valid opinion," Thelma said, equally sarcastic. "Now, you've dodged Mr. Spencer's question about whether it's in the Bible that children will fight this evil force wanting to attack heaven and earth?"

"The Bible says, "But you belong to God, my dear children. You have already won your fight with these false prophets, because the Spirit who lives in you is greater than the spirit who lives on the world. (1 John 4:4 NLT) So, yes, the children have the power in them to fight evil. And so do you!"

"An evil force we can't see, God help us! Michael, do you have some answers?" Henry asked, hopefully.

"We'll agree with whatever our pastor says."

Isaiah inwardly groaned.

⁓

"Tonight, we're broadcasting from our television studio in Washington, D.C. My special guest is, Pastor Isaiah Hillman," Jan Summers announced with a smile, but openly unsympathetic to the crisis the Miracle Children and Isaiah brought into the world.

"Pastor Hillman, the Miracle Child, Michael Spencer told the world one word, 'Believe.' I'm sure everyone now realizes that no Higher Power is protecting you and Miracle Children. The Earth Soldiers have known all along that this unseen god, and the place called heaven was just a dream you all experienced together, and no heavenly spirit ever really communicated with the children. So, what should the world do now? Believe what? Believe who?"

"We're still here. President Morrison and Susan Faraday are still here."

"They've been shot, are we to believe in some spiritual ghost who let that happen?"

"Ms. Summers, everyone isn't a believer, but to be honest our world has traveled far beyond belief. There's no one in this world today that hasn't experienced the presence of the Miracle Children. We have been moved physically, mentally, and spiritually beyond our mindset of belief. It's now time to put our beliefs to work, and the way to do that is through fasting and prayer. Jesus says in Mark 2:19-20, can the children of the bridechamber fast, while the bridegroom is with them? As long as they have the bridegroom with them, they cannot fast. But the days will come, when the bridegroom shall be taken away from them, and then shall they fast in those days. That time is here, now!"

"Oh, so now it's fasting and prayer?"

"These acts of deliverance have been in the world for centuries, but not many of us take advantage of them. To believe is to have faith in a truth that hasn't yet been revealed to you. Prayer and fasting solidifies our journey to open heaven again."

"So why didn't Michael tell the world to pray and fast, instead of telling us a word that became a waste of time?"

"Ms. Summers, I know you're still upset about that show, but you asked me, not Michael, what the world should do now. Michael had to open minds to believe, because believing is the power of faith. That was his calling, and he did a wonderful job to get people to believe for the first time, or to believe again, because many were stumbling around in darkness, including me, and I was ministering to a church!"

"Is that why you wanted to quit the ministry? You lost your belief!"

"No, it's not that easy to put into words. I wasn't accomplishing anything meaningful in my church. No great awakening took over my spirit, and members of my congregation started staying home. I needed a change, and so did the church. God knew the world was now ready for the change, however, He also knew it would take a fight to bring it about."

"And God's great answer is using children to fight a war he created with some mystical devil he created? I'm sorry, Pastor Hillman, but I don't think this fasting and praying theory of yours is the answer. Tell me, why didn't you fast and pray when you were stumbling around in darkness?"

"I did, and God answered my prayers by putting me on this journey with the Miracle Children," Isaiah commented, and Jan felt small-minded, but she still didn't believe anything he said.

"Do you feel like you're losing? The two agents who shot President Morrison and Susan Faraday are still missing, and they were willing to kill to make their changes in the world. The only thing you're saying is to pray. Who does the world pray to? A closed-door heaven!"

"We're in this to the end, so perhaps my words to the few unbelievers left in the world will give them the courage to change their lives. God used Michael to wake up billions of lost spirits with one Word. God got the world to listen and hear Susan Faraday's Prophecy of Love, and now through me, and other voices around the world, God is going to get the relationship He's always wanted with His children. The heavens may be silent, but God has many ways to communicate to his believers. When God is silent, He's working. Believe me, heaven is never silent; God will always hear His people. Flood heaven with your prayers, Our Father will hear you."

"You're calling for an International Prayer Vigil."

"That's why I've agreed to do your show. President Morrison and Susan Faraday are in Intensive Care, and the doctors aren't very hopeful about their survival, but I am. I'm praying that we all send our prayers up into God's Kingdom. We fast, we light candles, and we walk together as brothers and sisters in faith. President Morrison heard Susan's Love Prophecy, and he responded. He heard Leon and Alonzo Serna's dream of Educational Cities, and he responded. President Morrison opened the hearts and minds of Kings, Queens and World Leaders who've made changes in their countries because a little girl, Susan Faraday said we either learn how to love or stay hateful and die. The choice is ours. We have the power to stop evil in our spirit, our families, towns and countries. Wherever evil raises its ugly head, we stop it! We shine a light on it with our prayers and obedience, which is our connection to our God. Jesus is the Light. The light shines through the darkness, and the darkness can never extinguish it. (John 1:5 NLT) We have to protect our children before they cross the line into darkness, by teaching them about God's Commandments. In Proverbs 22:6 (KJV), it says: Train up a child in the way he should go: and when he is old, he will not depart from it."

"I agree we should raise our children with good advice and teaching. It's our responsibility."

"I'm glad you're understanding what I'm trying to teach about the light. If you know where Karen Watson and Earl Sisco are hiding, shine a light on them! Be warned, the Miracle Children and myself have declared war on all Earth Devils. Your evil actions have the whole world declaring war on you. You can't escape. We're coming after you. The Miracle Children, their families, and my family are going to fast and pray. Prayer works! The choice is yours on how you want this to end. I'm going to read, Psalm 91, starting at verse nine. (NLT) (9)'If you make the Lord your refuge, if you make the Most High your shelter, (10) no evil will conquer you; no plague will come near your dwelling. (11) For he orders his angels to protect you wherever you go. (12) They will hold you with their hands to keep you from striking your foot on a stone. (13) You will trample down lions and poisonous snakes; you will crush fierce lions and serpents under your feet! (14) The Lord says, I will rescue those who love me. I will protect those who trust in my name. (15) When they call on me I will answer; I will be with them in trouble. I will rescue them and honor them. (16) I will satisfy them with a long life and give them my salvation.' The Lord has spoken. Everyone, old and new believers in Christ Jesus, declare that same prayer and send it up to heaven. God Bless You!"

"Pastor Hillman, you've declared war on Earth Devils, and you don't even know who they are!"

"God knows who they are, and God will reveal who they are, and we will destroy them!"

"So you think its okay to put your family, the Miracle Children, their parents, and many other lives in harm's way because of what you've just read from the Bible?"

"We know God's power! We've experienced a journey into God's Kingdom, and we know that His Mighty Power will deliver the World into the New Day. God never instills failure in his children. You have to do that on your own."

"Let's hope you're right," Jan offered. She reached over and shook Isaiah's hand. "Thank you, Pastor Isaiah Hillman. You've been watching a News Special of 'Talking With Jan.' I'm Jan Summers, stayed tuned for your local news after this brief commercial break."

~

Ivan Stone, leader of the Earth Soldiers, yelled, "Damn fool. That preacher thinks a stupid prayer and fast will stop us! He doesn't have any idea who we are!"

"If he gets everybody praying, God may open heaven to them again," Earl Sisco shrugged, somewhat stunned and plagued with doubt.

"Earl, I have some good news for everyone. A big problem was created in heaven when those children were allowed to return back to the earth with new bodies. Hear me, if those children can live here on earth in spiritual bodies, so can all the other spiritual bodies who were banished into the lower light!"

"Lower light?" an Earth Soldier questioned.

"You've all heard, that if you don't believe the son, you'll burn in the hell-fires of Hades, not true. Spirits who don't want all that singing, dancing, praising, and worshipping will enjoy life in the lower light."

"How do you know all this?" Karen Watson asked, pleasantly delighted.

"Karen, our forces live in the lower light, and they are soon coming into this world with a mightier power beyond what some little children can amass. The Great Adversary is ready to attack heaven and earth, and deliver them both into our hands. So when we destroyed those children, our revenge will be accomplished, and you'll receive all the riches and power you've ever dreamed about. Earl, Karen, Earth Soldiers, the Great Adversary is on his way here with his army, and he'll take back all the power stolen by that jealous son. This is the Great Adversary's Promise, You Will Inherit The Earth!"

"I'm really excited about finally getting all that's been promised to us."

"We all are, Karen, and I'm glad we're all in this together. Earth Soldiers, we're not the bad people here. Those destroying our democracy are the ones joining forces with Judaism, Islam, Christianity, and other religious lunatics. President Morrison has done that! Those children have done that! And now, Our Roaring Lion, the Great Adversary will walk across the earth and share his power with us, and we'll take back everything the son on the cross stole from the lower light!"

~

"Throughout the world, people of many faiths, nations and cultures are accepting Pastor Isaiah Hillman's call for International Fasting and Praying," Alison Hewitt reported for the National News Network. "Young and old, rich and poor, are taking time to pray for the President of the United States, and Susan Faraday. Mary Chung has a report from China."

"Hi Alison, all along the Great Wall of China, over a million believers are holding hands, and praying for the President of the United State and the young prophet, Susan Faraday. The government wanted to stop it, but quickly realized it was a good thing."

"Thank you, Mary, our satellite is showing the marvelous event in China to our audience. We're also screening praise dancing from India, and the burning of candles from Africa to South America as believers walk for miles in prayer and song," Alison stated, as she watched studio monitors.

"Excuse me, I'm getting a news bulletin...is that true? My producer has just informed me that the Miracle Children have joined Pastor Isaiah Hillman's call for an International Fast and Pray Vigil, and all, one million, five hundred and fourteen thousand, Miracle Children from around the world have descended on Washington, D.C. Please stand by for our cameras...no, never mind, since the National Mall is only a few blocks away, I'm going to run down to the Mall and bring you this amazing, exciting event myself. Let's take a commercial break. I'm Alison Hewitt, National News Network!"

Alison rushed out of the studio and yelled for her cameraman to follow, "Rollie, let's go."

~

"Okay, Rollie, roll camera...Hi, I'm Alison Hewitt, National News Network, and only fifteen minutes ago, the

Miracle Children came together in our nation's Capital. They are all here at Washington D.C.'s National Mall. The last time the children were together to prepare the world for a New Day, a nuclear attack took place. I'm with Melissa, a Miracle Child from El Salvador. Melissa, tell the world how all the Miracle Children are able to come to America?"

"In the New Day, everyone will be able to do what Our Father God has blessed us to do."

"How will that happen? Will we have to die to get new bodies?"

"In 1st Corinthians 15:50-51, it says: that flesh and blood cannot inherit the Kingdom of God. These perishable bodies of ours are not able to live forever. But let me tell you a wonderful secret God revealed to us. Not all of us will die, but we will all be transformed. Our Savior, Christ Jesus was crucified, and then returned in his new body to show his disciples that there is life after death. You have to believe! There's no death of the spirit. The Lord Almighty says, "The day of judgment is coming, burning like a furnace. The arrogant and the wicked will be burned up like straw on that day. They will be consumed like a tree – roots and all." (Malachi 4:1)

"If you have new bodies why is Susan suffering?"

"She isn't suffering. The President of the United States didn't have a new body, so she's protecting him.

"How do you know this?"

"I can hear."

"You're hearing from God?"

"No, I hear Susan."

"And Susan is protecting the president until God sends His healing."

"Exactly."

"When will that happen?"

"Soon."

"That's so nice to hear. Thank you, Melissa," Alison hugged Melissa, and then turned and spoke into the camera. "I don't know about you, but I'm feeling the Miracle Children are here to prepare for something more than a song and dance. Stayed tuned to the National News Network for more interviews with the Miracle Children in Washington, D.C. I'm Alison Hewitt."

~

"Good Morning, First Lady Morrison," the Secret Service Agent said, as he stood and greeted Jennifer and Christian Sparrow when they entered the Intensive Care Room.

"Good Morning. I want to be alone with my husband for a moment."

"Yes, ma'am."

The agent exited the room and stood outside the room with other agents.

Jennifer knelt down in front of Christian, "Christian, is the president dreaming?"

"I don't know. I can only see the dreams of other Miracle Children."

"Oh, I didn't know that. There's Susan Faraday over there. Is she dreaming?"

Christian closed, and then opened her eyes. "No, her spirit is awake, keeping the president alive."

"Is there something we can do to help her?"

"Susan says for me to tell Pastor Hillman about her new dream."

"Do you see her new dream?"

Christian closed her eyes, "Susan is showing me a vision of many soldiers spraying children with water. Pastor Hillman doesn't like it. He picks up Susan and runs away."

"Anything else?"

"No, that's all."

"Why are soldiers spraying water on the children? Are they on fire?"

"I didn't see that."

"You said Pastor Hillman picked up Susan and ran away. Was he running away from the soldiers?"

"That's what it looked like."

"But it looks like he saves her, right?"

"She's already saved."

Jennifer nodded in agreement, "Yes, she is. Thank you, Christian. I thank God for you."

"I didn't have to come here to see her dream."

"I didn't know your ability was so powerful."

"I'm still learning. I don't know everything."

"God has blessed you with a mighty power, do good, I'm sure you'll learn everything," the First Lady smiled and hugged Christian.

~

"This is the road, Karen. The checkpoint is a mile up the road. Everybody, get into position," Ivan Stone informed the Earth Soldiers.

Karen drove a yellow school bus off the main highway, onto a narrow road. The bus stopped at the checkpoint, and Karen spoke to the security guard when he stepped out of the guard shack.

"I'm a new driver. I must have turned onto the wrong road!"

"Must have. No school down this road," the guard acknowledged.

Karen's arm was leaning out the window, and under her arm is a gun with a silencer pointing at the guard. She pulled the trigger and blood spurted out the guard's neck. Shock and horror covered the guard's face before he collapsed to the ground.

"All clear," Karen observed, and over twenty Earth Soldiers sat up in their seats and pulled black head covers over their faces so only their eyes were visible. Two soldiers, wearing black sweat suits exited the bus. One entered the guard shack, found the gate key and tossed it to the other soldier, and then he dragged the dead security guard behind the guard shack. The second soldier unlocked the gate and slid it open, which allowed the bus entry into the government-restricted area.

~

"National News Network has learned that a minimal security, government installation was attacked and robbed a few hours ago. The lone security guard on duty was shot and killed, and what's shocking about this installation is that it housed a poison called, Ricin. Ricin is so deadly that a piece the size of a grain of salt can kill an adult. It's six thousand times more poisonous than cyanide. Another horrible fact about Ricin is that there is no antidote. We at the National News Network wonder why such a deadly poison was stored at a minimal security installation? How much was stolen? What was the government planning on doing with the Ricin? Who stole the poison? Terrorists? Earth Soldiers? Who? I'm Alison Hewitt."

~

"How come we don't have this story?" Jan Summers hollered, as everyone in the television monitoring room felt Jan's anger. "She's grabbing all the headlines. How did she get this story? No other news agency has the story. She must know the people who stole the Ricin."

"It happened in Virginia. I think she lives there."

"Shut up, Dave. I don't need your analysis. Get me on the earliest flight to Washington. Did somebody get Isaiah for me?"

"He's on the phone, Miss Summers," an assistant replied, and handed Jan a cell phone.

"Good Morning, Pastor Hillman. How are you? Any comments from the White House regarding the Ricin robbery?"

~

"Emergency! How can I help you?"

"The Secretary of Defense is the Leader of the Earth Soldiers and Earth Angels," a man guiltily admitted, while talking on a roadside emergency phone. "They stole the Ricin, and he owns a secret cabin in Virginia. I'm sorry about what we've done, and what they're planning to do."

He hung up the phone, got back into his Jeep, and sped off. A motorcycle police officer, seeing the jeep speeding away from the emergency phone, turned on his red light flasher and raced off. The man wiped tears from his eyes as he drove to the side of the road and stopped. The officer approached and peered inside the Jeep.

"I saw you leave the emergency phone. Are you all right, Sir?"

"I'm fine. Thank you."

"What was the emergency call about?"

"Nothing. Actually, I thought I was experiencing a heart attack. It was just...It was nothing," the man lied.

"May I see your driver's license, please," the officer said, as he stared at the man's cell phone on the passenger's seat.

"Why? I have a problem with high blood pressure!"

"Step out of car, sir!"

"Officer..."

The officer drew his gun, "Sir, you best step out, now!"

He turned off the Jeep's engine and stepped out. The officer patted him down for weapons, and then looked around inside the Jeep. In the back, he found a black head covering. The officer handcuffed the man.

~

"Mr. Tucker, the emergency phone you called on, number two-nineteen, received a call minutes before the officer stopped you. The caller said that the Secretary of Defense, Phillip Hunter was the leader of the Earth Soldiers and Angels. We're wondering how the caller would know this?"

Mr. Tucker, somewhat nervous, remained silent to Martin Canaby's interrogation.

"Where is this cabin in Virginia?"

"I want a lawyer," Mr. Tucker answered, his voice filled with misery.

"Sir, we're having a National Emergency in the country, so wanting a lawyer isn't the correct answer."

An F.B.I Agent glared at Mr. Tucker, "We'll get you a lawyer, but I'm sure you know how serious Ricin is! The officer that arrested you found a black head covering in your car."

"You're in serious trouble. Help us with the location of Mr. Hunter's cabin, and information about his plans for the stolen Ricin, and we'll help you get the best defense lawyer?" Martin Canaby said, as calmly as possible.

"I'm sorry. I'm really sorry. Killing children...it's wrong," Mr. Tucker sorrowfully cried, as he bowed his head in shame.

~

An hour later, helicopters land on a field, and F.B.I. Agents, Secret Service and Martin Canaby exit and stormed through the front door of an empty cabin.

"Look for phone books, bills, location maps of any kind," Martin Canaby ordered everyone.

"Sir," a police officer motioned to Martin and pointed at the cabin's fireplace. It was filled of charred papers.

~

"What's up?" Isaiah inquired, when Secret Agents Anthony Anders and Carlos Silva approached him in the White House dining room.

"We need you to come with us, Pastor Hillman," Anthony said.

"Yes, of course. My wife and family are on their way here. Will it take long?"

"We'll make arrangements for them," Carlos said, but clearly concerned with what's about to happen in the world.

"What's wrong? Is it about the Ricin robbery?"

"Worse," Anthony gravely answered, and quickly ushered Isaiah out of the dining room, through a maze of corridors, down into the basement, and into a room where Mr. Tucker was being held.

"Okay, tell Pastor Hillman what you've told us," Martin Canaby said, still calm, though inwardly disgusted with Mr. Tucker and the Earth Devils.

"Ivan Stone stole the Ricin, and they're going to kill the Miracle Children."

"No, tell him about this Great Adversary and his army!" Carlos yelled at Mr. Tucker.

"Carlos, Mr. Tucker is cooperating, aren't you, sir?"

"Yes, sir, when Mr. Stone shot Kenny Cash we were all afraid for our lives."

"Mr. Tucker, we understand your fear, but we need you to tell Pastor Hillman what you know, so he'll be able to stop it," Martin Canaby said.

Mr. Tucker looked up at Isaiah, tears were rolling down his face as he whimpered, "I'm sorry, Pastor Hillman."

"I understand. The secret agent said something about a Great Adversary and his army. Who would that be?"

"Satan, Pastor Hillman. We've been told that when God allowed you and the children back on the earth, it opened the door for all spirits to live here."

"Mr. Tucker, spirits need bodies to live here on the earth."

"They're going to take over bodies of the unsaved!"

~

"National News Network has just received word that a National arrest warrant has been issued for the Secretary of Defense, Phillip Hunter. The bunker where the Ricin was stored was only known by a few on the Secretary's staff. His sudden sick leave is under investigation, and my White House source said the Miracle Children told President Morrison that Mr. Hunter held secret meetings with the Earth Soldiers and Angels," Alison Hewitt informed her viewers.

~

"Damn," Jan cursed into her cell phone, as a few passengers on her flight to Washington stared at her. "Sorry, I'm just upset about some personal news."

~

"Isaiah you declared a war on these Earth Soldiers! Why would you do that?" Diana Serna said in a meeting with others in a White House Conference Room.

"I did it to make them come after us."

"Come after us with this Ricin poison!" Mario Serna said, exasperated.

"Mario, they didn't have the Ricin when I said it, and understand that the Ricin was stolen to stop the changes the president and the children have called for in the world. The children threaten their lifestyles and businesses, so when they come it won't be after you."

"Isaiah, we're with our children, so what happens to them, happens to us," Diana Serna said, profoundly unhappy. "We're not going to let Leon, Alonzo, and the other children, wage a war against people using poison." She looked at the other parents, "Are we?"

Mrs. Faraday responded, "Yes, we are. My daughter is in the ICU because she's a Miracle Child. We believe God has a New Beginning for the world, and yes, we're going to fight. We will die fighting."

She broke out crying as her husband took her in his arms.

Mario frowned, "I'm willing to fight, but my wife and sons won't be in this battle."

"Dad, God gave us the power, not you!"

"What power, Leon! What power! I'm sorry, Mrs. Faraday, but your daughter's prophecy has opened up a can of worms. Look at what happened to her! Where is God now? He doesn't even talk to the children anymore! We're taking our sons back home!"

Isaiah held up his hand and spoke, "Mario, we all have the same questions as you. The Holy Spirit may not be talking to us, but He's watching. We've been told not to open a pathway to heaven for evil spirits to enter. God is watching. Everyone in heaven is watching. Susan and President Morrison are in the ICU's, and they are the signs to let the world know what will happen if we don't stop the attack here on earth. The Miracle Children are a light for all nations under heaven to see. If you can't see their light, you're walking in darkness! Excuse me, but right now, I'd rather be a light that Father God, Christ Jesus, and the Holy Spirit will guide!"

Isaiah walked out of the Conference Room. Evelyn, Paula, the Faradays and Spencers followed Isaiah's lead, and then, Leon and Alonzo rose and stared at their parents.

"Sorry, Mom, Dad, we have to follow our pastor," Alonzo announced, as he and Leon walked out of the dining room.

"Isaiah isn't telling us everything," Mario said, uncomfortable by what he's heard.

"You think he's not being honest with us?"

"Diana, they were told not to open a pathway for evil forces to enter heaven, that they had to stop the attack here."

"I thought he was being honest about that."

"Honey, before the Miracle Children came back to earth, thousands of terrorist cells were destroyed. God didn't close heaven because of some fools were going to steal some Ricin poison."

"What are you saying, Mario?"

"Something worse is threatening heaven and earth."

"You think it's the devil?"

"It must be, otherwise why did God tell the children to prepare the world for a New Day?" Mario shrugged, as he and Diana contemplated the horrors facing Isaiah, the Miracle Children, and the world.

~

17

Faith

Now faith is the substance of things hoped for, the evidence of things not seen.
Hebrews 11:1 KJV

"Pastor Hillman," First Lady Morrison whispered, as she approached Isaiah, who was praying in the White House Chapel Room. The chapel is painted white and gold that gives the place a heavenly light. Mounted on a white marble pedestal, is a beautiful painting of the anointed one, Jesus the Christ in a rich, gold-frame. President Morrison built the little chapel, though many in the nation thought it inappropriate, as he was elected to represent all people. The president responded, that he needed a place to pray, and perhaps the people who objected, should have a place of prayer in their home, so blessings would come into their lives, and then, they wouldn't have time to stop blessings from coming into his life, his family, and the White House.

"Pastor Hillman, I'm sorry to disturb you, but something is pressing on my mind."

Isaiah stood up from his kneeling position, "You're not disturbing me. I guess you've heard about the horror we're facing."

"Yes, I've heard about the robbery. Christian Sparrow came with me to see Aaron and Susan at the Medical Center. Susan was able to show Christian a dream where you saved her life. Isaiah, Susan is waiting for you to save her."

"Me?"

"Yes, she needs your help."

"I see…well, Michelle's faith brought Michael back to life. Let's see if God will work His Spirit through my hands. However, there's another major crisis we have to resolve. I haven't told anyone, but we'll have to let the world know what's coming."

"You think they're going to ship the Ricin to other countries."

"Ricin isn't the problem right now."

"What are you talking about?"

"Our return to the earth has allowed an opening for evil spirits to do the same. They're coming out of hell and possibly will be able to inhabit human bodies."

"You said possibly."

"High possibility."

"How will you stop it?"

"I don't know."

"God left you in charge of the Miracle Children. I'm sure you'll come up with an answer."

"Your fearlessness is comforting!"

"It's a comfort for me, too. Isaiah, I've read the Bible, God wins. Now let's go deal with Susan Faraday!"

~

"Pastor Hillman, Isaiah," Jan Summers yelled out as she ran down the Medical Center corridor, and four Secret Agents stopped her.

"I'm Jan Summers, I'm sure you recognize me!"

An agent looked at the First Lady.

"It's okay, Marvin. Let her pass."

"Thank you, First Lady Morrison. Good Afternoon, I've been waiting here hoping you'd show up," Jan said, and shook Jennifer's hand. "Is there good news?"

"As best can be expected under these circumstances."

"Yes, of course. May I walk with you?"

"With you and your cameraman?" Jennifer answered, feeling put upon by Jan.

"It will be a great inspirational story for the world to see you with the president."

"What do you think, Pastor Hillman? Want this show televised?" Jennifer turned to Isaiah, concerned.

"Yes, I think it'll be a great inspirational story."

"What if you...?"

"God wouldn't have brought Ms. Summers and her cameraman here for a failure!" Isaiah smiled, as they all entered the Intensive Care Room and Brian filmed President Morrison in his ICU.

Brian filmed Isaiah when he took a doll from a chair and placed it under Susan's arm.

"Let's all join hands," Isaiah said, enlightenment entering his spirit as he joined hands with Jennifer and Jan.

Jan pushed Brian's hand away, "You keep filming, Brian," Jan whispered, as Isaiah closed his eyes and prayed.

"Father God, Christ Jesus, Holy Spirit, we know you're watching us. We know you've gathered us together for your preparations to bring the New Day into our world. Father God, Susan Faraday has your Marriage of True Empowerment with Christ Jesus anointed in her mind, body and spirit. I know your Mighty Hand protects her, now let your power flow through my hand...Yahweh, f'binna sama koah..."

Isaiah's spirit is overcome, as his words are changed into tongues, an a white light, invisible to everyone, flowed from his hand and into Susan's body."

Meanwhile, Susan's spiritual body materializes in the room, and Isaiah sees her holding President Morrison's hand.

"Susan's spirit is here," Isaiah said.

Jennifer, Jan and Brian looked around.

"Your spiritual eyes aren't opened, however, I see her moving away from President Morrison as a rainbow light from her spirit covers her physical body."

Isaiah watches in amazement, as Susan's spirit is turned into a bright energy of light, and her spiritual body is reborn in her human body. A moment later, she slowly sat up and hugged the doll.

"Hi," Susan smiled, and looked around at everyone.

Brian, teary eyed, took Jan's hand, but she shook his hand loose, and whispered again, "Keep filming, Brian. Keep filming!"

A doctor is brought into the room to check Susan's heart, pulse, and temperature. Medical check completed, he stared wide-eyed at everyone and announced, "These children are amazing!"

Jennifer hugged and kissed Susan, before she questioned, "Susan, can you wake up the president?"

"I went back to heaven and God told me how to do it," Susan answered. She walked to the president's bed, closed her eyes and concentrated. A moment later, flames of fire burst out all over the president's body.

Jennifer screamed in horror, "Susan, what have you done?"

Susan took Jennifer's hand, "It's okay. It's God's Fire of Grace, and it will burn up all sickness, and it will also stop all evil spirits from entering his body."

As with Susan, the fire turned into a bright energy of light, and when the light dimmed, President Morrison opened his eyes and sat up.

The doctor questions, "President Morrison, are you feeling any dizziness…"

"No, I feel…really…clean. Renewed…I haven't felt this good in a long time!"

"Lets go, Brian," Jan said, stunned by the event, she rushed out the room, but before Brian followed, he nods to everyone his appreciation for the news story.

"Thank you," Brian thoughtfully said, before he walked out of the ICU room.

Isaiah turned to Jennifer, "You gave Miss Summers the news story of her life,"

"No, God did that through you, Isaiah," Jennifer said, and then walked over and took the president's hand and kissed him.

Susan spoke into Isaiah's spirit, 'God said your prayer has been answered on how to stop the evil spirits.'

'I know,' Isaiah answered in spirit.

~

"This is a great, mind-blowing, eye opening, Breaking News story. Larry, get me on the air before the other networks find out!" Jan hollered, running into her affiliate television network in Washington D.C. and handed the news producer a DVD.

"What do you have, Jan?" Larry queried.

"Larry, I'm going out to the news desk. Get me a makeup artist, quick!"

Jan hurried out of the monitoring room. It didn't take long before she sat behind the news desk and a makeup artist was brushing powder on her face and forehead.

"Five, four, three..." the stage director counted down, as Jan composed herself and looked into the studio television camera.

"Two, and you're on, Jan!"

"Good afternoon, I'm Jan Summers. And it's a Good Day for America. I've just left the Medical Center and we have this exclusive news story to show the world. Larry, run the DVD!"

Jan looked on in horror as everyone stared at a blank screen.

"What's going on? Get Brian in here!" Jan yelled, as the news manager cut to a commercial.

"Brian went out to lunch, Jan? Did he give you the wrong DVD?"

"No, no, I guess his camera couldn't film what happened," Jan lied; totally embarrassed by the situation Brian left her in.

~

"National News Network has this Breaking News story of Susan Faraday and President Aaron Morrison's miraculous recovery. Watch this Supernatural Miracle," Alison Hewitt announced, as the network screened Brian's DVD of President Morrison and Susan Faraday's miracle healings.

"We have a remote crew at the Medical Center. Ben Richardson, what new information do you have?"

"Alison, here at the Medical Center, there are tears of joy for the miracle recovery of Susan Faraday and President Aaron Morrison. I'm with nurse Patricia Sellers. Patricia, please tell everybody what you've told me!"

"Well...Pastor Isaiah Hillman told us that Susan Faraday visited heaven again, and came back with some very important news. God will never close off heaven to believers," Patricia Sellers happily smiled, as people stood and cheered and clapped their hands.

"What else, Patricia?"

"There was more, but Pastor Hillman said the Miracle Children will reveal it."

"Alison, I've heard from another source, that First Lady Morrison has stated that when God heard everyone's Psalm 91 prayer, He healed her husband and Susan. The Bible says that God doesn't show favoritism, (Acts 10:34-35) so what He does for one, he'll do for another. Happy days are here again!"

"Well said, Ben. Our audience will be happy to know that heaven is open to hear our prayers again. Thank you, Patricia Sellers and Ben Richardson at the Medical Center. This has been a Special Report from the National News Network, I'm Alison Hewitt."

A few hours later, Alison Hewitt brought another news exclusive by getting Michael and Michelle Spencer on her show.

"Michael, what is this fire power that Susan Faraday is able to produced?"

"I read the Bible to Susan, where John the Baptist said he baptized with water, he then said that someone is coming after him, to baptized with the Holy Spirit and fire." (Luke 3:16)

"The one who baptizes with the Holy Spirit and fire is Christ Jesus," Michelle confirmed. "I looked up the word fire in my mother's Concordance, and read that our God is a consuming fire. (Hebrews 12:29 KJV) God's fire will burn up all diseases, doubting hearts, lying tongues, people who have evil desires...everything wrong with this world!"

"Are all the Miracle Children baptized with God's fire?" Alison asked.

"We have different gifts, but unbelievers won't live in the New Day that God is preparing for the earth," Michelle answered.

"Will God's fire consume them?"

"No, the hellfire will welcome them!!! Where the fire never stops and worms never die!!!" (Mark 9:46 KJV)

Alison nodded, "Let's pray that unbelievers will hear you and turn their lives around."

"They better hurry up, time is running out," Michael announced.

"Today, with all that's happened, it's foolish to think that God didn't bless the Miracle Children as a sign for the entire world to see! We can no longer close our eyes to the truth; so open your ears to hear what the Words of God are telling you. Listen and hear God's Miracle Children, that God is preparing a New Day for those who love Him. Michael and Michelle, we thank God for your special anointed spirits. I'm Alison Hewitt, thanks for watching the National News Network."

~

"The F.B.I. and police forces are doing a nation wide search for former Secretary of Defense, Phillip Hunter and his Earth Soldiers. With the threat of the Ricin poison in the hands of these Enemies of the State, what are you and the Miracle Children going to do about it?" Jan Summers asked, while interviewing Isaiah, Leon and Alonzo.

"In celebration of President Morrison and Susan Faraday's great works and miracle healings, the Miracle Children are planning a Children Concert on the Mall this coming Saturday," Isaiah announced.

"What? A Concert!"

"Yes, a Spiritual Concert for the World. Everyone is welcome, even the Earth Soldiers and Earth Angels, who want to repent and be forgiven from all their sins."

"I'm thinking you're joking!"

"No, to say thank you, a Children's Concert will offer up Praise, Honor, and Worship to our Father God. Christ Jesus came into the world to save sinners, (John 3:17KJV) and his grace is open to all of us. After Saturday's concert that door might close, and may be too late for you to enter. Isaiah 55:6 and 7 says, "Seek the Lord while he may be found. Call upon him while he is near. Let the wicked forsake his way, and the unrighteous man his thoughts: and let him return unto the Lord, and he will have mercy upon him; and to our God, for he will abundantly pardon.""

"What are you telling us, Pastor Hillman? I'm always surprised by your answers. One minute you're talking war, the next you want to sing for your tormentors! I've heard from another source that you've been reported as saying heaven will never close its doors, now you're saying the door might be closing. You're confusing everyone!"

"Ms. Summers, you must not leave out words. I've stated that God will never close doors to believers. (Revelation 3:8) In Matthew 25, Jesus tells the parable of the ten bridesmaids who took their lamps to meet the bridegroom. (2) Five were foolish. Five were wise. (5) In short, the bridegroom was delayed. (6) At midnight they were roused from sleep with a shout, 'Look, the bridegroom is coming! Come out and welcome him!' The five wise ones had enough oil in their lamps to get to the marriage feast. (11) The foolish ones, had to go buy oil for their lamps and when they returned they found that the door was locked. They called out for the door to be opened, but the bridegroom answered, (12) "I don't know you!' Jesus ends the story with these words, (13) Stay awake and be prepared, because you don't know the day or hour of my return."

"For those of us who don't understand, please explain the story."

"I believe Jesus was telling a parable about the rapture, His second return; when the ones who obeyed the Word will be raised up, saved, and will never die. As the apostle Paul says in 1st Corinthians 15:51-53…But let me tell you a wonderful secret God has revealed to us. Not all of us will die, but we will all be transformed. It will happen in a moment, in the blinking of an eye, when the last trumpet is blown, and believers who have died will be raised with transformed bodies. And then, we who are living are transformed and will never die. For our perishable, earthly bodies must be transformed into heavenly bodies that will never die. Jesus is the Light, the oil is His anointing, and the lamp is our lives. The foolish people who don't prepare their lives for the Kingdom, will suffer the devil's horrible tribulation, you won't have freedom, and you will received the mark 666, and become a slave of the devil, and the ones who don't serve him will be killed. Jan, the devil's war is to hide the Light of Jesus. I believe it's now coming to a showdown. The announcement for a New Day has been on the earth for a few years now. Susan Faraday's prophesy has held it off for five years because politicians, businessmen, and religious leaders asked for more time to set up new laws, rules and regulations, however, the truth is they were stalling, because it's not about new laws. The Bible says we're saved by grace through faith, not of yourself: it is the gift of God: not of works, so no man can boast. (Ephesians 2:8,9 KJV) So while it's still daylight, those living in darkness and sin better seek forgiveness and Jesus, who is the embodiment of grace, or be prepared for the worse!!!"

"Leon, Alonzo, as Miracle Children, do you believe that our lamps are burning out as Pastor Hillman seems to suggest?"

"Aren't you tired of telling people the same thing for over a thousand days?" Alonzo asked.

"Yes, of course. Do you have something new to reveal to the world?"

"God is tired, too," Leon announced.

Jan is rendered speechless.

"Cut! Go to commercial!" Larry the news producer, yelled out. "Jan, you're looking like a deer caught in headlights. We gave you another shot with this story, but if we broadcast this interview the station will become a tool to cause more fear and panic in the world. I'm sorry, we'll have to broadcast another story."

"Larry..."

"Leon is misleading. God doesn't get tired!" Larry scolded.

"God gets tired of people's sins!" Leon said.

"Leon, we're not going to debate this, so just leave it alone. We've received word that we're linking up with the National News Network and Alison Hewitt. The station thinks it's best to have one voice on this story from now on. Okay, we're linking up with the White House in five, four, three, two..."

~

"Good Evening, I'm Alison Hewitt. I'm here in the White House Chapel with the First Lady, Jennifer Morrison and our Commander in Chief of the United States of America, President Aaron Morrison."

President Morrison and the First Lady smiled, and acknowledged Alison's warm greeting, "Thank you."

"We're more than happy to speak with our fellow citizens of the world," President Morrison happily smiled.

"The National News Network and I, thank you for this exclusive interview. First of all, how are you, Mr. President?"

"I'm fine, Alison, and feeling better every minute of my new life."

"You wanted to do the interview from the White House Chapel that your presidency has built. Is there a special reason for this?"

"It's an opportunity to thank everyone for their cards, gifts, and prayers."

Jennifer continued, "It's also allows us a chance to pray with everyone in the world."

"Have you always been a believer, First Lady Morrison?"

"I've always been a believer, and as a child, I've always wondered when the Egyptians experienced the plagues of blood, frogs, locusts, darkness, and then God delivered the Children of Israel through the Red Sea, and saved them from Pharaoh's Army, (Exodus 8-14) I've always wondered why God's Chosen People didn't stay true to God. Then in today's world, the Miracle Children are blessed to prepare the world for a New Day, and they are bombed, killed, brought back to life with new spiritual bodies, bringing many special gifts from heaven for the world to experience, and then there are people who still don't want to hear the truth. They still won't believe! What's wrong with us?"

President Morrison responded, "I'll say it's a lack of faith. People have lost trust in leadership. I want to pray and renew that trust and faith in God for America, as well as for the rest of the World. I know haters and unbelievers don't want to see the president kneeling and praying, so turn off your television if what we're about do, will offend you."

President Morrison and the First Lady joined hands and knelt down to pray.

"Mind if I join you?" Alison asked.

"You'll probably lose your job, but we would love for you to join us in prayer," President Aaron Morrison smiled, and took Alison's hand as she got into a kneeling position.

"My daughter is one of the Miracle Children, I need to join you in prayer," Brian said, tears in his eyes, he positioned his camera on a tripod, and then knelt in prayer next to Alison. Alison smiled and took Brian's hand in hers.

President Morrison prayed, (Matt 6:9 KJV) "Our Father which art in heaven, Hallowed be thy name. (10) Thy kingdom come. Thy will be done on earth, as it is in heaven…"

~

"Hello, God, maybe it's time for us to talk," Jan said, finally worried and fearful, as she watched Brian kneeling in prayer with Alison and the First Family on the television studio monitor. She had to admit, that God was planning something with the children, and even if it was just singing and dancing, this New Day, that the Miracle Children were preparing, has filled the whole world with a new spirit of joy, and she didn't want to be left out. She knelt down and prayed, "Hello, God, it's me, Jan Summers, I know we haven't spoken before, but if there's still an open door, please welcome me…and, I'll like to welcome you into my life, and as Pastor Hillman said, get my sins washed in the blood of Jesus. I believe you're really giving me a chance to change my unbelief…"

~

"Paula is very excited about tomorrow's concert on the Mall," Evelyn said.

"Paula doesn't remember the Children's Concert on the Hill, or visiting heaven. She won't really remember tomorrow's concert."

"You don't know your daughter, Mr. Know It All. Paula, tell Daddy how many Miracle Children are in the world."

"One million five hundred and fourteen thousand."

"What are there names?"

"Dee Dee Wise, Tuffy Williams, Joyce 'Piggy' Fergus, Reginald Gary, Vernon 'Wahab' Goodman, Lewis Barker,

Nathaniel Belson, Quincy Warr, Samuel 'Puggy' Morton, Diane..."

"Paula, are the children telling you their names, right now."

"I know them from heaven. Susan Faraday sees fire. Summer Wind sees a Bright Star."

"What did I see, Paula?" Isaiah asked.

"You saw the Holy Spirit as the Universe."

"Wow," Isaiah said in amazement. "Paula, when Jesus asked us to close our eyes and see God, what did you see?"

"The New Day."

"Oh...Susan also saw the New Day. Paula, do you know what's coming before the New Day takes place?"

"Yes, Daddy. I know."

"So stay in the White House and protect Mommy, okay?"

"What's going on, Isaiah?" Evelyn asked.

"We didn't tell parents before because we wanted to keep this information out of the news. Only the Miracle Children will be present on the Mall. For security reasons adults will be held behind barriers far away from the children."

"Isaiah, Paula is a Miracle Child, she has to be there!"

"Then I'll take her. You won't be able to come."

"You're so calm about this. What are you hiding?"

"Nothing, but for safety precautions, the restrictions will be strictly enforced."

"Then I'll stand behind the barriers. I want to see the concert live, not on television."

"The children will be on the Mall for six hours. There'll be protestors and people in the crowd who'll want to cause a National Disaster."

"You were with the children on their journey to Star Island...you entered Paradise, the Kingdom of God...Isaiah, you're not going to talk me out of this experience."

"All the Miracle Children in one location is also a chance for another terrorist attack."

"The whole world knows that and everybody will be watching to see what happens."

"I'm sorry, but you'll have to stay here in the White House."

"I told you I'm not..."

"I've given instructions to White House security not to allow you outside in the morning."

"You've put me under house arrest. You better tell me why, right now?"

"You don't want to know. Take my word for it."

"Who else, my parents, the Spencers?"

"Everybody. Everybody!"

"Why are you doing this? Please, don't do this. You're on television talking about the light, and then you keep me in the dark. Why, tell me why?"

"Come, look out the window and tell me what you see?"

"It's cloudy. Is that it? You think it's going to rain tomorrow!"

"It's raining now. Millions of dark smudges are coming into the world."

"Smudges!"

"That's what they look like, but they're really evil spirits, empty of all light, searching for human bodies to invade. You can't see them, but we can."

"You're not serious. You're only saying this to keep me inside."

"Please, don't even try to sneak outside. Paula has a new body, you don't. Tell her the truth, Paula."

"Don't go outside, Mommy," Paula agreed.

"Paula, Mommy is going outside, and your Daddy better not come home if he thinks he's going to lock me in some room. I'm a believer, I'm married to your father, but I'm also married to Jesus, and no evil spirit will ever take over my body! Not today, tomorrow, not ever! I'm covered with Jesus blood, so in the name of Jesus, I'll be safe. Amen!"

~

"The day for the Children's Concert on the Mall was sunny, warm and beautiful," Alison Hewitt beamed, while she stood behind a barrier. "Pastor Hillman, and one million, five hundred and fourteen thousand Miracle Children are gathered here, and as on their previous Miracle Children World Concert, the children are wearing clothes from their native countries. Many of the children have shook my hand, and said hello into our camera in their native tongue of Chinese, Spanish, Danish, Hawaiian, Zulu, and of course, English. Surrounding the mall are barriers with armed policemen, National Guards, and Secret Service Agents on Special Duty. At many strategic locations are fire fighters, paramedics, and motorcycle police officers. Also behind the barriers, are over a million spectators unafraid of what the day will bring. They have been checked, screened and searched for weapons, drugs, alcohol and other materials that can cause problems. Flying in the sky are three fighter jets circling the Mall. The public has been warned that the fighter pilots are ready to attack and shoot down all unauthorized aircrafts, helicopters, and the many Hot Air Balloons people threatened to fly over the area. I'm told that people are watching their televisions, viewing on the Internet, or have come together in homes, barrooms, stadiums, temples, synagogues, and churches to see Susan Faraday and the Miracle Children. Sad to say…quite a few others are watching to see if terror will strike again. To my left is Mr. Tony Dyson. Mr. Dyson, you told me earlier that you're not afraid and came out to show support for the children."

"My five year old granddaughter is a Miracle Child. She told me about being in heaven and seeing all the people and angels, and how beautiful God's home is. No, I'm not afraid, I'm saved and so is my family. And even though we don't see them, I believe God has sent his Holy Angels here to protect His children!"

"That's Good News. Thank you, Mr. Dyson, enjoy the concert. Now let's listen to Pastor Isaiah Hillman saying a prayer to start the concert. I'm Alison Hewitt, National Network News."

Isaiah was on a stage overseeing the large gathering, "Over the years, I've had many, many questions about the New Day the Miracle Children were preparing the world for. My questions were the same as yours. Why Children? Was God bringing the world to its Last Day? The only answer I've received was to save lives. That's it, Save Lives! Our God knows the answers to all our questions; *so don't put a question mark, where God has placed a period*. Though, we're less than two years away from Susan Faraday's five-year extension to change our world, the Miracle Children and myself know how this day will start, and we know how it will end. Did you hear me? I'll say it again, listen closely. *We know how this day will start, and we know how it will end!!! So again, hear my words; don't put a question mark, where God has placed a period!* If you're not saved in the blood of our Redeemer, Christ Jesus, then your time for questions is over! It's time to plead the blood of Jesus over your life and family and make that change. Let's pray, everybody together...*God be merciful to me a sinner, I believe Christ died for me and that His Precious blood will cleanse me from all my sin...*"

~

In the White House Chapel, Evelyn, Thelma, Richard, the Spencers, Sernas, and a number of parents and family members are in prayer as Isaiah spoke from a large television monitor.

Evelyn, stood up from praying, and started walking out of the chapel.

"Where are you going, Evelyn?"

"Daddy, I'm going outside."

"Isaiah said we'll be safe in here."

"Like the man said on television, I believe God has sent his legion of Holy Angels here to protect Isaiah and the Miracle Children. I'm not afraid, I'm going outside." Evelyn affirmed, and then walked out of the chapel.

A moment later, everybody else followed Evelyn's lead.

~

"...By faith I now receive the Lord Jesus Christ into my heart as my Lord and Savior; trusting Him for the salvation of my soul. Help me Lord to do your will each and every day. In Jesus name I pray. Amen! Now let's all give Praise to God in his heavenly dwelling," Isaiah finished the Sinner's Prayer, and looked out at the Miracle Children.

The Miracle Children shouted loud praises to God from the Mall.

"Hallelujah!"

"Jesus saves!!"

"God will bless you!!!"

Isaiah continued, (Psalm 150 NLT) *"Praise him in his mighty heaven!* (2) *Praise him for his mighty works. Praise his unequaled greatness.* (3) *Praise him with a blast of the trumpet!"*

At that moment, quite a few Miracle Children blew melodic riffs on their trumpets.

(3)*"Praise him with a lyre and harp!* (4) *Praise him with the tambourine and dancing. Praise him with stringed instruments and flutes! God's Miracle Children get ready to praise God with a clash of cymbals.* (5) *Praise him with loud clanging cymbals.* (6) *Let everything that lives sing Praises to the Lord!*

The Miracle Children screamed with joy, and the concert began as they sang, played their musical instruments, and danced in spirit as King David joyfully did! (2Samuel 6:16)

The crowd behind the barriers, yelled, shouted, and hollered with excitement when Susan Faraday came onto the stage and began her spiritual dance. They cheered even louder when Michael, Michelle, Leon and Alonzo came out and sang in four-part harmony:

Michael/Others: *"A great rain is coming*
A new rain for everyone
It's full of living water
Sent from the Father's Son
The heavens will deliver
The rain to everyone
Drink your hearts full
A New Day will come"

The Miracle Children:
"A New Beginning from heaven
Sent from the Father, the Son,
And the Holy Ghost
A rainbow will crown the earth
A New Birth for everyone..."

The Miracle Children's Concert on the Mall, had billions of people in the world coming under the spiritual influence of their great talents as musicians, singers and dancers.

~

A mile away from the Washington Mall, a car drove into the parking lot of Fire Station 86. Two men stepped out of the car and entered the rear door of the Fire Station. They looked around the empty station.

"They must be out at the concert," Rick said.

"I'll give the Captain a call to see if he's going to drive us to the Mall," Andre nodded, as they walked up the stairs to the station's living quarters.

~

"Keep alert," a firefighter said, as he sat in the cab of a fire truck parked at a north section of the Mall. Checking his watch, he started the engine and motioned for a fellow firefighter, who stood at a barrier to move it aside. The fire truck drove onto the Mall. A second fire truck followed.

~

"Slobs," Rick frowned, when he walked into the firehouse bathroom and saw some sprinkles of blood on the floor. He looked around, saw more blood on the shower stall door, and slid it open. He gagged at the sight of eight dead bodies dumped on top of one another in the tub. He stumbled out of the bathroom, "Andre! Andre, call nine, one, one! **Call nine, one, one!**"

18

The Battle

Neither can they die anymore: for they are equal unto the angels; and are the children of God, being children of the resurrection. Luke 20:36 KJV

"These children are liars. Kill the lying, fire-spitting demons!" Phillip Hunter, the former Secretary of Defense, shouted into a bullhorn.

Concert spectators, with demon spirits living within them broke through the police barriers and ran onto the Mall to attack the children.

Meanwhile, Ivan Stone, Karen Watson, Earl Sisco, and fifteen other Earth Soldiers, who wore firefighter's protective gear, rushed about and hooked up hoses to their fire truck's water tanks.

Isaiah seeing the demons coming, shouted out in spirit the code word, 'ATTACK!'

The Earth Soldiers watched as three boys simultaneously blew loud blasts into bugles, and as the soldiers pumped out the Ricin solution from the fire trucks, Isaiah and the Miracle Children disappeared!

The Ricin solution rained down on the three bugles, and all the other instruments the children left behind.

Ivan, Karen, Earl, Earth Soldiers, and over a million evil spirits that inhabited human bodies, looked about the area in shock and stupidity. In an act of more stupidity, the soldiers turned off the hoses so the solution wouldn't harm the demon possessed people on the Mall.

Phillip hollered at his soldiers, "Turn the hoses on and spray our enemies behind the barriers."

Panic ensued as Evelyn and many others ran for their lives.

Isaiah yelled out in spirit, 'LIFT UP...LIFT UP!'

Those running away from the Mall, all the godly people, were grabbed by an invisible hand, and transported to a safer place.

The people left on the Mall, who were demon-possessed, looked around in fear and saw only Phillip, Ivan, and his Earth Soldiers.

Suddenly, Susan and three other Miracle Children reappeared and hovered fifty feet above Phillip, Ivan, and the Earth Soldiers.

Ten thousand angels were protecting Susan, and the three other Miracle Children. Two children stared at the fire truck's gas tanks, while Susan and her partner caused a ring of fire to encircle the Mall.

In a flash, Susan, the three other Miracle Children and the angels disappeared, just as the fire trucks were engulfed in flames.

Ivan and his Earth Soldiers screamed in horror and tried to flee, but before they could get away, the fire trucks exploded and Ricin solution rained down on them. Though they were wearing fire protection suits and facemasks, the solution seeped into the suits breathing apparatus, and flowed like a worm from hell, and ate up their eyes, ears, flesh, and then seeped down, and melted their hearts, lungs and other vital organs.

The million-man army of demons, who escaped the rain of Ricin poison, were unable to escape the Ring of Fire that rapidly moved inward toward them. Then, came the eerily howls of horror from them, as the Ring of Fire burnt the bodies of Phillip Hunter, Karen Watson, Earl Sisco, and the army of unsaved humans that the demons spirits infiltrated.

～

After the attack on the Washington Mall, many Miracle Children returned to their individual homelands. They were unseen by human eyes, however, any unsaved human, whose body was infiltrated by a demon spirit, saw a Miracle Child being protected by many angels as they hovered over their city, town or village in Afghanistan, Angola, Australia, Burma, Botswana, Canada, China, Iran, Iraq, Rwanda, South Africa, United States and many other places of human habitation.

The demons watched in fear as God's Holy Angels sent Rings of Fire down on villages, towns, and cities, but the fire, racing inward, only engulfed the embodied humans with demon spirits. The fires didn't burn plants, homes or humans with saved spirits.

Many demons inhabited one unsaved body, so they fought internally to escape out of a body. The demons that were able to flee a burning body were unable to escape the Ring of Fire that burnt their evil spirit. Ugly, disfigured and howling souls fell into many dark pits around the world that opened up its mouth to receive them.

People were shocked to see their King, Queen, World Leaders, politicians, drug dealers, gangbangers, and other unscrupulous sinners burst into flames and cry out in horror as the dark pits of hell captured and sealed them inside.

Three minutes later, the demons were gone, and so were all the dark pits of hell!

~

An hour later, National Guardsmen, who wore protective gear, marched onto the Mall, and used flame-throwers to burn up the grass and whatever else the Ricin solution rained down on.

~

19

Tomorrow

And then at last, the sign of the coming of the Son of Man will appear in heaven, and there will be deep mourning among all the nations of the earth. And they will see the Son of Man arrive on the clouds of heaven with power and great glory.

Matthew 24:30 NLT

"Susan Faraday, I didn't have the opportunity to complete this special event," President Morris said to Susan, at a celebration being held in the White House Rose Garden, with special guests, the press, and the media in attendance.

"As President of the United States, I award you this Special International Medal of Honor. God Bless You."

President Aaron Morrison pinned the medal on the front of her pretty, yellow dress, and then hugged and kissed Susan Faraday as the crowd cheered and applauded.

Susan walked over and handed her new, hand-painted doll to the president's daughter.

"Samantha, I want NuNu's sister, NuNuYu to live here in the White House with you."

"Thank you, but she needs to be with you." Samantha tearfully hugged the doll, and then tried to hand it back to Susan.

"No, she will protect you. I'll make more dolls for other children."

Susan's parents, Michael, Michelle, Leon and Alonzo, Isaiah, Evelyn and Paula also hugged and kissed Susan, as Alison Hewitt announced the event for the National News Network, and her cameramen, Rollie and Brian filmed the ceremony so every man, woman and child in every village, town, city, and country around the world would forever enjoy a Special Susan Faraday Holiday.

~

"It's hard for me to believe they were so stupid," President Morrison said, as he enjoyed a cup of coffee with Pastor Isaiah Hillman in the Diplomatic Reception Room.

"Stupidity is too polite. They were so eager to come into the earth that hundreds of spirits would invade the body of one non-believer. Once the fires started, they became so confused and disoriented, the only thing they could do was fight each other trying to escape!"

"Thank God, they're all burning in the fires of hell," President Morrison smiled.

"Mr. President, we must stay alert! The Great Adversary, and many other demon spirits didn't fall into our trap, and they'll be searching for new bodies to live in."

"Are there still non-believers in the world?"

"There was only a million and a half Miracle Children to cover the whole earth. A lot of places didn't get covered, so Satan will find angry spirits in the world who are willing to let them in."

"Isaiah, we'll have to work harder and get everyone to believe and develop that intimate relationship with God."

"Yes, and we have less than two years to learn how to love one another."

"Love, the easiest virtue to attain, the hardest to maintain," President Morrison acknowledged.

The President and Isaiah sat in silence as they contemplated the future of the world.

"Isaiah, do you know what the New Day will bring?"

Isaiah pondered, before he answered; "Mr. President, Susan Faraday and my daughter told me they saw the New Day in heaven. I'm positive we all saw it, but didn't recognize it as they did. What I did see, and what I'll never forget was Christ Jesus' interaction with the children. He kissed, hugged, laughed, joked, and loved the children regardless of their race, religion or background. Watching Jesus, I know in my heart that Father God, Christ Jesus, and the Holy Spirit aren't interested in converting the children to a religion. They loved each child because of their pure belief. This revelation of "Our Savior" offered salvation to all nations of the earth, so give praise and worship to God, because the blood of Jesus will wash sin from every spirit as long as they believe."

"Amazing!"

"No, Amazing Grace," Isaiah stated. "My wife always talked about being married to me and Jesus. In the Kingdom of God, the Miracle Children, and myself were blessed to receive a Marriage of True Empowerment. This morning, I promised Evelyn, I would teach the world about being married to Christ Jesus!"

"Marrying a man, is it possible? President Morrison asked.

"Not marry the man, we must become one with His Spirit and walk in His Light and Love!"

"It sounds beautiful. Isaiah tell me more about this marriage…"

~

20

Revelation

The one sitting on the throne was as brilliant as gemstones—jasper and carnelian. And the glow of an emerald circled his throne like a rainbow. Revelation 4:3

Isaiah awakened, got out of bed and walked into his study. He sat before his digital camera and began recording his latest dream.

"February 12th, 2018, Susan Faraday's five-year prophecy concludes today, and my dream this morning was a vision of a baby sitting in a beautiful garden. I truly believe the baby is the same infant that Susan saw when Christ Jesus closed her eyes, and she had a vision of a baby near some water. I asked God who the baby was, and where was the water that Susan prophesized about? At that moment, I heard in my spirit a voice that told me to read Revelation 21 and 22. I prayed for wisdom, understanding, discernment, and then read both chapters, and when I finished, a new vision of the baby was revealed to me. This time, I saw the baby's full aura as he sat near to a river of crystal water, 'Living Waters of God' that you receive when you're baptized and born again. Susan and Paula were truthful when they told me they saw the New Day in heaven; and now, I'll confirm that the Miracle Children and myself also saw the New Day in heaven. Wow! The baby's full aura was the same aura that circled the body of the Holy Spirit. Today, those still unsaved, won't see the New Day. God revealed in my dream, that during the night, the pits of hell opened up and swallowed all unbelievers. They are gone forever! Praise God!!!"

Isaiah completed his visual recording, then knelt down and prayed:

Dear God,
Father within us, Spirit of our lives
In Jesus name,
I pray, we pray, all pray
And we Thank You, Father God
For hearing our prayers
And sending continuous Blessings,
Love, Inspiration, Guidance,
Knowledge, Wisdom, Patience,
Understanding, Strength, Deliverance
And Your Word into our Lives
We Thank You, Father God
For all the Wonderful,
And Loving Gifts
That You have bestowed on us
Thank You for our great talents
Our good health,
The wealth You share with us
Friends, family and love ones
You surround us with
Thank You for the good work

You provide for us
The opportunities You present to us
The success You share with us
The protection You surround us with
The cleansing of our Body, Mind, and Spirit
With Your Loving SPIRIT
Thank You for the blood of Jesus
That washes away our sins
Thank You, Christ Jesus
For You were wounded
For our transgressions
Bruised for our iniquities
The chastisement of our peace is upon You
And by Your stripes we are healed
Thank You, Christ Jesus
For walking the walk, talking the talk
And saving our lives
By bringing us into The Kingdom of God
Through Your Blood and Resurrection
Thank You, Father God, Christ Jesus, Holy Spirit
For the River of Living Water
Flowing out the Belly of our Heart
Full of Faith, Hope and Love
Thank You,
That the River of Living Water is so Full
That it overflows unto our
Family, friends, love ones,
And those You bring near
It overflows unto our churches,
Careers, businesses and jobs
Unto our gifts and special talents
And unto all that we are, have, and do
Thank You, Father God
For all Your Gifts, Love, and Favor

Seen and Unseen,
But always known by Your Word
Your Truth, Your Light,
Your Mercy and Forgiveness
Always known by Your
Grace and Your Promises
Always known by Your
Inspiration and Revelations
That flows into our hearts,
Into our thoughts, hopes and dreams
Always known by those You anointed
And blessed to be
Preachers and teachers,
Ministers and prophets,
Pastors and priests,
Evangelists and apostles
Always known by those You
Anointed and blessed to be
In positions of Leadership,
Power, Authority and Influence
Always known by the Seed of Abraham
The Children of God
Those who walk in Your Light
Do Your Will, and Believe
In Our Lord and Savior, Jesus Christ
Always known by
The Miracle Children
Who heard the Call of the Holy Spirit
Walked in His Light,
Did the Will of Our Father
And became Obedient to His Word,
Always known by the Holy Angels You send
To guide, provide, protect and direct our lives
Always known by the Kingdom of God

And The Kingdom of Heaven
Always known, Father God
By the many ways You reveal
Your Loving Spirit into our world
With Great Signs, Wonders and Miracles
Thank You, Father God
For this New Day and New Beginning
And we hope and pray
That in this New Time of our lives,
That our words, our deeds,
Our thoughts, and our actions
Bring Glory to You, Father God
To Your Kingdoms
Your heaven, Your earth
And all that is!
We hope and pray that on
This New Beginning of Time
Our words, our deeds,
Our thoughts, and our actions
Bring many blessings into our lives
To share and care for others
And do good work in the world
We hope and pray that on this
New Day of our lives
Our words, our deeds
Our thoughts, and our actions
Bring Joy, Peace, Love and Happiness
Into the Kingdom of God
Heaven and Earth
New Heaven, New Earth, and New Jerusalem
Thank You, Father God
For the seeds You've given us to plant
And we plant our seeds
In the Spirit of Your Love

Obedient to Your Word
And with Joy in our Heart
We plant our seeds
As tithes, offerings, and good works
We plant our seeds for
Health, Wealth, Love, and Creative Inspiration
We plant our seeds in the Garden of Heaven
Where thieves can't steal
Moths can't destroy
And rust won't corrode
We plant our seeds in the Garden of Heaven
In good ground,
Where Your Word, Father God
Will multiply our seeds
Some thirty, sixty, a hundred fold
And the seeds we plant in The Garden of Heaven
In good ground,
Multiplied by Your Word, Father God
Will produce an Abundant Harvest
Of Good Fruit, in Heaven,
In the World, and in Our Lives
So once again, Heavenly Father
Thank You for your Word,
That in due season,
You'll open the windows of heaven
And pour out a blessing
We won't have room enough to receive!
So now, I pray, we pray, all pray
And Thank You, Father God
For bringing us all together
To Your Glory
And forgive us, Father God
For not appreciating enough
The healing power

In Christ Jesus Precious Body
And the deliverance power
By the shedding of His Blood
So now, provide us with the wisdom
To discern how valuable the taking
Of Holy Communion is to our wholeness
And our path to righteousness in this world!
In Jesus name, I pray, we pray, all pray
Amen."

Pastor Isaiah Hillman finished his prayer, turned off the camera, and smiled with the knowledge that God had purposed a new adventure in his heart; now he would continue his journey with the Miracle Children and bring the **New Day…a beautiful promise from Our Father… an Earth without corruption…with clean new bodies… with a spiritual mind reigning with Our Lord God, forever and ever!!!**

"I am the way, the truth, and the life: No man cometh unto the Father, but by me." (John 14:6 KJV)

"See, I am coming soon, and my reward is with me, to repay all according to their deeds. I am the Alpha and the Omega, the First and the Last, the Beginning and the End." (Revelation 22:12-13)

"GLORY TO THE FATHER…TO THE SON… AND THE HOLY SPIRIT!   AMEN!"

End Part II – The Miracle Children

Ending Prayer

To all of you, who have read this book, we pray that your heart has been touched; we assure you, that the blessings from God will be in your life, and when you accept Jesus Christ as your only Savior, you will discover that Jesus is patiently waiting, with such a great love to invite you to the Great Feast of the Lamb.

As you fell in love with the most important person in your heart, we are sure memories will bring to your mind those exciting moments when you were nervous, had a pounding heart, waiting for the phone to ring to hear his/her voice, and meeting each other...we are sure it was your best time in this earth! An unforgettable time!

It's time to recapture those precious moments, by being married to Christ Jesus; the Holy Trinity; which are the Father, Son and Holy Spirit will anoint you; you'll experience the greatest wealth this world will ever deliver!

The wealth of Jesus, will bless you to help others by sharing your love, joy, peace, happiness, fortune and everything that God blessed you with.

The wealth of Jesus, will bless you with the power to speak to disease, poverty, stress, and the evil forces of darkness to be cleansed from your body, mind and spirit.

Our Ending Prayer for you is Deuteronomy 8:18 (KJV) "But thou shalt remember the Lord thy God: for it is he that giveth thee power to get wealth, that he may establish his covenant which he sware unto thy fathers, as it is this day."

Join us in our prayer for the world:

"Christ Jesus, my Lord and Savior, my greatest step forward in spirituality is to marry my spirit with your eternal love, peace and joy. Fill my heart to enjoy all the unearned and unmerited favor God has placed within me.

Open my ears to hear all the truth embedded in God's Holy Bible.

Lord Jesus, expand my vision to see through your eyes and receive the bridegroom's promise of eternal life in the Kingdom of God.

Today, Christ Jesus, my Lord and Master, I pray that my marriage to you becomes my New Day, knowing that your light will shine from me forever and ever. In receiving your precious love, I now pray that my walk will open the hearts of men, women and children...my family, friends and love ones to also receive the Bridegroom's Ceremonial Call to Marriage! Amen."

"I am the light of the world:
He that followeth me
Shall not walk in darkness,
But will have the light of life.
John 8:12 (KJV)

By having God in your heart,
God will always be in your life,
God Bless You!

Gerald Michael Daly
Sonia Orellana